# CW00458645

Jill Rutherford was born in \
adult life living in England. . ... me, she fulfilled a
dream of living 'The Good Life' on a smallholding in
deepest Wales and for nine years ran her own bookshop in
a nearby town.

Then she discovered Japan...

CHERRY BLOSSOMS, SUSHI and TAKARAZUKA

Seven Years in Japan

Jill Rutherford

Little Wren Press

Published in paperback in 2011 by Little Wren Press

Text and photographs © Gillian Rutherford 2011
www.jillrutherford.wordpress.com

ISBN 978-0-9569679-0-9

A CIP catalogue record for this book is available from the British Library

Set in Garamond
Printed and bound in England by Witley Press Ltd

Little Wren Press, 27 Old Gloucester Street, London
WC1N 3AX

This book is dedicated to my wonderful friend Ryoko, her family and to all my other friends and acquaintances in Japan who have generously given me permission to tell their stories along with mine.

Without you, none of this would have been possible. My heartfelt thanks to you all.

ACKNOWLEDGEMENTS

With special thanks to;-

Janet Coles who checked and helped correct the manuscript with unfailing generosity and offered advice where needed.

My Japanese teacher and friend, Yayoi Lidbetter who checked the manuscript from a Japanese point of view.

My friends at the Pickhams Writers' Group, who gave me the confidence to continue.

Matsubara san, a survivor of the A-bomb attack on Hiroshima who has generously given me permission to quote from her website.

AUTHOR'S NOTE

While I was living in Japan, I had no thoughts of writing a book about it. When I came back home to Britain, I had lots of stories to tell, that I wanted to tell.

To my surprise, people I knew, or met, didn't ask me questions or show any real interest in my time in Japan. If I ventured onto the subject, they would say something like, 'Oh, I bet that was interesting,' – pause – and continue, 'have you seen the new supermarket on the edge of town?' Or changed the subject to something similarly commonplace. I realised that it was not that they weren't interested, but that they had no idea of my life there and didn't really know what to ask.

I was frustrated, I never got to tell about my experiences or express my feelings about that time, and as I didn't want to be seen as a bore I clammed up even more than I might ordinarily do. However, I felt a deep longing to talk about it.

This book is the result of that deep longing and is based on my memory, the letters I wrote to friends and family and the aide memoires I made to myself at the time. The two years it has taken me to write has been a time of great happiness whilst I immersed myself in my memories.

I hope the reader will also be interested and entertained enough to be immersed alongside.

CONTENTS

FOREWORD: KIM LONGINOTTO
International Documentary Film Maker

I'm so pleased that Jill Rutherford has written this book about her experiences of this intriguing country and of the strange and extraordinary world that is the Takarazuka Revue Company. With all the odds stacked against her, she succeeded and survived in Japan.

When Jano Williams, my co-filmmaker, showed me an article about the Takarazuka theatre, I was really intrigued. The photos showed extravagant stage sets and glamorous performers in outrageous costumes. I remember one feather costume that looked about 2 metres high! The performers were all women - playing the male parts too. It seemed a perfect subject for a film about the changing roles of young women in Japan. The male role-players looked so confident as they swaggered across the stage in all their arrogant finery. The women playing those parts would have been changed by them, we thought.

I think that one of the most exciting, but also scary, things about making documentary films is that reality always subverts your assumptions. We went to Takarazuka and fell in love with the theatre but it was a much more complex world than we had anticipated. The theatre and its training school were run under a repressive regime. But then the survivors of this theatre school would take to the stage with such luminous beauty and grace.

When we made our film, Dream Girls, we had to embrace these contradictions and go on a journey of discovery. The experience of watching the performances was exhilarating and it was wonderful to see the Japanese women who were playing men looking so assured and powerful, revelling in their own athleticism and talent. The 'females' by contrast were much more held-in and subdued and would play more passive roles; an acutely traditional idea of a woman - in fact the female role-players would say that the 'male' players were able to be much more true to themselves - a wonderful contradiction.

When we were there in 1993, the theatre was run by middle-aged men who would choose the plays and decide the whole tenor of the performances and impose a strict regime of discipline and lifestyle on the performers. But once on stage, the 'male' players danced and sang with such conviction and aplomb that thousands of the female spectators would fall in love with them. Here in the West, we tend to see things as definite opposites. But there, housewives would sneak away from home and fall blissfully in love with their 'perfect men' - beautiful young women looking like the young David Bowie and showing a delicacy and sensitivity they felt was missing from their own men-folk. I could go on forever... Takarazuka intrigued and thrilled me, confounded and confused me. In the 16 years since we made our film, I'm sure that the company has changed a lot, but also that the Takarazuka theatre will still be an inspiring place.

Kim Longinotto

PRONUNCIATION GUIDE

The following tips will help with pronunciation:

a	as in apple
e	as in egg
i	as in eel
o	as in coffee
u	as in the call 'kooee'
ke	as in ketchup
ko	as in coffee
su	as in soup
tsu	as t - plus su as in soup (say quickly)
ou	as in door
ei	as in Kay
yo	as in yoghurt
chi	as in cheek

JAPANESE NAMES and USAGE

Japanese names are written in Japanese order, with the surname first and the given name second.

In their first usage, Japanese words are italicized, but not subsequently. Foreign words which are familiar to English readers are not italicized at all.

PREFACE

Two Ladies In Kimono

Takarazuka, western Japan, 1999.

I first saw them standing in front of a cigarette kiosk. Obviously, I couldn't tell what the two ladies in kimono were thinking. I'm not a mind reader. However, I am intuitive.

The incongruity of seeing these two traditionally and exquisitely dressed Japanese women, who exuded money and elegance, outside a soulless modern cigarette kiosk stays with me still, as does the image of their totally expressionless faces. However, I could feel the tension between them; within them - and tangible, at least to me. Something was amiss.

I watched them as I walked towards the kiosk, it was a matter of seconds but felt much longer. Everything seemed to happen in slow motion, my mind totally absorbed by them, each nuance accentuated by my curiosity and fascination. They had seen me also, but in true Japanese style, they gave no indication of having noticed this foreigner in a town where foreigners are as rare as kimono on a London street.

My eyes never left them as I got closer; it's easy to stare when people don't acknowledge your existence. They were of different generations and the younger woman, attractive and aged around thirty, said something briefly to the older one and without waiting for a reply turned and walked away towards the doors of the department store a few yards ahead. My instinct told me they were mother-in-law and daughter-in-law, as their demeanour suggested the ice of a relationship which should be intimate, but had failed.

The younger woman walked several yards ahead of me and went through the glass doors. She walked on traditional zouri sandals, an inch high, like elegant flip flops. To me, they seemed like an implement of torture. But this lady was a master as her smooth movements made clear. Her kimono only allowed her to take tiny steps but they became gliding, gracious miniature footfalls of infinite grace and beauty, like the smoothness of a humming bird hovering over a flower. Without effort she had moved quickly and I caught a glimpse of her face as she turned slightly towards me as she went through the doors. Again, I felt the tension of a woman close to breaking point, her face not so passive now that her mother-in-law couldn't see her, but only a tiny frown gave any indication of her feelings. It was the tension coming from within her I could feel, vibrations in the air which I absorbed.

During these few seconds, I was also passing close to mother-in-law who was buying several packs of cigarettes. Her kimono was exquisite, her figure slim and elegant, but her face was impassive and hard, accentuated by the ultra bright red lipstick on her long, thin lips, making her look like a badly made puppet. Stiff, unattractive and un-lifelike.

That evening, my friend and I had decided to eat in our hotel's restaurant. We were studying the menu when I felt, rather than saw, someone being sat at the next table. It was some distance away, and as I turned my head slightly to confirm my feelings, they sat down, still exquisite in their kimono, mother-in-law with her reapplied gaping wound of lipstick and daughter-in-law looking even more fraught.

It was during this meal that I developed to a fine art, the act of watching someone without seeming to (a well practiced custom in Japan). My eyes swept over the room regularly but only saw the two ladies in kimono, as I monitored their meal. They didn't speak to each other once during it. Their tension was now so tangible to me that my own stomach tensed and became uncomfortable.

The older woman spoke to the waiter and after he had cleared their dishes, I saw the younger one put her elbows on the table, cup her hands and rest her forehead in them her face looking down into the stark white and un-forgivingly clean tablecloth. She stayed like that for at least ten minutes, no movement discernable, while the older woman sat impassively looking nowhere, at no one, not even her daughter-in-law. But she did light a cigarette. So, the cigarettes were for her! Suddenly, I had a vision of a kimono thrown on a bed smelling strongly of cigarette smoke, stale and sad looking. But this woman looked strong, hard, unforgiving. And absolutely silent.

Without a word, the younger woman got up and left the table. I watched her glide elegantly through the restaurant, her movements still humming bird smooth, her face blank as she left her companion sitting straight backed and expressionless. My heart went out to the departing woman; I felt her pain and unhappiness as I wondered why she felt this way?

What had happened to her? Or, what had she done? What sort of life did she have with this stone statue of a woman for a mother-in-law? Was she really her mother-in-law? If she was, then it was not a question of disliking each other – but of hating each other.

Sadly, I will never know the truth. I didn't see them again, but their impression and little vignette will stay with me forever.

That true story for me, stands as a metaphor. I saw those ladies and wrote about them some ten years ago while on holiday and since then have come to realise that their vignette stands as a metaphor for Japan itself. For the country is a secretive place, tight lipped, blinkered and often cruel, and these things go hand in hand with the most exquisite beauty of sight and manners, and incredible kindness. Secrets and personal views are kept to oneself, even at great cost, while elegance of person and manners and the 'face' presented to the outside world is more important than personal happiness, efficiency and money. At the same time, it engenders fascination and mystery for foreigners looking in.

INTRODUCTION

The How And Why of It

What made two ordinary British women in late middle age cash in their life's savings and go to Japan for one year – and stay for seven?

We were two independent and responsible women who had worked hard all our lives in traditional jobs; administration and the book trade. Not usually the type of person one envisages taking a jump into the unknown without any resources or much hope of achieving our goals. The only things we had on our side were our strong wills, determination to succeed, courage, that we had to continually dig deep for, and a strong desire to live our dream.

How did all this come about? What had pushed us in such an unexpected direction? It may sound odd, but it was an interest in a Japanese theatre group that opened the way to a life change so drastic; so unexpected; and at an age so advanced; that I sometimes wonder whether it happened at all. I was a sensible intelligent woman, living an ordinary British style life, and apart from a general interest in theatre, there was nothing to warn me that an unexpected theatre visit in London would change my life unrecognisably. It was like an epiphany tied up in sequins, feathers, top hats and tails. I seemed to have no control over the events that spiralled me into an unknown world: one in which I had no qualifications to succeed.

This theatre company, called the *Takarazuka Revue Company*, plays a big part in my story. I had gone to Japan to see them in situ, in their own environment, and by chance the box office had sat me next to Ryoko, an ordinary Japanese woman, and that one event changed both our lives and took us into areas of the unknown; pulled and pushed us into undreamed opportunities. For, from that little acorn of a meeting, grew a big oak of dreams realised and ambitions achieved.

I didn't do all this alone, my good friend, Jan came with me and helped me through some of the unfathomable, unexpected, exciting and terrifying things that threw me around in one of the oldest, most puzzling and unadulterated cultures in the world. But the dream was mine and mine alone with Jan willing to help me for one year, after which she returned to Britain. But she too, had fallen under the spells of Japan and returned after eight months to join me again until the end of our adventure, seven years later.

Apart from Ryoko, I had no one in Japan who could help me achieve my dream of living and working there. I knew no influential people, had no qualifications needed to get a job, and as I was not rich, if I were to stay, I had to earn money. This was my dilemma. How does an unqualified and rather gentrified, middle class British woman survive in such an environment? Yet, survive I did, and through the trauma, drama and humour of my seven years there, help came from the most unexpected quarters. My ordinary Japanese friends, acquaintances, and even people I had never met, helped me to achieve my goals, build a Japanese life and succeed in opening my own prosperous and successful English conversation school. They gave me their time, energy and advice unflinchingly, and treated this strange foreigner – as

I'm sure they thought of me – like a wayward niece and took me by the metaphorical hand. Inside the most ordinary Japanese person, it is surprising how often you meet an extraordinary person waiting for the chance to clamber out and spread their wings. We were fledglings together. What we achieved was extraordinary and rare.

So many things happened to me and I met so many amazing people that I wanted to write about it before it got lost. You know when you throw a kiss into the air? It is well meant and much appreciated by the recipient at the time, but it is quickly forgotten and never thought of again. I didn't want my time in Japan to be like a kiss thrown into the air and lost. I wanted to capture and write about the people I met and their lives and passions. For to know the people is to know the culture. Therefore, this book is a vignette of some of the peoples' lives I met there, as they mixed and mingled with mine.

This is also the story of *my* Japan, the one I discovered; of my life there, full of the foibles of the author and the people I met. I've done my best to show the country as I saw it, warts and all. I've written it truthfully and unembellished, as it happened to me, funny or sad, poignant or silly – it's those human things in all of us that make a country and its culture.

I've sometimes offered my own conclusions about the country, but I emphasise that they are my own opinions and nothing else. This book is not meant to be an academic book nor an analysis of Japanese culture, although I do offer some of my own thoughts as I try to work out how and why certain things happened to me.

CHAPTER ONE

The Takarazuka Theatre

Strange things happen in life, which can change it forever but be insignificant at the time. They are of no importance and you don't give them a second thought until later when the events they unleash become clear. That insignificant seed for me was a television programme, although what was even stranger was that I rarely watched TV at that time. It was one of those odd coincidences that make you wonder about fate and your role in it.

At that time of my life, it was 1994 and I was 45 years old, I came home from work that particular evening tired and lack lustre and put on the TV and channel hopped. By an extraordinary quirk of fate, I stopped on BBC2 at the start of a thirty second clip advertising a programme to be shown later that evening. It was from a series of programmes about cultural oddities that happen in countries around the world and this one was about a theatre company in Japan. I was intrigued and decided to record it for later viewing. That was a decision that changed my life so utterly and completely and led me into the most interesting, mysterious and fascinating world that is Japan.

The programme was about a unique theatre company, called The Takarazuka Revue Company. All the performers are women, who play both the male and female roles on stage; each performer specialising in either male or female parts. It's big business in Japan with over 420 players performing drama, comedy and revues nonstop all year round in its home town of Takarazuka in western Japan, Tokyo and out on tour. The women who play the male parts are idolised and revered by millions of women fans throughout the country. A whole town has been built up around the theatre and developed because of it, with thousands of people depending on it for their livelihood. They also have their own TV station devoted to their shows. It is a unique and fascinating place in a unique and fascinating country. For me, the Takarazuka theatre represents the quirky Japanese attitude to life.

The theatre encourages the male impersonators, called *otokoyaku* in Japanese, to be sexy to attract the ordinary Japanese housewives who make up most of the audience. The fact that they are being attracted by a woman playing a man doesn't enter into it, as many of these housewives don't even consider the performer as female. On stage, they represent men; therefore, they are men in their eyes. However, the otokoyaku is as unlike an ordinary Japanese man as you can get, for they are usually kind, considerate, good looking and respect their womenfolk and give them importance and value – something the ordinary Japanese husband doesn't normally do. For the Japanese housewives who are fans of Takarazuka, this makes the enchantment complete and the Takarazuka theatre is regarded as mainstream family entertainment with generations of families going to see the shows together. Grandmothers, mothers and children, with only the occasional man enjoying the shows. It has something for everyone and everyone sees it differently, that's one of the joys of it. It can entrance the adult woman whilst at the same time, fascinate and entertain her children. It's regarded as a 'woman's theatre'. A theatre by women for women, although often, the back of the stalls are filled with hundreds of school children (boys and girls) whose schools organise trips to the theatre as a special treat. The shows that are generally put on are seen as upholding traditional Japanese family values where the hero always wins and the bad guy gets his comeuppance. Also, the performers themselves must be seen to be upstanding citizens in their personal lives. The performers work extremely hard and it's a restrictive and disciplined life for them, but the rewards outweigh the sacrifice for most. It's a respectable and honourable profession and many young women aspire to become a *takarajienne*. In a country that automatically subjugates its women as a matter of course, the Takarazuka theatre offers the chance for women to become powerful and have professional success, status and a career that gives them opportunities, security and adulation. This must be a very heady mix for the Takarazuka stars and many of the fans will experience this vicariously by supporting them.

Take a pinch of Follies-Bergère, Hollywood and Broadway musicals, couple it with Japanese imagination and flair for taking a concept and improving it, and you will have an idea of the spectacular shows one sees on stage as a matter of course. Imagine the women who play the roles of men idolised more obsessively by their fans than Hollywood film stars, with fan clubs who sacrifice themselves for their stars, spending all their money, time and energy supporting that star, and you will only have an inkling of the strange phenomenon of Takarazuka in Japan.

It was into this world that I was to step and live for seven years. Forever an outsider, because I was a foreigner, but nevertheless, involved on its periphery. I was also involved in the life of Japan, for the country is also a phenomenon. A strange, mysterious and compelling place. It has a seductive quality that draws visitors into its embrace.

These two worlds led me into unknown waters and changed my life forever. Beforehand, I had no interest in Japan, with its urban sprawl, overcrowding and industrialisation, even pictures of *geisha* parading in the streets, stunning cherry blossoms and picturesque food, didn't clip a nerve of interest in me. It wasn't until I set foot on Japanese soil that I fell and tumbled uncontrollably under its spells.

I was fortunate to share this passion with Jan. She's tall and slim, friendly with a ready smile and looked fifteen years younger than the sixty she had lived with the energy levels of a forty year old; always polite, sensible and serious, with an interest in politics and world affairs. Fortunately, she also had a lighter side which fuelled a fire of interest, that turned into a passion for the Takarazuka theatre and Japan to match my own. She was pivotal to me as she gave me a great deal of support and encouragement through all my ambitions and dreams of living and working in Japan.

Of course, my duel passions for Japan and the Takarazuka theatre didn't happen instantly. There were steps to be gone through, although it didn't take long for the first step to show itself as another quirk of fate awaited me. A couple of weeks after I had watched the TV programme and had virtually forgotten about it, Jan bought a newspaper. Normally, she didn't buy one, but for some reason she couldn't fathom, she bought one that day. In it was an advertisement for the Takarazuka Revue Company who were coming to London to perform for two weeks at the London Coliseum. As I had shown the video recording of the TV programme to Jan, she was as intrigued by it as I was. A quick discussion ensued and next day, we booked our seats to see the Saturday evening show. Having been a lover of theatre all my life, I was half way to meeting the Takarazuka theatre, but nothing had prepared me for the high speed extravaganza of glitz, glitter, feathers, sequins, kimono, cherry blossoms, evening dresses, top hats and tails that flew before me during that performance. Three hours of high level, energetic entertainment of song, dance and story left me breathless with excitement. At the end, I thought the roof would blow off the applause was so thunderous. The next week, we were both back to watch the last performance, we just couldn't keep away. I was worried that the show would not live up to my enhanced memories of it, but it didn't let me down and if anything, was even more wondrous than the first time round as I noticed so many other things happening that I had missed before. And do you know what? I really do think that the roof was raised up at the end of the final performance!

It was back to ordinary life for the next four years, with Takarazuka again a dim and distant memory. However, yet again, fate seemed to take a hand, when I met some people who had just returned from a holiday in Japan. Whilst there, they had taken the opportunity of visiting the Takarazuka theatre, having seen the London production, and brought back eleven videos of their shows. I was able to copy them to view at my leisure. That was the final step in my Takarazuka induction. I was hooked. I was able to understand more fully the size of the theatre company and the diversity of shows it put on, ranging from historical romances, great wars of bygone days, western musicals like *West Side Story, Guys 'n Dolls,* intermingled with Japanese historical stories involving Shoguns and samurai. I also realised that many of the performers were of world class talent and ability. As a general rule, give Takarazuka performers a world class production and they will give a world class performance, in their own unique style of course.

*

Finally, Jan and I decided to go to Japan for a holiday to watch some Takarazuka and get the flavour of the country. Whilst there, to my surprise, I also developed a passion for the country and people as well as for the theatre company, falling willingly under their enchantments. So much so that I wanted to go there to live, to experience Japanese life to the full. Every holiday I spent there (five in two and a half years), I was heartbroken at having to leave and took my body home but left my spirit there – the Japanese government only being interested in my body!

However, there was a major problem. If I lived in Japan I would need to work, but jobs for foreigners were closely controlled, and the only job open for most is teaching English. For that you need a university degree, alas, neither Jan nor I had one. But I wasn't so easily put off, and having every door resoundingly closed in my face by the authorities, I decided to go for a year's holiday. Japan was like a persistent itch that had got under my skin and the only time I could scratch it was in Japan itself. The odds were stacked heavily against me, many people said I was crazy and that I should give up the idea of fulfilling my dream. But I couldn't let it go. I wanted to experience the 'real' Japan, to understand more of its complex and fascinating culture. Fortunately, I persuaded Jan to come with me. I wasn't brave enough to go on my own. She was as entranced with Japan as I was and as keen to go. It was our moment of madness, of throwing all caution to the wind. We had our doubts of course, but decided not to air them too fully because once you do, they have a habit of increasing like weeds in a flower bed. So we went to Japan for our year's holiday, for if I was not allowed to work there I would jolly well go to live there for as long as I could.

CHAPTER TWO

Meeting Ryoko

The start of something, whatever it is, can be an exhausting business, and moving to Japan for a one year holiday was no exception. If I had known that I would stay for seven, I would have taken another suitcase. As it was, I struggled out of Kansai airport in Osaka, Japan's second most important city after Tokyo, with my one suitcase and almost collapsed as the debilitating heat of a Japanese summer attacked my body. It was difficult to breath the polluted air; the humidity seemed to soak into me and sigh as if it was snuggling in for a snooze. Jan and I were like foreigners to the slaughter, the slaughter of a Japanese high summer on my fifty year old body and Jan's sixty year old one.

We had been given advice from our Japanese friend, Ryoko, who told us that we should not start our adventure in the high heat and humidity of a Japanese August.

"It's too much to bear," she had said. In our ignorance we decided that we knew best, and now we had to pay the price for that flippant attitude.

Our year's holiday started in August 2000, but we had met Ryoko by chance about eighteen months earlier during one of our holidays and became friends, although I had no idea at this stage just how important she would be to me. She is typically Japanese, small and slim with stylish short, black hair that turns auburn in the sunlight. She was in her early thirties at this time, full of life, energy and vigour, hyper almost. Beautiful, sophisticated and modern, while at the same time, she has a beauty of face, posture and grace that has come down through the ages in that gentle and unassuming tradition of Japanese women. She is always laughing, especially when we are together as we share the same sense of humour, but at the same time she has an aura of serenity around her that disguises her courage and determination to improve herself and achieve her dreams. This was hidden in true Japanese style by her gentle ways and one had to get to know her to appreciate her core inner strength. Being a stranger in a country I didn't understand, she was a friend made in heaven for me as she gave me the most precious gifts anyone can give, her time and good will; generously.

We first met Ryoko during the second holiday to Japan that Jan and I took in 1998, when we found ourselves sitting next to her in the Takarazuka theatre. Jan was next to Ryoko's daughter Mika chan, three years old but already a fan as she sat there motionless, her eyes glued to the stage in awe and wonder. At the end of the show, Jan turned towards Mika chan, and smiled at her. This was all the encouragement Ryoko needed.

"Are you tourists?" she asked Jan.

"No, we're fans of Asaji Saki san," who was the top star of the show we had just watched. Ryoko started with surprise at this, and recovering her composure said in astonishment, "You know about Asaji Saki san?"

Jan smiled and said, "Yes, we've come from Britain especially to see her. We're very big fans of hers." At this, Ryoko stared at us in wonder. I'm sure she was thinking what strange creatures are these, who have come to see a theatre performer in Japan, but at the same time, she was intrigued and excited by it. As we made our way out of the theatre, we chatted with Ryoko, Mika chan's hand in hers.

Mika chan was very pretty and the epitome of cute. Small, perfectly proportioned and delicate looking, as her mother. Everyone dresses formally, whatever the occasion and Mika chan was no exception. Pretty dress, which was high waisted, making the white top look like a bolero, matching perfectly with the dark, velvet of the rest of the dress. Long white socks, black shiny shoes like the ones I used to wear as a child, no trainers for her. Her long hair parted into two plaits tied with pink ribbons. She was formal in her manner, polite and perfectly behaved, like most Japanese children. I often used to wonder what Japanese mothers did to their children to make them so well behaved. What was the secret? I would have liked to bottle it and send it back home.

We continued chatting together and I realised that I did not want this conversation to end, so took a deep breath and made a suggestion to this stranger, this beautiful woman with her daughter's hand in hers. It was nothing extraordinary, rather mundane in fact, but it was a suggestion that changed all our lives forever. I suggested that we go for a cup of coffee and continue our chat, if she had the time. Fortunately, she was delighted, the attraction and interest reciprocal, but she didn't accept my invitation. Instead, she said the words that I was to hear so often in Japan, the words that always made me so angry. She said that she would have to, 'ask her husband', who was waiting for her downstairs.

We exited the theatre, our feet sinking into the thick red carpet of the stairs and foyer which in turn leads on to a select mall with cafes, restaurants, seating areas and gift shops. Two thousand five hundred people can be seated in the theatre, with ten shows performed every six days (closed on Wednesdays). The theatre is mostly full every sitting. It's big business. There are millions of women fans throughout Japan, many of them travelling from other parts of the country to see their favourite stars.

The Takarazuka theatre follows the western fashion of the nineteenth and early part of the twentieth century, when it was popular to have women performing as men. It still thrives here, in this corner of western Japan, where it first started in 1913 in a small spa town called Takarazuka, at the foot of the mountains in the middle of nowhere. From there, the nowhere started to become somewhere as people flocked to this isolated area to see the shows. The somewhere started to become valuable as people wanted to live near the theatre and many people moved into the small town to set up family businesses to cater for the fans.

The fans grew, the traders grew, the town grew and the theatre grew. From a start of around a dozen girls in their early teens, the theatre was originally called, The Takarazuka Girls' Opera, the theatre grew and employs over 420 performers today. All of them work constantly. The town is now one of the most sought after places to live in this part of Japan. It is affluent, cosy, expensive, pretty (for Japan) and relies heavily on the theatre for its survival. It's my favourite place as there's always a buzz of excitement in the air especially an hour or so before every show, when fans exit the train station en masse and take the five minute walk to the theatre along the Hana no Michi (Flower Road) with its scores of cherry blossom trees lining every inch and the masses of flowers below them all gently bobbing for one's attention. It's a road of beauty and calmness in this country of high speed living. The fans themselves are also calm, like nuns going to mass. They all seem to glide serenely towards the theatre, no one speaking loudly or being exuberant, most dressed formally with designer labels in predominance. Everyone is perfectly behaved, respectful of others, but underneath, one can feel the excitement within. For a Takarazuka fan is usually a passionate fan, albeit in that understated, calm, Japanese way.

The theatre has a very interesting history. It was started by a railway company called the Hankyu railway. The founder of the railway, Mr Kobayashi, had built a railway from Osaka into the countryside to link up with a small spa at the foot of the mountains in Takarazuka, which is about twenty miles from Osaka. It was the end of Mr Kobayashi's line, but unfortunately, not many people were using it and he needed something to encourage them. Being a great lover of western theatre, such as the Follies-Bergère, he started his own theatre modelled on western revue. As they had nowhere to perform, the theatre started its life at a swimming pool. From there, they eventually built a theatre, which has been rebuilt and expanded several times. Over the years, Takarazuka has developed its own unique version of popular, western style theatre, and for most people there's no half way measures. You either love it or hate it.

Loving the Takarazuka theatre as both Jan and I do, we were doubly delighted to meet Ryoko, who was also a fan and, we felt instinctively, was a nice, decent woman, but more than that, she could speak English. The day we met her the foyer was crowded with women, their high pitched voices like the raucous babble of excited starlings, the after-show buzz animating everyone. It was difficult to find her husband with all the women milling around but we found him eventually, waiting patiently beside one of the foyer's formidable cream coloured pillars. He was very handsome and looked more like a film star than a husband, dressed in an expensive mustard coloured shirt and white slacks. His upright carriage, composure and slim figure cutting a dash amongst the hurly burly of the foyer. Black hair parted in the middle, in the latest Japanese style, aged about 30, he looked a million dollars.

He glared at her watching us approach. His wife and child escorting two strange and large (in comparison to them) foreigners. Foreigners, even today, are not that common in this part of Japan and at that time, they were rare. Therefore, I think that Kenji san was registering shock more than disapproval. At least, that's what I hoped.

He said something fast and strong to Ryoko, who giggled with her hand automatically going up and covering her mouth, Japanese style. Oh dear, I thought, this is the end of a possible friendship. But I was wrong. Kenji san was just being Kenji san, and cracking a joke. He has a droll sense of humour I was to discover. Ryoko spoke to him in rapid Japanese, smiling all the time and nodding towards us. Kenji san listened intently, he laughed, nodded, looked at his watch, spoke back to Ryoko in mild, gentle tones.

Ryoko introduced us and Kenji san bowed, holding his handbag in front of him like a shield. Like many Japanese men, he carried a man's handbag. Soft leather, small and long, no handle, like a clutch bag. He was the picture of elegance, and like his daughter, he wore shiny, stylish shoes. No trainers for him either.

He spoke to us in Japanese, as he spoke no English, and pointed to the coffee shop behind him. We settled ourselves inside and had lots of questions we wanted to ask each other. Ryoko, sitting upright with her ramrod straight back, popped her head on one side in that way of hers, with a smile and in halting English said, "Why do you like Takarazuka?"

I laughed, "Yes, people often ask me why I like Takarazuka so much. It's a hard question and there are many reasons." I gathered my thoughts and made a start, hoping that she would be able to understand me.

"At first," I continued, "I was attracted to the novelty of having an all woman cast, and was fascinated by that and how it alters the performances and the way one perceives things. As a general rule women cannot usually be as aggressive as men even when they try to be, and therefore, even if it's a story about war or violence, it's gentle and any aggression shown is soft compared to men's performances on stage and I found that appealing. And then, the more shows I saw, the more I realised that it is deliciously old fashioned. The shows are like old Hollywood musicals, full of wonderful tunes which actually have melodies that please the ear. It's relaxing compared to real life, and most shows have a happy ending, and all is right with the world." I paused, gathering my thoughts again, while Ryoko was following my every movement with great intensity. I carried on, "It's a place apart, like a dream world where you never run the risk of having a nightmare. It sweeps you along in a bubble of make believe and encourages you to leave the real world behind when you step through the doors of the theatre. It sells itself as the 'theatre of dreams' and that it certainly is. Also, many of the performers are world class in their own specialised way. It's very interesting to see how performances differ between them and their personalities can come through. It's almost unheard of in our theatres to have a cast of eighty performers in every show and that gives the performances great excitement and intensity, especially in the revues. It's the revues I really love, they lift me up into a different world and leave me feeling elated. The glamour and sparkle of it, the skill of delivery with the wonderful singing and dancing, everyone knowing their right place and no one falling over each other, for as you know, the stage can get very crowded sometimes. It's a skill I marvel at every time."

Ryoko, I'm pleased to say, followed this rather complicated (for her) answer.

"Yes, I see," she said slowly. "I can understand your view of Takarazuka, but how did you know about Takarazuka and Asaji Saki san? I'm very intrigued by this."

"I saw a TV programme about it in 1994," I explained. "It was a documentary about different cultural aspects in countries around the world, and for Japan, they'd chosen a documentary about the Takarazuka theatre called *Dream Girls* made by two English women, Kim Longinotto and Jano Williams. Seeing that programme changed my life."

"Changed your life?" Ryoko said, with eyebrows raising.

"Yes, because I had no interest in Japan before and I had never had the desire to visit it, but now, I'm a dedicated fan of the Takarazuka theatre and this is my second visit here in eight months. I've fallen in love with Takarazuka and with Japan, and I already want to come back again for another visit soon."

"You had a dream to come to Japan and watch Takarazuka," she said earnestly. "Was it easy to come to Japan for you?"

"No, it was very difficult for both of us because we don't speak the language and neither Jan nor I are rich people, so we had to save very hard because Japan is an expensive country. It was difficult and somewhat traumatic, but I am here because I just couldn't stay away. I just *had* to come. It has become a great passion for me. I think I can say that Jan feels the same way as I do." I looked over at Jan as she nodded her agreement.

"You're living your dream," Ryoko said in a slow and wistful way. "How I envy you. To live your dream is wonderful."

"I hadn't thought about it exactly like that, but I suppose you're right, yes, I think we're living our dream." I pondered this thought for a moment, in fact, we all did.

Silently gazing into space, reflecting on our dreams, was the moment that cemented our tenuous acquaintance; that turned us into embryonic friends. For we all had dreams and an overriding desire to fulfil them. We recognised ourselves in each other.

It started the most amazing and incredible friendship. Ryoko became my mentor, advisor, critic, business partner and more than anything else, best friend. Also Kenji san became our sponsor. A fateful meeting indeed. But at this time, it was all in the future and unknown. Now, this day, we only had one thing on our minds.

In three days time it was to be the retirement show of Asaji Saki san. After sixteen years in the Takarazuka Revue Company, she was to retire, because this is a young person's theatre. The work of performing demands the three disciplines of acting, singing and dancing, but once performers hit their middle thirties, they are 'encouraged' to retire from the theatre as they are usually no longer able to keep up the energy levels and dancing skills needed. A little bit like ballet dancers, they have a best before date. It also gives a chance for the younger performers to climb up the pecking order.

Asaji Saki san was a male impersonator, an otokoyaku. She only played male roles and had trained for the role of a male from the age of sixteen, when she entered the Takarazuka Music School to train to be a *takarajienne*, which is what a Takarazuka performer is called. The young women who enter the music school are usually aged between 16 and 18. They go through a vigorous and militaristic training for two years in all the performing arts. It's hard, demanding, and they have to devote their life to it. It's not for the faint hearted.

Tickets for any top star's *Sayonara* show are like gold dust. There are only two such shows, so only 2,500 people can get in to see it in the Takarazuka theatre and another 1,750 people in the Tokyo theatre. Unbelievably, Jan and I had high hopes of tickets for this show, but we were awaiting confirmation. The ticketing system for Takarazuka is complex and indecipherable to foreigners, at least it was for us, and it took us about five years to finally resolve it into logical sequences. Ryoko took us by surprise when she said that she and Mika chan had tickets. Therefore, we arranged to meet three days later for lunch at the same coffee shop before the show started at 1.00pm. All the shows in Takarazuka are daytime shows because most of their fans are housewives, and that's when they are usually free.

On the day of Saki san's Sayonara show, Jan and I joined the excited throng of fans walking up the Hana no Michi, which always gave me a thrill, and when we got to the theatre, we were amazed to find thousands of fans milling around. Far too many to fit into the theatre. Some of them were camped out around the periphery. It was very hot as it was the beginning of August, the killer month of 30-35 degrees centigrade coupled with heavy humidity to weigh it down. It's the humidity that really knocks you out. It saps energy levels like a leaking sieve.

We met Ryoko and family as arranged and went into the coffee shop. Ryoko did her best to order something edible for us. Both Jan and I are vegetarians and found, to our astonishment and disappointment that this Buddhist country, this land of healthy food like fish and rice, was now in an out of control spiral of thinking that meat is good. 'We must eat meat every meal'. In restaurants, the choice is usually between meat, for meat read beef or pork, some sort of fish, shellfish or shrimps. We ordered rice with shrimps, ate the rice and gave the shrimps to Ryoko and Kenji san. It was then we discovered that the Japanese love to share food.

After lunch, we were due to meet our 'mole' in the ticket office. Before each holiday to Takarazuka, we had written to the theatre and asked them if we could buy tickets for the shows prior to our arrival, offering to pay by bank transfers or credit card. A simple business one would think, it was the ticket office after all, but we never received a reply and always arrived in Takarazuka without any tickets, having no choice but to adopt a hope for the best attitude. Each time we went to the box office to make enquiries, a Mr Suzuki would appear and magically produce two tickets for us which were invariably for good seats in the stalls. Although he never replied to our letters, 'too difficult', he told us, he always obtained two tickets for the dates we had stipulated. Although, of course, we didn't know it at the time, which caused us considerable stress.

Buying tickets for Takarazuka shows can be very nerve wracking for confused foreigners, and for a Sayonara show, doubly so. Suzuki san had told us he would do his best, sucking his teeth to emphasise the difficulty of obtaining tickets for such a show, 'but he couldn't promise'. Therefore, with that hope for the best feeling in our stomachs, we climbed the stairs to the box office at the appointed time, which was 12.50pm. The show started at 1.00pm. We usually got our tickets at 12.30pm on the day of the performance. Why did Suzuki san tell us to come this late? What was happening?

We got to the box office and asked at the desk for Suzuki san, *onegai shimasu*. Mr Suzuki please. We knew him quite well by this time as he had been given the job of dealing with us, the foreigners, as he spoke some rather fractured English and none of the other staff could speak any at all. I'm not sure if he relished this job, I think not really, because it seemed to make him rather nervous and I know that his colleagues ribbed and teased him about it.

But, reluctantly or not, Suzuki san duly appeared from the back office and asked us to wait. 12.52pm, 12.55pm. Please hurry. What's the problem? He fiddled about in drawers and cupboards and finally, took us to the end of the counter, away from the other customers who were queuing and hoping for tickets.

"We don't want them to know that you are getting tickets from us," he said in a conspiratorial voice. "I don't think they would like it". I looked over to the queue of about thirty people, all looking a little frazzled and frowning our way.

Suzuki san whispered, "Let me go first, then follow me downstairs after thirty seconds." He was flushed and looked anxious. His anxiety fed itself into my veins as surely as a blood transfusion, and I paled considerably. I grew more nervous, wondering whether we were going to be attacked? Mobbed? Would people try to steal our tickets from our grasp? Would we actually get any tickets?

Of course, follow him we did, as he disappeared into the distance like the rabbit in *Alice in Wonderland*. We couldn't keep up, he really was moving apace. We approached the long escalator as he got off the other end and disappeared into the throng of people in the main foyer. We saw him turn left, but when we got to the end of the escalator, we couldn't see him in the crowd. We continued walking left, and suddenly my arm was grabbed by Suzuki san who was standing hard up against the wall. He looked up at us and said, "Eleven thousand yen," out of the corner of his mouth.

I said, "Pardon." He repeated it, a little louder in English with his thick Japanese accent, "Eleven thousand yen. For the tickets," he added quickly. I felt something press gently into my groin area and I looked down astonished to see a long white envelope was waving back and forth at the end of his fingers.

"We have tickets?" I gasped, overjoyed.

"Yes, I got them for you, it was very hard, but I got them. I couldn't let the other people know because they have been waiting all night to get tickets like these, they are returns, people who have bought the tickets but at the last minute cannot come."

"Oh." So that's how he got our tickets each time.

Jan and I rummaged in our purses for the eleven thousand yen. We didn't know at this stage that one was supposed to pre-prepare one's ticket money in a pretty envelope ready for a quick handover. Therefore, in our clumsy western way, we rummaged for the money and came up with the correct amount, thank goodness: there would have been traumas if we had to have change.

He passed the white envelope from his groin area to mine and said, "Don't let anyone see me give you these tickets," his eyes swivelling sideways and back to me, as I felt the envelope wiggle around.

"No," I said bemused, "No, of course not." I took the envelope from our private places and then I gave the game away by bowing to him and saying a profuse thank you.

But he had already gone. Back to the escalator and the queues of people waiting for returns. Most of them would be disappointed, but not us. Another gigantic leap of faith had paid off without mishap.

We got to our seats in the dark as the show had already started. The formula is always the same. Starting with a play lasting about one and a half hours, which could be a modern play or an adaptation of historical stories, followed by an interval of thirty minutes and then a revue of about an hour. As the plays are all in Japanese and difficult for us to understand, we were fans of the revue. A spectacular performance of high speed song and dance extravaganzas. One's senses are bombarded with colour, action, music and extravagant costumes, at the end of which the grand finale takes place, and all eighty or so performers in the show descend the extraordinary Takarazuka staircase, which appears on stage as if by magic at the end of each show. It fills the stage with its 40 or so steep and narrow steps and looks incredibly dangerous, but the performers dance along it with impressive abandon, smiles fixed and eyes straight ahead, and I have only ever seen one mishap, where a performer got her foot caught in her long dress and fortunately slipped backwards, rather than forwards. Only her dignity suffered. Performing on this staircase is a skill for which they should get Oscars.

In a flurry of lights, feathers, sequins and fantastic costumes the performers will parade down this staircase and along the front of the stage to the accompaniment of suitably stirring music. This will last for five minutes or so, at the end of which, the final curtain will come down to the sweet habit the performers have of waving to the audience as the curtain falls. It always left me breathless and in awe.

For a takarajienne, it's a demanding life, but one that can give its equal in rewards. It's one of the reasons I love this theatre, for it gives women a chance to be something and achieve something in this land of male dominance.

Sayonara shows, which usually only top stars are entitled to, are performed after the normal show. It is paid for by the star herself and includes her favourite numbers from her shows as a top star. Together with her troupe, she will perform for about forty minutes or so, enabling the fans to reminisce and shed any tears they want to, for tears are a frequent friend at Sayonara shows. After the show is finished the star takes her many bows, makes a speech, is presented with flowers, sheds some tears, takes more curtain calls, until finally, it's over. All she has to do now is leave the theatre for the last time.

Asaji Saki san was known for her dancing, She was a superb mover, her grace, elegance and strong character defining her role as a male impersonator. What you have to understand about a Takarazuka otokoyaku is that the player is not meant to be a substitute man. The idea is that she takes the best part of maleness and combines it with the best part of femaleness. The grace and elegance of the female must be combined with the authority and strength of the male. The Takarazuka otokoyaku epitomises the ideal Japanese man in the eyes of the female Takarazuka fans.

The show over, we met up with Ryoko and family in the coffee shop. We were all in a state of high excitement and settled down to await the final departure of our star from the theatre. That was why there were so many fans gathered outside, they were waiting for her so that they could say a final goodbye. Thousands of fans were lined up around the pathways and the concourse of the theatre, many of them spilling out onto the road outside for as far as the eye could see. We waited in the cool of the air conditioning in the cafe, looking out of their large windows onto the sea of fans outside, and where we knew Saki san would walk past later, but soon it was closing and we were asked to leave. Kenji san, who had not seen the show but met us afterwards, decided to be chivalrous and had a discussion with the staff, asking if we could stay in the cafe although it was closed. This cafe fronted onto the foyer of the theatre, which was still open, and had no internal walls or doors. Just a few pot plants to make a barrier between the foyer and the cafe, and a rope with a 'Closed' sign was all that was needed to keep people out. Everyone respected that it was not their space to invade, and nobody did. To stay inside, in the cool, was a life saver for Jan and me as we hadn't adapted to the intense heat. I think Kenji san was afraid we would faint if we had to wait outside for a couple of hours.

A fan will usually stay loyal to her performer from start to finish, fickleness is not encouraged, and if you belong to your star's fan club, then you will be expected to 'do your bit' to support your star. Attend her tea parties, wait for her at the stage door, send her flowers and presents, write her letters of support, buy her promotional material and mementoes, videos, DVDs etc. The more products a star can sell in the gift shops, the more the management understand that they should keep employing her, although one of the major ways the management gauge the popularity of a star is by the number of flowers she is sent by fans. On opening and closing day of each show especially, expensive bouquets of flowers, orchids and the like are sent to the stage door addressed to the performer of choice. In fact, Takarazuka town's nickname is 'Flower Town', and you see rivers of flowers everywhere. The cafes and restaurants have many baskets and bouquets of flowers outside and inside their premises. After all, if you get a few hundred bouquets sent to you in one day, what do you do with them? You can't take them all home. Therefore, the fans spend a fortune on sending flowers, and then spend the evening, once the number of bouquets have been counted, taking them around to their favourite eating places. 'A gift for you'. Don't come to Takarazuka town if you suffer from hay fever, it will cripple you.

At last, our star appeared for her final walk as a takarajienne. She made her way from the back of the theatre on her journey down the pathways to the main concourse where her car was waiting. Security consisted of one old man who walked near her and a young woman, her fan club 'boss', who led the way. This is Japan. Security is not an issue because every one of her fans knew that they must not approach her or try to touch her. The golden rule of Takarazuka. Respect the performers' privacy and dignity, or else be ostracised. That's one of the reasons I think performers are a bit scared of foreign fans. You cannot guarantee what they will do or how they will react. Rightly so. They do not understand the rules that the Japanese play by – or if they do, they are not constrained by them.

These final moments are heart wrenching for loyal fans, and Saki san's fans were no exception. This is one time when the fans can let their hair down and behave like screaming groupies. They take advantage of this permitted lax in decorum and when she came into sight, a huge scream went up as nearly a thousand women who were nearest to her let out their emotions and screamed out her name and things like, '*Mariko san* (her nickname), *ai shiteru.*' Mariko san, I love you. They jumped up and down, waved frantically, screamed their adoration and sayonara. The noise of so many screaming women felt like razors in my inner ear. Saki san, in her turn, never lost her dignity, elegance or her delight in waving back, until finally it was time for her to get in her car and drive past the many fans lining the road outside. Again, there was no security whatsoever, no one misbehaved and Saki san was able to make her slow progress driving by the fans, waving and acknowledging them without any worry about safety. It's one of the things I love about Japan, the absolute confidence that people have in others to behave in a respectable, responsible and unselfish manner. It's a joy.

There is nothing to compare with the phenomenon of the Takarazuka theatre. It is unique. It is also a world of two halves. The performers and the fans. The two depend on each other for survival, although they are completely separate. The gods and the worshippers. Divided from each other, but both living in a world of fantasy. To see the dedication of the fans who belong to fan clubs is to marvel at the amount of time and money they devote to their star.

We made a point of watching the national television news that night. Saki san's retirement would be on it. Takarazuka is that big.

CHAPTER THREE

Living in Japan

During the first week of our year's stay, our priority was to find a flat to live in so that we did not lose a big chunk of our money on hotel bills. Ryoko helped us with everything. Before we arrived, she had chosen many suitable properties in the area we wanted to live in and all we had to do was to view them and say yes or no.

In the company and car of a rental agent, youngish, extremely affable, with so much boundless energy you could feel it in the air around him – and whom Ryoko had carefully chosen – we went in the terrible heat and humidity, to view flat after flat. Unfortunately, we had to say a sad, 'No, sorry, not suitable', for two full days. Even though we were travelling around in the agent's car, which had air conditioning, Jan and I were wilting under the pressure of the heat. However, with great joy, at the very end of the second day, with my energy level so low, it wouldn't even fill a finger, we finally saw one that would suit us.

Our priorities were that the flat be a reasonable rent and in a quiet position in a good area. This flat fulfilled that criteria and was on the top floor of a three floor block, at the end of the block and away from the small sparsely used road, making it semi detached and quiet. All our needs were met and we were happy.

We had been looking in an area along an eight mile

strip between Nishinomiya Kitaguchi and Takarazuka, following the Hankyu railway line – we didn't want to be far from the railway as that was our major means of transport. All of this area looked much the same, and had been farmland prior to the coming of the Hankyu railway. Now it is a non-stop mass of concrete; roads; houses; apartment blocks, shops and railway lines. All jammed in extremely close proximity to one another. You really have to get on with your neighbours in such a place. There is hardly a green square to be found that isn't someone's garden. Public parks and play areas are few and when you do find them, they are the size of a postage stamp – but they are an oasis for wildlife, teeming with birds and insects which often made me gasp in surprise at the abundance of butterflies, cicadas and birds flying around. At night, small bats would come out from the roofs of people's houses via overflow pipes or air bricks – you could actually see them – and fill the air with the little flutters of their wings if you listened hard enough.

The houses varied between the older traditional style with smallish gardens, interspersed with new ones, of varying quality and attractiveness, which sported minuscule gardens and finally, blocks of modern flats, almost universally uninteresting. As all the local roads are extremely narrow, parking is off road, with people giving up their precious garden space to car hard standings. Every house has one, even the smallest. There are no pavements except on main roads, with people and traffic mingling together without animosity, each accepting the others right be there (what else could they do?)

Cutting through this concrete civilization were many wide river channels gouged deep into the ground. They started up in the mountains that surrounded this area sweeping down in a more or less straight line to the sea, some ten miles distant, slicing communities in half. They were like slashes of nature and a total necessity for wildlife and people, the latter of whom would walk up and down these riverbanks with their dogs, or jog or take the children for a walk or have a family picnic or barbeque. It got very crowded down there sometimes. I realised later that there was a normal river nearby and that these extra channels were dry for most of the year and brought into use in the rainy season where they became flash flood channels with thunderous water rushing down them in a ferocious fight to get to the sea. The power of that water was awesome with the river beds going from dry to full flow river in a matter of hours. It was nature in the raw in the middle of a concrete civilisation, controlled by man, but at the same time uncontrollable. Many a time I used to stand on one of the bridges and watch the power of the water.

It was just past one of these channels that we found our flat, not far from a small pedestrian bridge joining the two halves of the community. But the glory of this area is that although, in reality, it is a concrete jungle, every opportunity is taken to plant trees and shrubs, which abounded along roads and in everyone's (yes everyone's) gardens, softening up the views and making one feel human.

We had to have a sponsor for the flat, someone who would vouch for and accept responsibility for us. We had initially thought that Ryoko would do this, but we discovered that as she was a housewife, albeit with a part-time job and income, she was barred from becoming our sponsor. Although women are still considered second class citizens, (picture Britain circa 1950s) things are improving slowly for Japanese women and they have achieved the status of being eligible to sponsor someone if they earn a sufficient salary. The fact that most women are housewives or on a low salary which automatically disqualifies them is not an issue to most of the men in government. The law is there even if the social pressures mean it is not relevant to most women's lives. Fortunately for us, her husband, Kenji san, disobeyed his father's strong advice, which was, 'Never become a sponsor of another person, it can ruin your life'. Kenji san had held this advice high in his esteem throughout his life, and had never sponsored anyone until he met us and took the difficult decision to throw off his caution and sponsor two foreign women he hardly knew. It was a gigantic leap of faith for him, but he had trust and faith in his judgement of our character. That was enough.

We had also made a gigantic leap of faith by trusting Ryoko and Kenji san. We all knew, instinctively I think, that we could depend on each other. We had identified that our inner core values were similar, and that we could trust one another, even though we didn't know the other well in person. We were all taking a huge risk, but especially Kenji san because he would be held responsible for absolutely everything we did in Japan, financial as well as moral. He was an ordinary salary man (an office worker) in a design company, and he would have to pay any debts we incurred if we were unable to meet our obligations.

The help Ryoko gave us in finding our flat was incalculable. We would not have been able to find our way through the labyrinth of complexity that is house and flat rental. To start with, our Japanese was still very basic, in fact, it was almost non-existent. Both of us had tried hard to learn over three years of intermittent study, through books, tapes and even found a Japanese lady to help us. But to no avail, both of us failing miserably, with the convolutions of the language winding us up in verbal knots and leaving us confused and frustrated. Japanese is considered one of the world's most difficult languages. Finally, we gave up and headed out to Japan linguistically backward.

There are 126 million people in Japan crammed into a very small area of land. Two-thirds of the country is too mountainous to build on, the mountains being incredibly steep, therefore the flat plains between these mountains are in high use with everyone crowding onto them. Consequently, houses, shops and businesses are all scraping bums and tums, vying with each other for space. Every inch of land is used to its utmost. This is why we were so particular with the position of our flat, we wanted some space around us. In some rentals we visited, you were only feet away from your neighbour's window and in fact, could hand each other things through them if you'd a mind to. This flat was in a distant suburb of Kobe, called Nigawa, and was very conveniently placed being about fifteen to twenty miles from the cities of Osaka and Kobe, in an area called Kansai. In terms of travelling times, we could be in central Osaka or Kobe in less than half an hour by train. And even more importantly, it was only six minutes on the train to our beloved Takarazuka town, a distance of about four miles.

The flat we chose was also surrounded by open space, at least one hundred feet on one side, in a narrow strip, and twenty feet on the other. The remaining side overlooked our neighbour's roof, some twelve feet away, but at least we could look out over his flat roof from our own veranda to the sea of roofs beyond. However, as with all things in Japan, we were to find out later that whatever provision you make to your own private foibles, it will be made useless by the unexpectedness of an unknown culture when those same open places acquired six new houses, built over the following few months.

But on that first day, as we were looking around the flat with the agent, strangely, Ryoko kept asking us in a worried voice, "Will this do?"

"Yes, it'll have to," I answered.

"But how about the kitchen?" she kept asking me looking even more worried.

Unfortunately, Japanese kitchens are a throwback to an age of austerity. If you think of a design which would hinder and make any cook's life difficult, you have an idea of the traditional Japanese kitchen. Most of it is made up of a very large, deep sink, about three times the size of a normal British one and has a plug hole big enough to lose your hand down! The rest of the kitchen consists of a few cupboards and drawers attached to the sink unit and that's about it. For people who rent their home, it means that one has to go out and buy one's own kitchen cabinets (a la 1960s) with a pull down flap as a work surface. Cookers are minute affairs, more reminiscent of one person bedsit cookers. Usually gas, they have two rings and a small grill underneath. It sits on a shelf near the sink. If you have the space, you can buy a cooker with three or four rings, but for many people in flats, space was limited and two rings were the norm.

Ryoko was truly worried. She kept asking me, "But what about the kitchen? Is it all right for you? It's old and not nice."

I kept answering, "What choice do we have? This is the kitchen that's here, the rest of the flat is ok."

"Oh, really?" Ryoko would say. I was to hear that phrase a lot over the next seven years.

It took me a very long time to realise that, as the Americans have taken to saying, we were reading from different scripts. The phrase could have been invented for Japan and its dealing with other cultures. My British culture had moulded my mind and way of thinking one way, and

Japanese culture had moulded the Japanese mind the opposite way in all things. The trouble was, I didn't realise the extent of this, and neither did my Japanese friends and acquaintances. We therefore got ourselves entangled in webs of misunderstandings with great regularity. Daily culture shocks became a way of life. The smallest daily event could flummox me.

I had to continually fall back on some advice a friend in London had given me about Japan. 'You must make a giant leap of faith and have confidence in it'. I was to use this advice over and over again, and I was never let down. My giant leaps of faith were always honoured, although not always in the way I expected.

The problem with the script regarding the kitchen, only came to light a few years later when we decided to move. By now, Ryoko's English was much better and our understanding had moved on eons, so we were able to understand the ramifications of changing tenancies.

When someone terminates their tenancy, the landlord will make sure that the flat is clean and he will change the tatami floor matting (the beautiful and delicate straw matting beloved of the Japanese). He will do nothing else. He will then get his agent to show all interested parties around and ask them what they want altered. He then decides which tenant he will let to and which alterations he will do to comply with the wishes of the new tenant.

Ryoko knew this, but didn't know that we didn't know it. We didn't know this and didn't realise that Ryoko was referring to this custom when she kept asking us, "Is this all right for you?" Therefore, we ended up with a flat that had no alterations done to it whatsoever. We put up with an old, unpleasant kitchen, ancient, well used cupboards, old decor and toilet for seven years. Unnecessarily as it turned out as we could have had it all renewed for the same rental price!

During our settling in period, Ryoko was on hand to help out far more often than she had anticipated I think, although she never let us down and took a great deal of time and trouble to help us through our confusion. Once we identified the fact that we could not find any second hand furniture, as those kind of shops didn't exist, she took great delight in taking us to the cheapest shops which would give us reasonable quality. The Saty and Daiei department stores would become our favourite shops, no brand names for us, although brand was king in Japan. At a time when several brand names were struggling for survival in other parts of the world, Japan came up trumps and saved many a famous name from collapsing or hitting bad times. Everywhere you looked there were brand shops selling goods at incredible prices. Two thousand pounds for a handbag was not uncommon and young Japanese women aspired to own such things. Status was also king. Buying the image was big business. One could find young women queuing from the early morning to be the first customers of a new brand outlet. All willing to spend a great deal of money to be the leader in their social circle and own the latest high-status fashion accessory.

The Japanese have an interesting habit of using words from other languages, called 'loan words', and changing them to suit their own language. Therefore, a department store becomes, *depaato*, television becomes, *terebi*, air conditioner becomes, *air con*. If it's not shortened, it is lengthened by the addition of extra vowels. Brand becomes, *brando*, friend becomes, *friendo*, knife becomes, *knifeu*, football becomes, *footuballu*. (Most words end in a vowel.)

You may have noticed me using the words san or chan after someone's name. The Japanese always use the friendly term 'chan' after a girl's name and 'kun' after a boy's name. Adults graduate to the honourific 'san' or extra polite 'sama' after their names. (The nearest we have to these terms are Mr and Mrs, sir or madam.) It is imperative that these polite terms are always used with someone's name, only family or extremely close friends would omit these terms when addressing someone. Even close friends often keep using the polite 'san' after their friends name, depending on the person. Politeness is everything. If you are not polite people don't respect you and everyone feels that you have let yourself down. Also, one has to remember that names are said in reverse, with the family name first and the given name second. However, just to confuse you, women are often addressed as '...chan' even if adult. It's regarded as a term of endearment by friends and family.

It is interesting to note that Ryoko instantly asked us to call her Ryoko, not Ryoko san. She insisted. She in turn, never called us Jill san or Janet san. Always just Jill and Janet. That immediately put us on a special footing of intimate friends or the intention of being intimate friends, although we didn't realise it at the time.

As it turned out, we were very lucky with our choice of flat because it was so quiet and the neighbours were friendly and kind, all except for one neighbour who always said the right things to us in a tone of voice that left us in no doubt that her real feelings were Grand Canyons away from her words. Fortunately, we didn't see very much of her and one of my neighbours said that, 'She's just such a person'. That's a lovely Japanese saying, 'So and so is just such a person'. It covers just about everything without saying anything negative or implying criticism, a major factor to bear in mind in Japanese culture.

The rest of the neighbours were dears, they made us feel

very welcome, especially the Takase family. They immediately invited us to their place for tea. It was a formal affair with cakes and English tea in bone china cups, and we sat around their large kitchen table all cosy and snug. Mrs Takase was rather large for an older Japanese lady at around five foot four inches tall, with a good girth of soft flesh. She was cuddly, soft and unthreatening to her core. Efficient in a gentle way, doing her best to understand our English conversation with her husband. His lean and spare physique always looked relaxed, and, as his wife, he was quick to smile or laugh. He was about the same height as her, his hair still black but receding a little with a few flecks of grey fighting to get out. Both gave out a pleasant, quiet, gentle personality. We discovered that Mr Takase was an English teacher at a state school, so I think he had a strong core somewhere if only for survival, but he never showed that side of himself to us.

Fortunately he spoke English well and he was to be a rock on which we often had to seek shelter. He never forced himself upon us but was always willing to help us and show unselfish friendship when it was needed.

We invited them back to our place for tea. A few weeks later, they entered our flat in typical Japanese fashion, eyes straight ahead, not looking around. It is polite in Japan not to acknowledge anything about your hosts home, so there is no showing anyone around, it's just not done, probably because they may have better things than you and that would make you feel inferior. Or conversely, you may have better things than them, and they feel inferior. Either way, the guests do not make any comments about the host's home.

Frankly, the inside of most Japanese houses look much the same. Every house or flat I visited, or could see into, had a similar layout, with the same doors and windows mass produced and installed. The interiors had a stark, unfriendly, clinical look, emphasised by the ubiquitous, harsh fluorescent lights which always seemed to be installed in each room. Internal walls were invariably painted a uniform off white with the woodwork painted white or light grey. They were almost always cluttered as there was not enough space to store one's belongings. Mostly bereft of furniture, and what furniture there was, I always found most uncomfortable. Comfort has a whole different meaning in Japan.

The main differences between homes being in the size and quantity of rooms, and how modern the bathroom and kitchen facilities are. Plus, the most important difference of all, the status of the area lived in. To have a small house in a fashionable area is preferable to a large house in an unfashionable area, but as truly Japanese as Mr and Mrs Takase were, they couldn't suppress a little "Oh," of surprise when they saw that our flat was virtually empty. Apart from a light green plastic covered sofa, a small low table and our futons (stored away in the huge built-in cupboard in our living room), that was it.

They sat down, Japanese style, on the floor, legs neatly tucked under themselves and unfortunately, Mrs Takase leaned on our 'table' to rearrange her position. It slid across the tatami mat at an alarming rate startling her. "Oh dear, Takase san, please be careful," I said, feeling embarrassed. "I should explain that this 'table' is in fact the box that our air con came in. We don't have a table so we covered the box with a table cloth and it works well, but you cannot put any weight on it."

They were looking perplexed, but too polite to make any comment in case it implied criticism of us. I explained to them that as we were only going to be living here for one year, we did not want to waste any money on things that we could do without and would have to try to get rid of before we went home. With those words hardly out of my mouth, Mr Takase rose in one smooth and graceful movement saying, "Just a moment please, I will be back shortly," and disappeared out of the front door. A couple of minutes later, he returned carrying a low, plastic table in perfect condition. "It's our old table," he said as he grinned at us, "please use it while you are in Japan. We don't need it."

"Are you sure, Takase san?" I managed to get out as Mrs Takase said something in rapid fire Japanese. Mr Takase translated. "She says that you are most welcome to it because it is only in storage in our cupboard. We would have great pleasure in lending it to you."

"*Domo arigato gozaimashita.*" Thank you very much.

Unfortunately, there was another shock awaiting Mrs Takase. As I prepared the tea, I had to explain to them that I had bought a teapot in honour of their visit, but the only one I could find, with my limited knowledge of the area, was at the *Hyaku en* shop – one hundred yen shop. One hundred yen at that time was equivalent to fifty pence in Britain and it was similar to our one pound shops; one of the few things that were cheaper in Japan. Sometimes at these shops one could buy a real bargain, probably some unfortunate person's bankrupt stock, but other times it was tat. Of course, when I was looking for teapots, it was tat.

She took one look at my pathetic, small luminous blue teapot and showed suppressed horror at such inelegance and disappeared downstairs to her flat in a flurry of indecipherable Japanese. She came back clutching a Wedgewood teapot and milk jug saying that we were welcome to use them for as long as we liked. "Use them until you leave Japan," she urged. We were astonished. Here was this delightful lady giving us her precious Wedgewood teapot and jug, a big smile of pleasure lighting up her face.

She really wanted us to have them.

Of course, we had to accept them, and we were absolutely delighted with this unexpected offer, but it was an expensive teapot and we were afraid to use it in case we broke or damaged it. So it lived in our cupboard for a long time before we felt that we could return it to her complete with packets of luxury tea as a measure of our thanks.

*

We had only been in the flat for about six weeks when we experienced our first earthquake. We were settling in quite well, getting used to sleeping on futons, cooking in a small space with no work surfaces. Cooking on a mini cooker. Coping with the kitchen sink. All was going well.

I was just putting out our lunch when the doors in the flat started to rattle, making an urgent and pulsating noise unlike anything I had heard before. Puzzlement did not last long. The whole building started to sway back and forth, like a ship in a swell. My stomach flipped, my heart lurched. I was in a true panic for the first time in my life. An earthquake.

I had read many articles offering advice on what to do to save your life and had made a plan following that advice, which gave one various options like hiding under a table to protect yourself from falling debris; standing under a door frame as it should be the strongest part of a structure; rush outside immediately; open all doors and windows so that you are not trapped inside by warped frames. In reality, most people just freeze, and in the panic of the moment, that is exactly what we did. We froze and waited to see if it would stop. It didn't. The floor swayed upwards, back down and upwards again, over and over. It was terrifying.

The most awful thing about it was not knowing what

else would happen. Was this just the beginning and a giant hole of horror was about to open up, or would it come to an end without further mishap?

Jan and I had instinctively rushed to the sink and held on to it, as if it alone could save us; watching with incredulity as our world moved around us. The table slid across the floor, things fell off shelves, pictures went askew. It seemed to last forever, but in retrospect, it probably lasted twenty seconds or so. When it finished, still clutching the sink, we looked into each other's ashen faces and unasked questions passed between us with frantic eyes. Are you OK? Has it finished? What do we do now?

Two minutes later found us still clutching the sink, but finally we decided that the danger had passed and I rushed out onto the balcony to see if there was any damage. I imagined houses down, people lying in the street under piles of debris, cars in disarray, all the things that you see on the news after an earthquake. I looked around but to my amazement everything was absolutely normal. A man walked by. A mother with a baby in a pram sauntered past. In the distance, cars went up and down the road. No damage, no panic, no anything in fact. It was as if it had never happened.

We finally sat down twenty minutes later to eat our lunch, both of us still feeling queasy, when, in a macabre coincidence, the moment the first mouthful of my lunch hit my stomach it all started again. The room swayed as before, things slid around, but this time it was over in a few seconds and peace and stability were restored. I was fighting to keep my paltry mouthful internal and not sure if I could manage to do so. "Relax," Jan said, "that was an aftershock I think, it's probably over." I wanted to believe her so much. We sat there in silence for several minutes until we felt confident enough to breath easily again. Stiff and terrified, we tried to get back to normal.

The myriad feelings during those two tremors will remain with me forever. The feelings of mortality, violent death and of an immediate fear so overwhelming that you are too paralyzed to help yourself, were, at first a great shock; and then a realisation that this is normal, as life here is lived on a knife edge. Any moment, it could be wiped out by the force of nature. It makes everything exciting, energetic, pulsating and alive. You can feel these underlying emotions, the will to make the best of things, the thrill of life is in the streets and in the way of business and the way of living. It's catching, it's addictive, it pushes you to achieve that little bit extra, or at least, it did for me.

This was to be the first of many earthquakes I experienced, and made me realise that this particular tremor was a small one, nothing to worry about. In fact, if you were outside, or on a train, you would probably have not felt a thing. As we were on the top of our block of flats, we felt the swaying of the building much more than the people below us. Buildings are built to sway, if they don't sway they crumble and fall down. But really, knowing that was never a comfort during the scores of earthquakes I lived through. Everyone of them still instilled abject terror in me.

CHAPTER FOUR

My First English Lesson

One of the endearing, although sometimes frustrating, things for me about Japan is that you never know what is going to happen. For example, things you think are all arranged do not happen in the way you had planned them. People will change your plans for you without consultation if they think their plans are better for you and they will take for granted your compliance in what they have changed or planned without you. I am not talking of major alterations, for example if I had arranged to go to a certain place, it would still happen but I might meet different people to those expected, or extra people would join us, or I might end up in a different building in that location because it was deemed better or more interesting. It has mostly been my experience that these assumptions have been made with my good in mind, never the other way around. People want to be helpful, it's just that they don't tell you about it beforehand.

This is the Japanese way. To do something for someone else is deemed to be a self sacrificing thing to do, and self sacrifice is looked upon as a virtue. If you tell the other person beforehand, then you are boasting about it and it is not genuine; at least that is the conclusion I came to after seven years of having things done for me without my knowledge or permission. The person on the receiving end is expected to accept all that's done for them with good grace and joy – which was sometimes rather hard for me.

A friend of mine, Yuko san, would occasionally come down from her home near Tokyo and spend a weekend in Osaka. We always met up and went out for a meal together and this was when she started ordering things for me in restaurants without asking if I wanted to eat it. She would say with pride that it was her pleasure to take the trouble to think about me and my stomach and what was good on the menu for me to eat. I hated it. I could accept many things about Japanese society, when in Rome and all that, but when it came to my stomach, I wanted to eat what I fancied, not what someone else thought I should eat. We had conversations about this and she could not understand my reluctance to eat what she had chosen for me. She would say 'but in Japanese society it is a great privilege for someone else to do something for you, or to choose what you eat. It shows that you think a lot of that person and have spent your time and energy thinking about them'.

I would try to explain to her in simple English, as her English was not so good at this time, that although I understood her point of view, I had to follow my own culture as far as this was concerned and it was good for her to understand that in other cultures it was considered arrogant to order something for someone else without asking them what they wanted to eat first. I wanted her to understand the difference as it could possibly cause her problems on her visits to other countries.

She had trouble with this concept, as did I with the Japanese one. Yuko san is very earnest and I know that I upset her by this, but this is one area of Japanese culture that I could never accept. We finally agreed to differ, but we were both very careful with each other in restaurants afterwards.

Another example of changing plans without

consultation, was a meeting I had with Yamamoto san. She was a delightful person, always smiling and agreeable, although she stuck to her principles with a grace and charm I envied. Small, a little round, her short black hair always immaculate, aged around 40, teeth a little too large, but the smile and shine in her eyes and her soft, gentle voice were the things you really noticed about her.

Yamamoto san was an acquaintance I had met several times socially at the Takarazuka theatre, as she was also a big fan.

One day when I bumped into her, out of the blue she asked me if she could come to my flat for an English lesson. Her English was miniscule but we could understand each other with actions, gesticulations and a few words uttered here and there and we laughed a lot together, so I said that I would be delighted.

It would be my first English lesson.

At the appointed time, the Japanese being very punctual, my doorbell rang and I answered it fully expecting to see Yamamoto san, but there was a totally unknown woman standing there, smiling broadly and waving to me through the open door (the Japanese love waving). I thought, Is she selling something? But then I saw Yamamoto san standing behind her, beaming her toothy and engaging smile.

I was thrown off balance somewhat by this unexpected arrival because I had been in Japan for less than a year, and at this stage of my Japanese 'education' I was not used to the practice of changing arrangements without telling the recipient. I invited them in and they both entered my small *genkan* (indoor porch) and struggled to take off their shoes. They had so many large bags with them, at least three apiece, that much jumping up and down and overbalancing went on, coupled with squeaks, much laughter and several little staccato, "Oh's" as they sorted themselves out. Many

Japanese women love to squeak and squeal whenever they think the occasion warrants it, but I was still a novice at this and was rather thrown by all the unnecessary drama. Feeling unsure of myself and confused, I put my hand out and took one of the bags from Yamamoto san, it was heavy and something clinked inside. I was a bit worried, and annoyed too, about this unexpected happening. This wasn't what we had arranged. Who was this woman and why was she here? I was not to know that this kind of unexpected happening would be part of my ordinary life for years to come.

I soon found out what was in the bags as the stranger opened one of them and pulled something out and presented it to me with another squeal of delight. I took it from her; it was a large Tupperware box and she gestured for me to open it. Struggling with the lid, I got it open to find a perfectly arranged pasta salad inside, looking very pretty and smelling delicious. Another box was presented to me in the same way, and another and another until all the bags were empty. My new kitchen sideboard, bought second hand from a departing foreigner, was now covered with many bowls and boxes, together with packets of miso soup and noodles.

I was rather overwhelmed and totally confused by all this food being so proudly presented to me. This was an English lesson with Yamamoto san and suddenly, the focus had changed and I was here with a stranger and surrounded by food. Why? I didn't know. This was my first experience of this kind of thing. A culture shock.

I took a covert and studied look at the other woman and found her to be elegant and beautiful in her own way. Not conventionally beautiful, like many Japanese women, but quietly beautiful, the kind that grows on you with time. Her body was as slim as a pencil and her back as straight as a flying arrow, so it didn't surprise me after introductions were done and it was obvious that I had no idea who this woman was, that Yamamoto san asked me if I had an *Otome* magazine, "Ah! Otome have, yes?"

"Ah, yes, Otome," I replied as I realised that this stranger must be a takarajienne. As there are so many performers in the Takarazuka theatre, it is difficult to keep track of everyone, therefore, the management produce a who's who of performers, which is an annual, glossy, full colour magazine, listing all performers together with picture and details of each person. Their likes and dislikes etc. It's a way of sorting out who all the newcomers are, who has retired, and who is where in the hierarchy of the theatre. (The word otome means, old fashioned young woman who likes the traditional life and crafts, such as knitting.)

I found the magazine and handed it to Yamamoto san who immediately turned to the correct page and showed me this woman's picture. She was in the higher echelons of the theatre by way of her age, she was in her forties I guessed, – the older you are, the higher up your status goes – although she was not an important performer. She was what I call, essential middle management. The shows rely on strong, convincing performances from the mature performers. The actresses are divided up into five troupes, named Flower, Moon, Snow, Star and Cosmos Troupe, with around eighty members in each and a great many of the performers are the youngsters coming up, just learning their craft and therefore, it is especially important for the established performers to be able to lift up the shows into the realms of credibility. This woman was one of these.

I needed to find out why she was here and why all the food! I took a deep breath, as I was feeling a little nervous at having a real, live takarajienne in my flat, and asked in my most diplomatic voice, *"Tabemono wa?"* (eating?) Oh dear, bad Japanese and bad English, but it was understood at once by both women, who nodded eagerly, smiling broadly.

"OK, *ato de,*" I said.

"Hai, ato de," they said in unison. Yes, later.

We put the food in the fridge and settled down. I was unsure whether my unexpected guest was here for an English lesson or just to meet me, so I asked her, "English Lesson?"

"Hai," she answered enthusiastically. Yes.

I was feeling nervous anyway, as this was my first English lesson, but now doubly so, because I had to do it with a takarajienne. It was also unexpected because I had planned what kind of lesson I would do with Yamamoto san, having gauged her English level, but now I had to think on my feet, change things, and I desperately wanted to impress at the same time. I calmed myself and tried to ascertain what the takarajienne could understand in English.

Nothing! OK, not to worry! Ha!

My brain was on overload and I could see that my first English lesson was going downhill before it had even started. Telling myself not to panic, keep calm and move slowly, give the impression you know what you are doing (another ha!) I decided to revert to the safe haven of an English grammar textbook, the production of which made their eyes widen in horror and their bodies went rigid. Not a good idea. They were probably remembering all the boring English lessons they had had at school, with its endless pounding of grammar and learning long lists of English words.

I tried to look relaxed as I threw the book across the room, making them laugh, and decided on something much easier. Standing up, I said, "Stand." We all stood and said, "Stand." I sat down and said, "Sit." We all sat down and said, "Sit." Then they fell into a shower of giggles and we were off. I tore off some paper from my writing pad and gave them a piece each, and we drew our bodies on it and wrote in the names of the parts in English. We did the usual places and then some more personal ones. More fits of giggles, including me this time, and the ice was well and truly broken and we all realised that we liked each other and would get on well together. A takarajienne is only human, as is a foreigner. That was something we both discovered that afternoon.

I was having some trouble pronouncing the takarajienne's name and she asked me to call her by her nick name, which I shall say was Fumi san, and we spent the next two hours doing all sorts of silly activities like running on the spot and practicing the r sound in running. The Japanese have great difficulty in pronouncing r's as they do not have this sound in their language. They have a sound which is something like a cross between an r and an l, so unfortunately, they constantly make the mistake of saying things like lunning instead of running and lice instead of rice. We spent some considerable time on the alphabet and getting the pronunciation correct and by the time we had finished, they were pronouncing the English alphabet just perfectly. Takarajiennes can learn very fast and remember what they are taught, which is a great advantage when learning another language.

By 6.00 o'clock our tummies started to rumble, and as Jan had just returned from her shopping trip, we took to the kitchen, which was all of four foot away from the living room. Yamamoto san took charge and instructed us as to her wants. Jan and I acted the parts of kitchen assistants, fetching saucepans, spoons, ladles etc on request. Fumi san elected herself head taster and nodded her agreement or emphatically said, "No no, more tamari," her judgement being perfect we discovered later.

Happily, we found out that Fumi san liked to quaff her wine as much as we did, so we spent a very jolly evening eating and drinking for several hours, and then watched some videos of Takarazuka shows in which Fumi san appeared. It was great fun and led to a few other English lessons, until unexpectedly, for me, Fumi san retired from her troupe and I didn't see her again.

*

One of the things that can change everything for you in a country such as Japan, something that can ruin all your best laid plans, are germs and viruses which are different to the ones we get in the west. Many foreigners succumb to these viruses and I was one of them. I had seven colds in five months! Each cold was severe and took me about 10 days to get over and all kept me housebound. No sooner was I out and about again than I would go down with another one. All you have to do, in overcrowded Japan, is to travel by train, any train as they all tend to be full, and you will catch a cold sooner or later. Finally, I consulted a German doctor who had lived in Japan for years, "Did I have seven different colds, or was it the same cold which didn't quite go away?" I asked through my adenoids.

"No, I think you had seven different colds," she told me in impeccable English, "it's quite common for foreigners to get frequently ill like this. You have to build up your immune system to cope with the different viruses here. Once you've done it, you will go back to the normal one or two colds a year." She was right, and I only got three more colds over the next six years.

However, because of these colds, I was beginning to feel that I had been cheated out of about half of my holiday as now it was almost time to return to Britain. Jan was committed to returning home after the year was up as she had family responsibilities to fulfil but I wanted to stay on.

We discussed the problem at length and decided that I would stay on alone and take the consequences, whatever they may be.

Therefore, I was casting around in my mind as to how I could extend my stay and, out of necessity, fund it. With these thoughts in mind I talked to Ryoko, with whom I was spending a lot of time, and we had discovered that we both had ambitions but lacked confidence and knowhow to put them into practice. Fortunately, we could both understand the other's problems.

That was why Ryoko was so important to me. She helped me and had faith in me, she recognised that I could achieve my dream, that I did have the determination and talent to succeed as an English conversation teacher even though I didn't have the academic qualifications. For let's be clear here, I am talking about teaching adults who have already had at least six years of English lessons at school, and many of them have had ten years or more. What they did not have was very much speaking practice. At school, the balance of English lessons were weighted towards writing with a little reading and pronunciation practice added on. Another problem was that many of the teachers' pronunciation was not good, and in some cases decidedly bad, and the students could not be confident in their own pronunciation skills. This left a lot of them traumatised when faced with having to speak English to a native English speaker.

Many students told me they had to learn twenty English words a day at school, for the next day they would be tested on them. The test was a written one, and although they did practice speaking the words a little in class, it was not enough and they felt very anxious about pronunciation. As there was little reinforcement of the new words, by the end of the week they had forgotten the words they learned at the beginning. And so the cycle continued. Teaching to pass the written test, with little expansion or understanding. Fortunately, over the past few years, teaching practices have improved and the children today are taught in a more balanced way with lots of speaking and listening activities using CDs and assistant teachers on contract from English speaking countries.

I would be teaching adults, mostly aged thirty upwards, who had suffered the old style English lessons, and in such cases the English conversation teachers' job is to help their students transfer their knowledge of English into intelligible speech. It requires training to do this effectively of course, but one doesn't need to have a university degree and a degree in English grammar to help them. Most Japanese adults consciously know English grammar, in principle, better than the average English speaker does. The skill is in giving the student the confidence to speak even if they make mistakes. A harder task than one might think.

Many Japanese people are terrified of making mistakes and would rather struggle and utter a painful English sentence word perfect, but taking several minutes to do so, than to jump in and utter a murderous melody of fractured English. This is down to the education system which does not encourage students to experiment and demands perfectionism every time. It has left many adults in a vacuum, who continually toil to string English sentences together and hold any kind of conversation, but at the same time, they can read English with good understanding.

It's a huge problem for the older Japanese, but it's good news for any native English speaker who would like to teach in Japan. I had grown to like and respect the Japanese people during my several holidays and I knew that to live and work in Japan was what I wanted to do. I also knew that I could do it. I didn't let the lack of a university degree stop me. I couldn't let it stop me because I wanted this so much. I was determined to achieve my dream.

So, I strode out, buttoning up my small amount of confidence into a tight ball, not letting it out to be stamped upon by un-carers, but waiting until the right moment to let it fly and soar with the person who would understand and care. Ryoko was that person.

There we were, Ryoko and I, both ambitious and determined but suffering from the 'ordinary woman's' syndrome. How does an ordinary woman get out of the crippling cradle of always being told that you cannot achieve because you are a woman, or because you do not have the right qualifications? This especially applies in Japan, whose culture is eons behind the west's in women's equality.

How to gain the confidence to start? How to continue to build on that confidence so that you can persuade other people that you are worth paying for your professional services? This was our challenge.

This is what we did for each other. We encouraged and offered advice. We helped each other, all above and beyond the normal calls of friendship. We recognised in the other the same needs and the iron wills of determination to succeed and that we could conquer our fears and other people's prejudices. And succeed we did. After six years, I had my own English school which employed Jan and me and one part time teacher, and Ryoko had her own English school for pre-school children, which besides Ryoko and an assistant, also employed a native English speaker on a part time basis.

But it took us a while to get there!

I remember sitting on a train with Ryoko. We were going on yet another journey to buy some pieces of equipment for my kitchen. Sitting side by side, gently rolling with the train,

Ryoko, quite out of the blue told me that she had decided to open her own English school. She explained that although she had been teaching English to children for over ten years – and taught with several native English speaking teachers – she was always an employee and had no confidence to open her own school; but she had been so encouraged by my example of living my dream that she had taken all her courage into both hands and decided to follow my example.

"I have discussed this with Kenji, and he is backing me all the way. He thinks it's a great idea. I am very encouraged, what do you think? Do you think I can do it?"

I was astounded by this news and that she was asking my advice. I admire Ryoko so much, she thrives on hard work and challenges. She's a super-woman to me, and this woman was asking me what I thought. The fact that my opinion mattered to her was so pleasing to me I told her a little story about my youth.

"When I was young, maybe twenty or so, I thought about my life and which road I should follow. I decided that the worst thing that could happen to me was to find myself, when I was old, looking back on my life and having regrets, thinking, I'm sorry I didn't do so and so. To be dissatisfied with my life through lack of trying new things, from playing it safe, how frustrating, dissatisfying and just plain boring. I didn't want to waste my life because of fear of failure.

I was a timid young woman, painfully shy and unsure of myself and this decision gave me the confidence to go out into the world. To leave my family and become independent. I didn't do anything extreme, I just never let the fear of possible consequences dictate my decisions. That's one of the reasons I am in Japan now. Living my dream. Many things could go wrong. I refused to let these worries dictate my actions." I paused for a short while, gathering my thoughts, and continued, "However, I didn't have a family who relied on me like you have Ryoko, although if Kenji san is willing to support you, then I think you should go for it. As long as you don't run the risk of bankrupting yourselves, or ruining your health and if it's really what you want to do, then go for it, grab it with both hands and don't let go until you have succeeded."

This rather pompous lecture was accepted by Ryoko with her usual grace and politeness and she said, "Oh really? I think so too. I am encouraged by you. I think I am the type of person who can take a risk and go against what other people say. You have given me courage, I will do my best to make my dream happen. Yes, I *will* do it!"

We sat there, side by side, swaying with the rhythm of the train, feeling sagely important. Both nodding our heads, lost in our private thoughts of living our dreams and making things happen. We were content.

About two weeks after this conversation Ryoko astonished me by announcing that several of her friends wanted to take English lessons with me, but were too shy to do so, (which, I discovered, is the normal ploy used when someone doesn't want to do something like take your English lessons – never be direct), but they said that they would be happy to send their children to me for English lessons. This came right out of the blue and I could only say very negatively, "But I've no idea how to teach children."

"Don't worry," said a calm Ryoko, "I will help you," and a little smile played on her lips.

"How?" I asked in a little bit of a panic.

In her usual calm and measured way, she answered, "We will do them together." And with that, we did!

However, I had one major problem to overcome before we could begin. My visa. I was on a holiday visa and would need to change my visa status. This was not a simple thing for me, not having the right qualifications to start with.

I now had possibilities on the horizon and Japan had weaved itself even further under my skin and I was more under its spell than ever and really wanted to open my own small school and teach English. I knew that I would enjoy teaching. I liked the Japanese and the way of life and was desperate to stay on. I enjoy a challenge and I put all my energies into this. I researched all the rules of visa applications, and talked to as many other foreigners as I could and clutched at any advice they could give me.

I'd joined a group called FEW (Foreign Executive Women) which was designed to bring together foreign women in Japan to network and help each other in a difficult culture. We met once a month at the Hilton Hotel in Osaka, and it was here that I met Kelly. A big, black, engaging American woman, with a personality as big as her kind heart (which was considerable). In her fifties, she'd been in Japan for over twenty five years. She offered me the hand of friendship, which I gladly clutched. We often went out to a bar after the FEW dinner with several others, and it was here that I told her of my current dilemma.

"Kelly," I said, "I'm so stressed and anxious, I don't know what to do about renewing my visa. I'd like to get a visa that will allow me to work, but every avenue I explore turns out to be barred for me as I don't have a degree. I'm desperate to stay on. I don't know what to do. Did you have such visa problems when you came here?"

"Honey," she said in her loud, rich, deep voice, "did I have trouble with my visas? You're looking at the original 'trouble with her visa girl'. I spent years struggling with my visas. I got myself one of those cu-l-tu-ral visas, (she spread out the word, cultural, in her American twang), where you study a Japanese art, but are allowed to work part time. The trouble was, they only lasted a year or two and then I had to find something else to study, or take my studying on to advanced level, to enable me to get a renewed visa. I spent years shaking in my shoes at the visa office in case they refused me. I know *all* about visa trauma." She patted my hand sympathetically, whilst lighting a cigarette at the same time.

I asked her incredulously, "Did you do that for twenty five years?"

"Not quite, but more or less honey."

"How does one get a cultural visa?" I asked in great anxiety, and *very* earnestly. (I must have been such a trial!)

"Honey, I don't know now. This was years ago and I did every cu-l-tu-ral thing in Japan. Want to know about the tea ceremony? Just ask me, I studied it for years. Want to know about *ikebana*? Ask me about that too, again I studied it for years. How about drum playing, kimono making, rice planting, tofu making, walking in clogs? Just ask me," she said with a distinct twinkle in her eye, "I've studied everything there is to study that would get me a visa – and then some!"

I felt like a little twerp talking to Homer, the great one, the one whose knowledge is all powerful, and I felt humbled.

"What are you studying now?"

"Honey, one day, when I went on one of my regular trips to the visa office, clutching my documents to prove my latest cu-l-tu-ral enterprise, and shaking in my shoes as I always did on these occasions, fear of refusal tearing at my guts, the immigration officer looked at me, flipped through my record, looked at me again, and I thought, 'Oh God, he's going to refuse me, after all this time, it's over'. I started to quake even more, yeh, I did, I was so scared. I didn't want to leave this country, I wanted to stay on. I know I sometimes moan about things, but you know what? It's a darn sight better place than most other places and that includes my own beloved America." She stopped talking and stared into space for a few seconds, lost in her memories, and then, starting a little, she went on, "Anyway, he floored me by saying that he thought that living and working in Japan for twenty years, which I had been at that time, was long enough and that he was going to give me a permanent resident's visa. Oh, my, I almost collapsed, my joy was so overwhelming. So yes, honey, I know your dilemma and I sympathise, but I think that most of the people I studied with will have retired, or are even dead. They were ancient when I knew them. I think we have to look at what's available now, but often, one finds these places by word of mouth. You should talk to the other women at FEW. See what they're doing."

In fact, I had already talked to many of the other women at FEW and had discovered that I was the odd one out, who didn't fit the mould because the others had their visas through their companies or as spouses here with their husbands. No one I met had my problem, except for Kelly. Finally, with Jan having already returned home to England, and with about two weeks before my visa ran out, when I was desperate and was almost giving up hope, it was time for the next FEW meeting and I was to gain my first experience of the extraordinary things that seem to happen in this country.

Dinner was formal and I found myself, quite by chance, sitting next to a woman I had never seen there before, or since. We chatted and I eventually took a deep breath and asked her about her visa. This is not as easy as it sounds as it's a bit like asking someone you've just met what kind of underwear they like. It's very personal and one has to tread carefully because people who do have trouble with their visas can get very touchy about it. Fortunately, this woman was sympathetic and told me that she had exactly the same problems as me for years on end. Nowadays, she was studying ikebana with Sato san, who was willing to guarantee her for a cultural visa. She generously said that she would recommend me to Sato san and ask her if she would be willing to take me on as a student. "She's very fussy who she accepts," she told me, "I can't guarantee that she will take you as a student, but I will try." I could have kissed her feet.

An 'interview' was arranged with Sato san, which lasted about an hour, where we chatted about ourselves, our lives, our aspirations and the Takarazuka theatre, which seemed to tickle Sato san's fancy – a foreigner being such a loyal fan of the theatre. After the interview, thankfully, she did take me on as her student and my visa troubles were over for the next two years. I would study ikebana with Sato san and would also be allowed to work for up to twenty five hours a week. I felt like I could have kissed the immigration officer too, and that's saying something.

With the freedom that the visa gave me, Ryoko and I started our kids' class in her front room (children in Japan are always called kids) with six of them who came once a week and sat on her sofa whilst Ryoko and I started the exciting task of introducing them to the English language. This was where I discovered that Ryoko has a talent worthy of an Academy Award for keeping kids entertained, interested and therefore malleable and pliable. She controlled those kids effortlessly and never stopped smiling and joking, even when stressed.

I had a lot to learn. I was so nervous in front of those six kids, aged between 6-10, that they must have wondered who was this strange creature, this foreigner. Actually, they were equally nervous of me. I was, I think, their first encounter with a foreigner close up. They had probably never spoken to one before.

They sat there, three girls and three boys, the girls with their eyes down, peeping up through their fringes, the boys almost as shy except for one. Masaki kun was full of himself. Ten years old and with more confidence already than most kids manage to achieve in a lifetime of childhood. He was, what is known today, as a challenge. Short for his age and bordering on the tubby with his jet black hair cut very close to his head, he tried to dominate the class by being a loud mouth, a joker, a kids' champion. But surprisingly, as the lessons went on, he displayed a superior intelligence and an absorbing interest in learning English. He was hungry to learn and his mother obviously fed him enough protein to increase that hunger week by week. He ate English, he was like a sponge, he was desperate to learn. And yes, I warmed to him.

The others were sweeties, especially the girls, who were soft and gentle, but fiercely intelligent, although they always withheld their personalities even at this tender age. One of the problems with teaching Japanese children is that they are sometimes too tired to concentrate on the lessons. This is because they have so much pressure put on them by their families to do well at school that many of them are enrolled at private schools, called *Juku*, in the evenings and/or at weekends to give them the extra push their families think they need. In fact, in my experience it can be detrimental to learning as they are too tired to think. Regardless, sometimes, children as young as seven or eight are studying at Juku until 10.00 or 11.00pm after having done a full day at school. The Japanese schooling system is based on teaching students to pass exams, rather than learning through understanding, therefore, these children are always having to work hard to memorise facts.

Many Japanese people told me that they thought their

race lacked common sense, and to a degree I think this is true. Or rather, their common sense is very different to ours. The upside down thinking of the Japanese shows up well in the education system and how they exhaust their students and expect many of them to work anything up to 16 hours a day on their school work.

I have a theory that this is all pre-planned by the authorities to keep the kids in order and obedient. After all, if they are always exhausted and only have time for school work, they cannot get up to much mischief outside school. Independent thought is frowned upon and not encouraged, in fact it is ruthlessly eradicated whenever possible. Human rights and freedom of spirit have a long way to go. The strain can be overwhelming for some kids and it pushes the occasional child over the edge into madness or withdrawal. Some just cope, some withdraw or develop hard shells, and some flip. An horrific story of a child flipping happened a few years ago when the severed head of a six year old child was left in front of a school's gate one morning. The whole nation was in an uproar of panic. There must be a maniac around. No one was safe. Find this person fast. They did find the person, it was another child. A child who went to that very school. It seems that the child in question was under such immense pressure from his family to succeed and pass all his exams and get into a top echelon school that the stress pushed him into insanity. He kidnapped a mentally retarded six year old boy, killed him, cut off his head and left it outside his school in a sort of bizarre statement and pleading for help. It sobered the nation up for a while with some discussions going on as to what should be done about the burden put on children. But little was done to change the system that created this awful event. You have to want to change the system to be able to change it, and my impression is that the Government does not want to change the system. As we all know, you can only rule for as long as the people let you, and the Japanese are well known for their passivity and the refusal of the masses to go against authority. This attitude has been part of society for millennia, I don't suppose it will change any time soon.

Ryoko and I wanted our small English class to be based on fun and games. We knew the strains these kids were put under in their schools and outside, so we made a special effort to make everything as much fun as we could. Again, Ryoko was a master at this, she really had a talent for keeping the children in order but at the same time giving them the luxury and relaxation of having a jolly good time. Again, I followed her lead slavishly.

Our front room school was a Juku of sorts. A very basic one, but Juku none the less, because the kids came to us after their school day finished. Our lessons started at 5.00pm and lasted for an hour and a half. No wonder the kids were tired sometimes, but tired or not, the girls often outshone the boys, much to the latter's chagrin. Boys are everything in Japan. A high pedestal awaits them. There they will spend their lives, top of the heap, ruler of their families, expecting all female members to kowtow to them and wait on them to extraordinary degrees with the women subservient in all things. It's like stepping back in time and the strange thing is, the Japanese women seem to like it that way, or at least, they don't demure in public. In our kids' class, I tried to encourage the girls and gave them equal attention to the boys, but it was strange for them and once or twice there were tears because they were only little. Once, I had to tell Masaki kun (the loud mouth) to treat the girls with respect or he would have to leave my class for good. He knuckled down and didn't seem to resent it, mostly because he was thick-skinned I think. His confidence in himself, and his place in the world as a superior boy had already been cemented in.

The other two boys were sweeties, thank goodness. Jun kun, handsome even at the age of eight and Takahiro kun, not so handsome but with such a sensitive personality, he was my favourite. He was a serious little fellow, with thick flowing hair, who was doing his best to learn his English as diligently as he could, while his classmate, with his pretty face and good looks that any film star would envy, was just as sensitive but in a completely different way. He hid this sensitivity under a barrage of jokes and good nature.

It was interesting to see the machinations of the kids and I suspect that, because I couldn't speak or understand any of the Japanese being said, I relied on my observations and became astute in reading body language and underlying emotions.

In these lessons I deferred to Ryoko in everything. She was the boss, I, her willing assistant. I learned from her, absorbed her knowledge and copied her shamelessly. She taught me how to teach kids, Japanese style. She gave me confidence and encouragement and I diligently studied all the things Ryoko taught me. At home, I would pore over books on teaching children and also enrolled for several seminars put on by experienced foreign English teachers to help new foreign teachers who were teaching English to Japanese children. It was a hard time for me, but we both felt a great responsibility for these kids and wanted to give them the best lessons we possibly could. After each lesson we would stay on and have a long meeting, sorting out next week's lesson and developing our own style and in the end, Ryoko went so far as to develop her own curriculum. But I'm jumping ahead, because I was still an embryo, swimming, sinking and bobbing up again, searching for what I needed to give the best possible lessons for our young students, while Ryoko was looking for ways to expand our partnership, to share our knowledge and realise our dreams. For although my teaching experience was limited at this time, we both realised that we worked very well together and my lack of experience didn't detract from my other qualities of dedication, commitment and a determination to do the best job I possibly could to help these kids. If the children had known of the effort and hard work we put into their lessons, they would probably have run a mile!

We decided to open up another, separate class, in a community centre although the one that Ryoko had picked out for us was not ordinary. This was the doyen of community centres in the area, being up market with a high reputation for the quality of the classes and teachers.

Ryoko always had great dreams, and quality and high status were paramount for her. She was not interested in working in a low-status situation of any sort. The best schools, the best buildings, the best teaching methods were her watch words and I concurred, although this philosophy did cause us problems, but I was always very grateful for it as it meant that we were always respected wherever we went because we presented the right image. Image is all in Japan. If you have the right image you can do wonders.

So, having chosen our community centre, all that was left was to be accepted by them; a difficult task. First of all, we had to decide what kind of class we would open. Again, I deferred to Ryoko. She had very definite views and had obviously been thinking about this for a long time but, without the confidence to go ahead and do it, she had put it on the back burner. Now she had a pal, a person of similar mind, who could match her in determination and who was willing to fail if necessary in order to succeed. Me!

We decided to move away from older children's classes and to open a Mothers and Babies class and this threw

Ryoko into top gear, she was like a small, slim whirlwind of activity. Her ideas tumbling out of her so fast that many got lost in translation and only came to light again during our many long meetings. We would meet either at a coffee shop, or in our homes, and chat for hours, and even then, we hadn't finished. We both had so much inside us, that needed the outlet of the other person. We fed off each other. We bounced our ideas off each other. We discovered each other's cultures, foibles, oddities and finally, deep inner thoughts and ambitions. Basically, we were a match made in heaven and met at the right time for each of us. We were both ready for the challenge the other person posed and for the opportunities that opened up for us together. Neither of us could do it alone. We needed each other, we had found each other, we both got on together superbly. This ordinary Japanese woman living in a country of 126 million people and this ordinary British woman who lived half a world away, had, unbelievably, found each other and prospered.

CHAPTER FIVE

Koyasan – A Buddhist Town

Before Jan returned to England, one of the joys of living in Japan was the fact that we could learn about an interesting place and then make a plan to visit it at our leisure – between my many colds of course. One such place was Koyasan (Mount Koya) in Wakayama Prefecture. Over one thousand years ago, a monk called Kukai, later known as Kobo Daishi, came back from two years in China and brought *Shingon* Buddhism to Japan. It was to change the face of Japan and make him one of the most revered people in Japanese history.

In 816 AD he chose Koyasan to make his headquarters. It is nearly three thousand feet above sea level, a valley nestled within a series of mountains which Kobo Daishi poetically called, 'a valley in the folds of eight lotus petals', because he thought the surrounding mountains resembled a lotus blossom. From those small beginnings, Koyasan has been a major place of pilgrimage for Shingon Buddhists in Japan throughout the ages. So much so, that a town has grown up around the temples. There are more than two thousand temples, shrines, towers, stupas, assembly buildings and an ancient and mysterious cemetery over one thousand years old. One thousand monks and priests live there together with about five hundred religious students and four thousand residents of the town, many of whom cater for the visitors. It also has an ambulance and a police car. A sort of religious theme park that has been there for over a thousand years.

Koyasan is a place one couldn't invent, as I, for one would have difficulty believing that such a place could exist. But it does, and Jan and I had the chance to visit it for a weekend. A small group of foreigners had got together and arranged a tour of Koyasan with a Buddhist monk and an overnight stay in one of the temples. Five of us would travel together, two middle aged French women, one elderly American woman and Jan and I. We had only met one of the women before, Francine, who arranged the trip.

"Call me Frankie," she had said on first meeting, her French accent softening the name and making it seductive. She was about forty, bony, with a head of orange hair that was short and spiked in the middle like a punk. She should have been far too old for such a hairstyle, but for some reason, it was her. She was great fun. The other Frenchwoman paled in comparison and I have to admit that I cannot conjure her up at all, but Maxine, the American was a force to be reckoned with. Tall, overweight and overbearing, with a firm grasp of her own 'superior' abilities, (but not unlikable) she had come to Japan two years earlier at the age of sixty two, 'to earn money for my retirement', she told me. She also confided that the first thing she had done was to get herself a Japanese boyfriend. "He's younger than me," she twinkled, "he's only 60! He wants to marry me – can you believe that? I told him to get real and not be so silly." She added, "Can you see me as a little dutiful Japanese wife! Bahh!"

We all got on well together, sharing the same excitement of going into the unknown. We chatted easily on the train, little knowing that this would be the only opportunity for us to get to know one another as our every second in

Koyasan was going to be filled to capacity with no opportunity for our own spare time or relaxation. A typical Japanese style trip in fact with so much packed into a short time that there is no time to absorb detail or replenish energy levels.

Travelling to Koyasan was easy for us, all we had to do was get the train from the centre of Osaka to Koyasan, included in the ticket price was a cable car and bus ride. The train travelled through urban Japan for about forty five minutes. A mixture of closely packed apartment blocks, houses, commercial buildings, factories, roadways, flyovers with the occasional small field of rice or vegetables squeezed in amongst the concrete. Most of it was dreary and dull and became mind numbingly boring after a while and one ceased to notice it. However, suddenly the urban sprawl began to thin and fields of crops took its place as we entered the countryside. It was then I started to realise just what an enormous undertaking it would have been for the pilgrims of old to make a visit to Koyasan. They would have travelled on foot mostly, with only the richer people able to afford horses. Even then, the trek would have been extremely arduous.

The train climbed relentlessly into the mountains, curving its way through thick tree-lined gorges, with a road running alongside the railway track. Several pathways followed the road and some disappeared into the dense woods like helter-skelters threading themselves through the tall, closely packed trees; pines mostly, but some broad leafed too. From a distance they looked like giant Christmas trees, triangular in shape, conical hats on trunks. Even though the sides of the mountains were almost vertical the thousands of trees stood proud and magnificent, gods of the plant kingdom singing out in a silent opera of nature.

There were no towns now, only hamlets or small

villages, very rural and traditional. They looked very dull places, all of them placed on small plateaus of land amongst the towering mountains. One place looked much like another and I couldn't see any evidence of shops or places of entertainment. Just small fields of crops, many tiny orchards, interspersed with the odd house, or small collection of houses. Grey, box like and modern looking, with postage stamp gardens and the fields starting right outside their garden walls. I could understand why most of today's population prefer to live in the towns and cities.

Finally, after a long, slow grind upwards, we arrived at Koyasan station where we transferred to the cable car situated at the end of the platform. Climbing up at what seemed like a 45 degree angle for a mile or so, my relief at reaching the top was short lived as we boarded the bus which was to take us the last part of the journey. It started off with a groan and grind and slowly took us along the final part of the road. It was so narrow that the bus took up the space of both lanes on bends, and as it was almost one continuous bend, I found myself hoping that nothing would sweep carelessly along in the opposite direction.

Arriving unscathed, we entered Koyasan and I realised the enormity of the place and how it had evolved through the centuries. The bus passed temple after temple lining the roadway, which surprised me as I had not envisaged them to be situated along the road like a row of hospitality inns. It was not a piece of planning made in heaven, but I realised practical and necessary as the pilgrims and monks have to have access. So I made a conscious decision not to notice the cars and buses which droned past continuously, hoping that the fumes would be swept miraculously heavenwards to be absorbed by the thousands of trees which made a halo around the town.

Our temple was situated on this busy roadway, but on

entering through the temple gate the outside world was left behind. All was calmness, peace and serenity, and it enfolded me in its embrace, leaving me childlike and willing to be led without protest.

As we walked across the raked gravel of the courtyard, the wooden buildings of the temple surrounding us, our guide for the weekend appeared at the main entrance and called a welcome. Although he was a Buddhist priest, he was in fact a Frenchman named Andre, of average height and looks, a little pasty, but slim and very fit looking, aged about forty, wearing his monk's loose trousers and jacket. His shaved head looked as if he polished it every morning. However, the one thing that made him unique was his eccentric English with words tumbling out of his mouth with such rapidity and volume that they seemed to bump and bang into each other in a match to the death for utterance. In the process, their pronunciation was squashed and their clarity deformed, until what reached the listeners' ears was a nonsense. This was punctuated by the odd arrow of clarity and understanding, but was then, alas, soon lost again in the renewed torrent. At best, his English was highly original, his pronunciation imaginative and his grammar a war zone. But with practice I was able to understand his verbal idiosyncrasies enough to get the gist of things.

He asked us to take off our shoes at the entrance and put them on the shelves provided. He laid out pairs of large red plastic flip flops for us to change into as shoes were not allowed in the temple. We all knew that this was a perfectly safe thing to do as regardless of where you go, temple, restaurant or museum, no one would steal your Gucci boots and leave you their trainers in return.

The five of us followed him into the temple, where we tried desperately to keep up as he sped ahead. I left my flip flops behind with annoying regularity as my feet found them hard to grip, but as I struggled along I was able to glance around me. We had entered a lovely old building of paper and wood which was built around a secluded and serenely beautiful garden. A glazed corridor ran alongside the garden, giving one the opportunity to converse with nature every time one moved around the temple. Opening off the corridor on the other side were many traditional tatami mat rooms, as usual, devoid of any furniture except for a *kotatsu* (a small electrically heated table that kept the sitters legs warm) and many small, flat, floor cushions. Each room was full of Japanese people on a pilgrimage trip to Koyasan, laughing and chatting away. Family and group rooms, where everyone slept together upon the floors on thin futons.

Andre led us into an adjoining building saying that as the temple was full this weekend, we would stay alone in this separate building. "It will be better for you," he explained, "because all toilets are unisex in temples." (I'm not sure if he meant we would frighten the Japanese or vice versa!) He went on to explain that he and his wife lived in the main building and during the summer and spring, when the guest rooms were full, it was so noisy that they couldn't sleep. "They party all night," he said with his eyes raised.

We had two rooms between us, each with the ubiquitous kotatsu and floor cushions. The building was large and empty and we echoed around it somewhat, although we felt perfectly safe.

I liked Andre, and admired his ability to live in such a difficult place. In winter it is very cold and life is spartan, but if he had a major fault, besides his eccentric English, it was his long windedness. It he could make thirty seconds worth of speech last five minutes, he'd do his best to last six. This meant, that when we started our tour, the amount of places that we could easily have covered was cut short dramatically as we listened to his incredibly detailed explanations delivered in his unique tongue. A crash course in Buddhism was not what we expected, but it was what we got. Consequently, we were so bombarded with information that we forgot most of it.

The town itself was compact with a main road running through the middle which was lined with many restaurants, cafes and gift shops, all of varying sizes and quality. Some were so big you could easily get a couple of coach loads of people inside, albeit squashed up in Japanese style, while others were more sedate. You could buy any memento from a Buddha to a Koyasan cookie. The cookies were doing brisk business when I was there and I tried some, they were delicious but very hard and sweet. If your teeth were not so good, you'd have to suck them for a while before being able to chew on them. The road itself was old and narrow and inflicted with a ceaseless barrage of cars and buses, which made it difficult to walk along the narrow pavements. The traffic noise and fumes made me irritable as they were so out of place. But this is Japan, where everything one does is usually done in the company of thousands of others and Koyasan was no exception. One just has to accept that fact and do what the Japanese do. Forget the irritating or ugly things and concentrate on the beautiful or interesting things. Therefore, don't see the traffic, just focus on the beautiful building beyond it, or the beauty of the tree which is mostly obscured by electricity cables.

The temples were exquisite places but there were so many of them that the ones we had time to visit have all gone into a pot in my brain and got mixed together. I remember; serenity; beauty; calmness; incredible craftsmanship; simplicity of line; superior quality; statues; gods; cleanliness and order. But these have become so mixed up in my brain, that I couldn't isolate any even if I wanted too, which I don't. It is the overall impression and feeling that is important – to get the feeling of Koyasan into your bones – if you can take that essence away with you, it can stay with you for life. It has for me. I immediately become calm and stress free whenever I think of it, regardless of where I am or what I am doing. That's the magic of the place. Koyasan has been a mightily important place for the Japanese for over a thousand years and one can see why. It has helped shape their unique character, morals and values.

We finally came to the cemetery, which I was really eager to see. This *has* remained in my memory very clearly. It is over a thousand years old and houses approximately two hundred thousand old tombstones and monuments, is about two kilometers long by one kilometer wide and many important people in Japanese society have been buried here over the past one thousand years. *Okunoin* cemetery awed me. The atmosphere and the sheer scale of it alone, makes it unique. It was surreal, mysterious, intriguing and compelling. To enter, you have to cross the first of three small arched bridges. Each one gives you a chance for enlightenment, therefore one should put one's hands together, with fingers intertwined, and bow to show respect. As I walked over this bridge, I felt dwarfed and insignificant under the one thousand year old trees which towered over me, so high that it hurt my neck to look up. They made a roof in the sky almost blocking out the sun, ensuring continuing coolness underneath. They also gave the graves an otherworldliness with shafts of sunlight striking some and others next to them in shadow. This light moved around, ever changing the shape and emphasis of the graves. The graves themselves followed the contours of the land like a moving caterpillar, some raised up in glory and others snugly tucked into hollows which looked like fairy grottos. I was enchanted.

The graves were packed close together and seemed higgledy-piggledy, with no planning or forethought. Huge memorials with steps leading up to them next to tiny graves with just an obelisk to mark them. Anyone can be buried here, if you pay the price. Make no mistake, this cemetery is not for the poor, the common folk, but anyone who wants to buried near the monk, Kobo Daishi, who started it all, can do so if they pay for the privilege. Kobo Daishi himself is buried here, high up, overlooking the rest of the dead.

Our first stop was right at the beginning of the cemetery at the memorial to the unborn child. There were five or six small statues of the god Jizu lining the side of the memorial, each with a little hat, shawl or bib tied to it. Andre's explanation was hard to follow, delivered as it was in his flowing and confident, but gloriously eccentric English. Upside down and back to front phrases competed with mispronounced words which at times, were almost impossible to understand – as an example, China was pronounced 'Jeena', let's pause here, would be, 'here, pause let's'. I tried to think of a paragraph I could write in Andre English, but it was impossible. His style is his alone, and is much too difficult to emulate; but I'm sure you get the picture. Think Andre, think confusion. Although, by now, we realised that one didn't have to worry too much because he would repeat it again sooner or later in his enthusiasm to pass on as much information as he could muster the energy to communicate, which, we were to realise later, was inexhaustible.

The belief is that an unborn child, or one that is born dead through miscarriage or abortion, has a soul. This soul is now wondering around without a body and very unhappy, so the god Jizu must go along and collect all the unborn souls and take them to rest. Whenever you see these small statues of Jizu he has pieces of clothing attached to him, and you see him absolutely everywhere and in the most unexpected places. On street corners, in buildings, in dense woodland, in shrines, wherever. He always has these clothes placed on him and the reason for that is because of a little tale of evil that results in reward. A long time ago, a wicked woman (it's always a woman!) who had never done a good deed in her life, one day came upon the god Jizu, who was very cold. She stopped and put her shawl around him to keep him warm. When she died, the god said that although she had been very wicked throughout her life, she did one good deed, which was to give her shawl to Jizu. For this, she would be forgiven all her other sins and pass into peace. Consequently, now everyone puts a shawl, or a hat or some other item of clothing on him.

The trees lining the pathway through the cemetery towered above us, like peaceful giants. Their trunks bare for a hundred feet or more, ending in a top knot of thick green foliage. If the wind was blowing, one was not aware the trees were moving unless one looked up. Their trunks had a satisfying red bark, which peeled away in chunks, curling over and giving them an untidy look. Mostly, they are cryptomeria, cedars and umbrella pines, they made the pathway very still and dim, adding to the mystique. Was this a cemetery within a woodland, or a woodland within a cemetery? I wondered which came first. Either way, the trees feed off the people underneath and in return, protect them from the elements. Little sunlight shines down through them and what light is there is muted and grey, misty without the mist. Lichen covers the graves which indicates that it's a healthy place as lichen will only grow in good, clean air.

Some of the trees had roots that were above ground, standing three or four feet proud of the earth, and into the nooks and crannies of these roots, people had put offerings to the gods. Small dolls, food, coins, little twee objects, sat there sheltered and still. Someone had left peanuts along the way, filling up many of the small offering bowls. Andre, in an action that surprised us, took the peanuts out of a bowl and ate them, saying, "Mmm, fresh, some try?" We all shook our heads, a little shocked I think.

Here's a tip for any budding plastic surgeons. We passed a statue of the founder of Koyasan, Kobo Daishi, small and squat as it sat on a rock. It's chubby face was painted over in various shades of bright red lipstick, especially the cheeks, lips, eyes and nose Andre explained that if you do not like a part of your face and would like to change it, take out your lipstick and paint onto the face of Kobo Daishi the section of your face you want to change. This kind priest will then take on the feature you want changed. The afternoon we were there, the overriding dissatisfaction was with cheeks and lips, as these parts of his face were painted over so many times, you could see the lipstick standing proud. A nice psychological boost to the spirit.

We reached an area that was so surreal I wouldn't have been surprised to see fairies gamboling behind each gravestone. It was eerie, with the shadows and dancing light, but strangely friendly. The cool atmosphere and the undulating ground made this place even more supernatural than other areas. Deep hollows lay calm and mysterious with moss covering every inch of ground causing some damper areas to shimmer as the light moved across it. Higher areas offered brighter colours, the moss looking a psychedelic green compared to the colours in the hollows. I didn't feel ill at ease, as it looked charming more than anything else, and indeed, I took myself off the main pathway and into this fairy dell and through into the thicket beyond. As I walked further in, it became very dark with the trees becoming thicker and I was starting to feel uncomfortable and a little scared. The deeper I went the more the coldness seeped into me as there was no sun here. The higgledy-piggledy graves took on a different shape and atmosphere. The fairy dells looked more of a menace than an entrancement. I was alone and I had ventured in quite a way. I felt a slight panic as I retraced my steps and was very relieved to get back to the civilization of the pathway.

The history of women at Koyasan is sadly like the history of women throughout the ages. Denied the basic human rights of freedom to choose their way of life and to make a contribution in any meaningful way to society, the arts, or indeed to Buddhism. They were banned from Koyasan for over one thousand years. Not only banned from becoming monks or priests, but banned from even entering Koyasan, which would not have its soil polluted by the soles/souls of women. It was not until 1872 that women were allowed to enter and then to become monks and priests themselves and to be buried here. Today, there is even an all woman temple and women can become priests or monks in any of the other temples.

By now, I noticed that everyone in our party had a glazed and vacant look in their eyes, except for Andre, who continued his nonstop verbal deluge when, suddenly, he said a very interesting thing. Standing at the grave of one monk, he talked of him 'self mummifying'. My head jerked around and I asked, "How could he do that?" Andre looked a little annoyed that his flow had been interrupted, but he rallied round and explained that when a monk, or priest, wants to take the final meditative stance, he chooses his spot for continual meditation, stops eating and gradually reduces the amount of liquid he drinks. Eventually, his body will start to dry out and he goes into a trance. His body is then placed inside a coffin which is buried in the chosen spot. I don't know how deep the coffin is buried, but a straw is placed through a hole in the coffin and up through the earth into the fresh air. I couldn't understand from Andre whether this was for air, to take the moisture out of the coffin, or both. Either way, it's a horror.

A bell is also placed in the coffin which the monk rings from time to time to let the others know that he is still alive. There are stories of monks lasting for up to one month in their coffins, the bell still being rung. Gives a new meaning to, *For Whom the Bell Tolls*.

At last, we finally made it to the grave of Kobo Daishi himself, aka Kukai. History tells us that at the age of sixty two, and according to his own prediction, he went into the meditative posture and self mummified. Whilst still alive, his disciples then placed his body into a cave that had already been chosen for the purpose, and afterwards built his tomb above it. History also says that 50 years after his death, the reigning emperor, Daigo, granted him the posthumous title, Kobo Daishi, meaning Great Master who Spread the Buddhist Teaching, and the night he bestowed this great title, Kobo Daishi himself appeared to him in a dream and spoke this verse, 'In a hut on Koyasan my sleeve is rotting, but under the moss is a bright moon'. Make of that what you will, but the Emperor decided to send a new robe to Kobo Daishi, which was placed on his body. Every year since then, a ceremonious robe changing takes place on the 21st day of the 3rd month of the lunar calendar. In fact, the monks do not believe that Kobo Daishi is dead. They believe that he is 'resting' awaiting the coming of another Buddha. The monks leave food for Kobo Daishi twice a day, although no one tells you if he has eaten it or not.

Kobo Daishi's tomb is approached by many steps and when we reached the top, Andre had prepared a lovely little scenario for us. He handed each of us a stick of incense, which we lit and stuck into the ash of the incense tray, and then he gave us a copy of a sutra to chant in front of the tomb. We grouped around him and he led off first in a deep baritone voice, strong, clear and bell like, we followed his example and chanted as best we could considering it was a first experience for any of us, and it was in Japanese. The magic of the chant was unfortunately a little lost on me, as I was stood next to the incense tray and the smoke from it tickled my throat making me cough. However, I managed to get in a few chants at the end, and it did have a mesmerising effect on me. I can see why a chant, if done with determination and a clear mind, could affect your mental state. It was a unique experience, and one that I will always be grateful to Andre for arranging. He told us that he has chanted his way into seeing the gods of old, visions have appeared before him and his eyes have moved to look in different directions at once!

It was time to leave, and as we made our way out of the cemetery we passed the more modern section. National companies have plots here, where company employees can choose, if they pay the high fees, to be buried. These plots are marked by a symbol of the type of company it is. One company has a space rocket as its centerpiece, another one has an orange, and a coffee company marked its plot with two giant, marble coffee cups. They stand either side of a flight of marble steps and if you go up and stand on tip toe to look inside the cups, you will find that they are full of coffee. Or at least, dark brown marble substitutes for the coffee, but it's fun just the same. I put my hand on the cup and it was warm. I assumed it had been warmed by the sun, but in a place like this, one can never be too sure!

Arriving back at the temple, it was time for our bath, or *ofuro* (honourable bath). This is a must when staying at a temple. There is no discussion or getting out of it, you take your bath either before or after dinner. We took ours before, "To beat the rush after dinner," said Andre, "as there are eighty women staying here tonight it will be a little crowded in the bath!" Bath and bathwater are all shared, so the ritual of the bath must be obeyed. (Unlike the toilets, the men have their own separate ofuro. Thank goodness.)

You undress in your room and put on your *yukata*, a sort of wrap around kimono that is more like a dressing gown than a kimono. As it was really cold by this time, we were also given an extra one to wrap around ourselves. Stepping into my flip flops which I had left at the door to my room (no shoes of any kind are worn on the tatami mats), our group gathered together and took the long walk down the corridors to the ofuro. I felt strangely vulnerable in my thinly covered nakedness, with the cold of the corridors biting through the cloth, but nonetheless, felt obliged to comply. Andre had told us to be quick because we were running late and the Japanese guests would soon be ready to take their baths. The ofuro seated six people comfortably and ten people if you really want to get intimate. The thought of eighty women trying to fit into it with us, speeded us up like a Charlie Chaplin film.

Once we reached the ofuro area, we entered the ante room where you leave your yukata and inhibitions behind. Wrap them up with your yukata they will do you no good here. Naked and extremely cold, with goose bumps the size of boils and nipples like ramrods, I felt hesitant and unwilling as I entered the ofuro proper.

This was a small room, spotlessly clean with a deep sunken bath, Roman style, with steps leading down into it. Along one wall was a row of four fixed shower heads with four small, low stools placed under them. These were for us to sit on whilst we showered as the shower heads only came up to thigh height. Too bad if you have bad knees. When I sat on the stool my knees came up to my shoulders and I felt stupid. You are expected to wash yourself very thoroughly whilst sitting on your stool, including all your 'secret places,' which can be difficult for a westerner not used to this kind of intimacy with strangers. Being a good citizen and sensible to the health and wellbeing of the other women who would be following, I dutifully washed all my bits very thoroughly, ignoring the other women in our party who were doing the same thing and trying to ignore me.

Once thoroughly washed and rinsed, I stepped down into the *ofuro*, where to my shock, I found the water was so hot it almost scalded me. Standing at the top of the steps, with the women who were already in the bath looking up at me, had an amazing effect on my ability to get in and under fast. I felt a fool standing there wriggling and exclaiming, so I mentally tucked my nerve endings into their little sacs and ploughed in. After a while, I adjusted to the heat and it started to do its healing work on my aching limbs and muscles. If you are lucky and there are not too many people in there with you, you can stretch your legs and let them float, which was blissful. If the bath is full, you would have to sit there with your knees under your chin I should imagine. Not a pretty sight.

All of us were out in about five minutes, unable to stand the heat. My skin had turned red and my head had started to swim. However, my trials were not over yet as I made my way back to the ante chamber and picked up the ofuro towel, which is supplied by the temple, and discovered that it was about the size of a head scarf and very thin. Large, western bodies were not meant for towels like these, and I struggled back into my yukata still wet in many places. The Japanese love their ofuros, it's a national pastime, but for me, it was a trauma and most certainly not relaxing.

Whilst we were busy in the ofuro, the monks had been busy in the kitchen and our dinners awaited us in our room. Our group shared one room for this meal and all exclaimed at the beautifully laid out food arranged on small red lacquered trays. There were two trays per person and we ate seated on cushions placed on the tatami mat floor with our trays in front of us. They were on small legs and stood about six inches off the floor. The beauty of food and presentation are something only found in Japan and is one of the pleasures of this country. Beautiful, healthy food. I felt the stress of the day evaporate as I sat down, still scorching from the ofuro, desperately trying to keep the heat inside my yukata as the cold night air tried equally hard to get in.

Because this is a Buddhist temple, the food is always vegetarian, gourmet vegetarian. Called *Shoujin Ryouri* in Japanese, it is cooked very skillfully without the use of meat, fish, onions or garlic. It was superb. Tofu, (soy bean curd) *miso* soup (soya bean soup), *tempura* vegetables (fried vegetables in a delicate batter), *tsukemono* (pickled vegetables), rice, bamboo shoots, and a flask of hot sake. Koyasan is famous for its tofu and the recipe is secret and passed down from chef to chef.

Andre told us that the monks had to eat in the kitchen and while we were in the bath he had eaten a bowl of rice and drunk three flasks of hot sake in ten minutes. That's pretty impressive as sake packs a powerful punch. Unfortunately, he insisted on joining us while we ate our dinner. He sat on the floor, and gave us a verbal concert of all his idiosyncratic speech and knowledge of Buddhism. But it didn't matter because we had switched him off. He didn't seem to notice.

After dinner, we were all exhausted and ready for our beds; it was 8.00pm. But Andre had other ideas. Even though the temperature was plummeting as we spoke and we were all very cold, (he told us that the doors either end of the temple were always left open so that guests could come and go at will) he insisted that we accompany him to the prayer room, even though we were still in our thin yukatas.

He explained that we would gather there the next morning at 6.00am and take part in the service. It was the highlight of everyone's stay, he told us, and we must know what was expected of us. So we reluctantly tripped down the corridors in our flip flops once again until we got to the prayer room. It was a room of darkness, for although I would guess, it had at least one hundred lanterns hanging from the ceiling, all of them lit, each one only gave out a faint glow, less than a match, and it left the room in dim darkness where one could only just see a couple of feet in front of one. The room was about thirty by forty feet long and was divided into two. The front section was empty and assigned for the pilgrims to sit in, while the other part was crammed full of things, although it was really hard to see as everything was painted black, even the floor. There were many black, floor to ceiling shelves, covered in neatly stacked, small, black boxes with a name engraved on the front of each one in gold lettering. Andre told us that these were the names of peoples' ancestors and that anyone, as long as they paid the fee, could have their name engraved on a box. The idea was that when the priests prayed in this room, a bit of it might rub off onto their spirit.

Entering this area was like stepping into a black void, but we all trusted Andre implicitly and followed him. He told us when we came to a step and we felt for it with our feet. We moved slowly and hesitantly, following him around as he told us that we, together with the other pilgrims (over a hundred of us) would walk around this room tomorrow morning as part of the ceremony, and that it would be just as dark, so it was a good idea to pay attention!

He explained that the Japanese pilgrims had each bought a prayer stick, or sticks, at the temple today, and the priests had written the name of their chosen ancestor on it. These would be neatly bundled together and would be ceremoniously burned in a special burning pot with lots of incense and oils. Whilst the priest was doing this, we would all file past him, look reverently at the fire and give our offering. For a change, the offering was not money, but a pinch of tea.

My eyes having adjusted a little, alighted on the only colour in the room. Stacked on narrow shelves were about a dozen rows of identical and very attractive small pastel coloured bags, with a little flap at the top. Like rows of expensive sweet bags. They made me want to pick them up and open them. Instead, I asked Andre what they were. His eyes lit up as he said, "Ah, they are the esophagi of dead priests!" (I was reassured to hear that they were dead before removal.) He explained that the priests' esophagi are taken out and kept because, it is claimed by those in the know, that they look like a Buddha.

In Japan they have a very hands on attitude to death. After cremation, your remains are brought out to the family. It is the skill of the people who do the cremations, that they can bring out the remains 'just right'. This means that the flesh has burnt away and all that is left are bones. The bones should be white and surrounded by ash, and not discoloured in any way. When these remains are brought out to the family, the body is still on the tray that it was cremated in, it will not have been touched. Family and relatives then pick out the bones with giant chopsticks.

Grisly, but this is the traditional way, which is still practiced today. Could anything be more intimate than this? You definitely get to see your friends and relatives in every light in this country. The bones are then placed in a container and buried, or kept by the family. For the priest, his esophagus is removed and put into one of these colourful bags and then placed in the temple. Again, the skill of the cremator is in bringing out the esophagus in one piece and not damaged by the fire. This is one aspect of Japan that I do not want to experience. Having your bones picked over, to me, is the ultimate invasion of privacy.

At last, we finished our visit to the black room and Andre said, in his idiosyncratic way, "Tired, rooms back." Everyone understood this instantly and perked up immeasurably making for the door in something that resembled a stampede, but a moan went up when he said, "But, go before I say..." he stopped, looked at our crestfallen faces, and I think he finally realised that he had said enough. "Go," he said, looking a little sorry that we wanted to leave him.

He escorted us back to our rooms, and asked one of the French women, Frankie, who had made the mistake of admiring some artwork in the temple, if she would like to come to see his wife's art work in the foyer. We realised that the invitation was really meant for all of us, as we saw his arm encompass our group in an arc, but we all ignored him and scuttled into our rooms like rabbits into a warren, so fast that you could only see our backs before the doors slid shut with a bang. Frankie was not so lucky, she hesitatingly said, "Yes, OK, I'll come and look."

I sat down on my cushion, at my kotatsu table and arranged my legs under it, switched on the electricity and it heated up in moments, warming me up. I made some notes and drank some cold water, which was all that was available. After about an hour, I was ready for bed, but annoyingly, I had to go and empty my bladder first. Everyone else was in bed and it was very quiet in our quarters. So it was with a certain degree of trepidation that I ventured forward in my ever ready flip flops, down the corridor for 100 or so yards to the toilet block at the end of our building.

Having discovered that all toilets in temples are unisex, I was a little nervous in case I encountered a little old Japanese man. I knew I would frighten him to death, and he me!

I was lucky, no men in sight. "Thank goodness," I thought, but just to be on the safe side, I was in and out very fast. The entry into the toilet area was large, at least twice the size of a normal doorway, and in fact, didn't actually possess a door, which meant that all the stalls and urinals were on display to anyone who happens to walk past on their way down the corridor. Maybe, because they are unisex, the idea is that there will be no privacy at all for any 'inappropriate behaviour'. Must be simpler to have separate toilets, there were enough of them around.

As I made my way back up the corridor, feeling pleased to come out unscathed, suddenly, a figure appeared in the distance. It hung around hesitatingly, saw me, and then hurried in my direction with determination. It was Frankie.

"Oh, thank goodness," she said, with her shy smile "I got lost, is this our section?"

I said incredulously, "Have you only just come back from seeing the artwork?"

"Yes," she uttered the word sheepishly, "I got lost, and have been wandering around for ages." I escorted her back, and she disappeared gratefully inside her room.

The next morning at 5.15 on the dot, Andre knocked and woke us all up with pots of Japanese tea. I think we were all awake anyway, none of us having got much sleep due to the cold and the thin futon on the hard floor. Sleeping on nails might have been more comfortable, at least there would have been the occasional gap in the nails to look forward to. Stiff and cold, we got up and dressed straight away. No hanging around, we had scorched in our bath the night before, and we followed the Japanese example and didn't wash in the morning.

All we had to do was visit the loo and clean our teeth. I scuttled down the corridor, confident now, about using the unisex. I left my towel and toothbrush at the washing area which was just outside and opposite the toilets. The washing facilities are also communal and unisex, the sink big enough to hide bodies in. About twenty feet long, three feet wide and deep. A row of ten taps were dispersed along the length of the sink. This was the first time I had ever seen taps lagged on the inside of a building. Each tap and pipe leading to it was wrapped in a layer of two inch thick padding and bandaged over. It must get *really* cold here in winter.

Again, I got in and out of the toilet in glorious isolation, and was happily cleaning my teeth at the giant sink, when I looked up and saw two old men rushing down the corridor towards me. One looked desperate and had his trousers open and half way down his bottom before he entered the toilet. Ugh! I have never cleaned my teeth so fast and never thought I could move so swiftly up a polished corridor in a pair of plastic flip flops. I might have looked like a penguin running along the ice, but it's a wonder what you can achieve in adversity.

We were ready and in the prayer room by 5.40am, before any of the Japanese folk arrived. This we had to do to ensure that we got our places on the half dozen chairs that were there. Everyone else had to sit on the floor on their knees. We sat on our chairs near the corner of the room, right up against the back wall, but even then, we looked incredibly conspicuous and I felt very out of place and uncomfortable as the Japanese people started to file in. No one looked at us directly as they settled themselves down on their knees. Everyone left a little space between their neighbour and the line behind them, but then it was realised that the room was full and there were still many people waiting to get in. Everyone did a soft knee shuffle and without getting up, closed the gaps between their neighbours and the lines behind them, in a noiseless action that seemed to be second nature to them. Without fuss, instruction or complaint, it was completed in half a minute. It's wonderful what the Japanese can do on their knees and was worthy of a well rehearsed chorus line. I was fascinated.

Suddenly, a bell was rung by a priest. It clanged for about five minutes nonstop whilst another priest started the fire which would burn the prayer sticks. Bells rang, cymbals vibrated, gongs were struck, a dog barked outside, and the priests started to chant. Then the rhythmic chanting began in earnest.

At this stage the people nearest the fire got up and made a bow facing the entrance to the black room. This was to help people get rid of their ego, leave it at the door, it's not wanted in here. This was the little file past that we had rehearsed the night before, and we were very glad that we did. Our turn finally came and we did everything impeccably and didn't shame ourselves by behaving inappropriately.

We all shuffled around the black room and down the step, feeling for it with our feet, following the people in front. It was uneventful and I'm not sure what it was we were supposed to be doing or feeling. Andre's English had defeated me. The Japanese people looked very earnest and dour about everything, and I assumed they were communing with their ancestors' spirits. But they may have been thinking, 'Bloody foreigners!'

The monks were still chanting, their orange robes glowing in the darkness, and intermittently bells and cymbals still rang out. The fire was spectacular, with the oils making whooshing flames and the incense was pungent and sweet. It lasted for two hours and like all religions, it was a show to sooth the masses and it succeeded.

It had been a memorable two days spent in the extraordinary company of Andre, an earnest and devout man, who despite his idiosyncrasies, I liked and respected, although the one thing that stuck in my mind from all the information that poured out of him was his statement that he was very disillusioned with the Japanese priests and monks. He had discovered that generally, they don't fully understand the doctrine of Buddhism. This was because it is not a vocation here, it is a job. A family business. The eldest son of a priest or monk, duly becomes one himself and carries on the business. Some even own their own temples. Consequently, many go through the motions and carry on the traditions when their hearts and minds are elsewhere. Deep understanding and philosophy is not studied. Andre said, "I speak to them in the evenings, and we debate the doctrine of Buddhism, and it becomes very clear that they do not understand what I am saying to them." If his Japanese is as idiosyncratic as his English, I can only say one word. Quite!

CHAPTER SIX

The Funny House and The Takarazuka Theatre

Still backtracking a little, before Jan returned to England and in between colds, we were going to the Takarazuka theatre regularly. At that time, the show and the troupe changed every six weeks, (now it's every four weeks) and many fans went on a regular basis to see each one, some fans seeing the same show many times over. We were no exception.

Yu san was a Takarazuka fan who had approached us in a restaurant one evening, introduced herself and left her card. Brash, brazen, loud, dominant, always smoking and liked to drink, think honest market trader and you have a fair idea of her personality traits. But she drove around in a flash car, got the best tickets to see Takarazuka shows and she took us under her considerable wing.

Tall and always dressed in expensive high fashion, the wrong side of forty and extremely thin. Her hair dyed an orangey colour as is the way with Japanese hair, which refuses to dye the nice blond colour aimed at. In fact, she was everything that most Japanese women are not. She also had that unfortunate habit of doing things for you without telling you, making and changing arrangements without consultation, and getting information out of her was as easy as walking on water. But she spoke good English, so she was our friend. (Finding a fan of Takarazuka who spoke English was even more difficult than walking on water.)

Prior to meeting Yu san, Ryoko and her husband Kenji san, had taken us to a 'special' Takarazuka restaurant. It's a 'you're only accepted there if you are introduced' kind of place. Takarazuka is like two worlds, the world of the Takarazuka performer and the world of the fans and the two rarely mix. However, what does happen is that performers will meet 'special' fans (i.e. long-standing, loyal fans) in restaurants for tea or dinner and chat to them in the safety of a public space.

The Funny House restaurant was such a place, where special fans were welcome and where minor performers could go and eat in peace and safety away from the hustle and bustle of the normal Takarazuka restaurants. Many ordinary fans do not know of this place, tucked away in a side street, well away from the theatre. It is on the ground floor of a wooden house built in the Dutch style. Inside, it has an old European style decor which was very smart and unusual when it was first opened 40 or so years ago, hence its name, The Funny House. It has not been touched since. No extra lick of paint, no new tables or chairs, no extra polish, it just is. It has a patina over it – a preserved history. The dingy walls, the peeling plaster, the rough wooden floor, the cracked counter, the rickety chairs, the tables that squeak, the low lights. If you think this sounds unpleasant, please think again, for it's like an old friend, a character out of Dickens, full of quirks and foibles, with a heart of gold. The old wood, untouched since inception adds to the deepness of the character. Two walls are covered in large, full colour posters of the latest Takarazuka shows and Takarazuka magazines are piled up on a table for fans, or performers, to leisurely flip through. Great discussions sometimes went on around tables of fans who were looking at the magazines and discussing the merits of this star, or that one. Young Takarazuka students, training for their dreams, often came in and ate dinner and checked out the magazines. It was a home from home, a place out of this world, a place left behind. I loved this restaurant and always felt that its arms embraced me and welcomed me to its bosom. I felt comfortable, reassured, secure and loved there. The Mama san, almost twice as old as her restaurant, always welcomed me with open arms and a smile of pure pleasure, her big old eyes lighting up. She had big, round eyes, most un-Japanese like, and a sturdy, but now soft and flabby body. Always impeccably dressed in a style of a bygone age, she made me feel at home.

This restaurant became very important to me, it was part of my life and I went to it once a week for years. The outsider or the uninitiated, unsure of its stature, could be put off entering by its ambiance, but for me, that was part of it. You became part of this secret place because you knew that the chef, Ko san, the Mama san's nephew, was one of the best chefs around and his food good, nutritious and all freshly cooked in a mixed menu of western and Japanese. If they were very busy, sometimes, you would have to wait an hour or more for your dinner, but nobody minded, again it was part of the charm. You knew that Ko san was working hard in the kitchen, as he had no help, and everything was being freshly cooked. The patrons of the Funny House would just hunker down, order in the beer, and start in on the merits of Takarazuka shows, performers and anything else that took their fancy. Passion was the key, no one sat there in misery with the wait, you came to the Funny House to continue your passion for the Takarazuka theatre, and when the food did arrive, it was ambrosia.

The Funny House was intriguing and untouched by outside life. For me, it was a rabbit warren of mystery.

Sometimes it was teeming with customers, other times it was empty, but mysterious phone calls would come with clipped conversation in Japanese. Then suddenly, there would be lots of activity in the kitchen. Ko san, tall, willowy, with pony tail and goatee beard, dressed casually in jeans, sweat shirt and trainers, would do his magic in the kitchen and parcels of food would appear on the counter and suddenly (at least to me) the waitress would take off with them. They were delivered, I found out later, to performers wherever they were at the time. At the theatre with late rehearsals or at home and exhausted.

Into this mysterious place, Yu san invited us to meet Miyuki san. She was a young Takarazuka performer who had expressed an interest in meeting us and Yu san knew her, as she knew many Takarazuka performers and staff through her business interests. Although, being Yu san, she never told us what those business interests were. "Just business," she would say in her gruff voice and turn around and talk to someone else.

We met one evening for dinner, Jan and I, Yu san, Miyuki san and her mother. Young Takarazuka performers are well protected by restaurants like the Funny House, by the other performers and by their mothers. At that time, I hadn't realised that I was also under that same protective wing, until one evening, a male customer, alone and rather drunk, which in itself was rare, suddenly got up off his counter stool and swayed over to me, put his arm around my shoulder and started speaking to me. Before I could react, both the Mama san and Ko san had shot like whippets to my table and put their hands gently on the man's arm. The Mama san started to speak to him in soft, gentle tones, goodness knows what she said to him, but it worked like a charm. Whilst she was doing this, Ko san was very gently guiding him to the door and within one minute he disappeared out into the cold night air without one cross word or any aggression. The Mama san and Ko san came over to me and apologised profusely. I realised then, why the Takarazuka performers felt safe there. Nothing can harm you at the Funny House. I was astounded and very pleased that they felt that they needed to protect me too.

I also met many takarajiennes there as I was introduced to them by the Mama san. I began to realise that the takarajiennes felt safe at the restaurant because the Mama san would only introduce them to people she recommended. She was implying that I was a safe person to speak to, that she had vetted me beforehand. Unfortunately, my Japanese speaking ability always let me down as I became lost in the intricacies of the language and unable to converse with them with any real meaning, which always left me feeling frustrated, because although I always managed to get over the points I wanted to make, it was the answers I had so much trouble with. Our conversations were usually short as the takarajiennes were coming to the Funny House to give the Mama san some of the baskets of flowers their fans had given them for the opening or closing of their show and they would be off to the next place soon. Often, this would take place at 10.00pm or thereabouts, making it a very long day for the takarajienne, who would have been at the theatre quite early in the morning. Sometimes, the Mama san would take a picture of me and the takarajienne and several of them have gone on to become top stars, so I feel very privileged to have been given such a rare opportunity by such a delightful lady.

I guess that Miyuki san was about twenty years old, not tall, and therefore a female player as, generally, only tall performers get to be male players. She was very pretty, poised, gentle and fun. A sweetie in fact. Her mother was more woman of the world, thin, bordering on the gaunt, but impeccably dressed, pleasant and politeness personified.

Yu san translated for us and we got on well, deciding to meet again at the Funny House. After which, Miyuki san and her mother invited us to their house for dinner one evening. At least, that's who we thought had invited us, and for that reason, but remember, this is the ever secretive Yu san translating. We only ever got half a story, half of the information. If we were lucky.

The day of the dinner came round and we met Yu san as arranged and got into her other car, a people carrier. We expected to go to Miyuki san's house, but instead, we drove around Takarazuka picking up women here and there at pre-arranged places. So seven of us were going to Miyuki san's house for dinner? Strange. Of course, we got no information out of Yu san.

Finally, after about a half hour drive, we drove into Miyuki san's driveway and there were gasps from everyone. She lived in a mansion! Modern and sweeping, with lots of pillars and glass, it was like something out of *House and Garden* magazine. (I found out later that Miyuki san's father was a rich man.) We drove up the curving drive and got out of the car. Miyuki san and her mother were there to welcome us. It was the right place then.

The hall was huge, up to a height of forty feet or so, with a grand semi-curving staircase to one side. Giant white orchid plants were everywhere, costing over £100 each, there were at least 10 of them on show in the hallway alone. I felt very small and insignificant giving our small gift to Miyuki san. Unfortunately, we had decided on a plant, and it looked paltry compared to the extravagant wealth surrounding us, but it was accepted in the spirit in which it was given and put in pride of place in the living room. This large, long room was virgin, with white walls, white carpets, white sofas and chairs. Here too, white orchids abounded. We sat down and chatted for a while and were introduced to grandmother, who was living with them. It was at times like these that I wished so hard that my stupid brain could get to grips with the Japanese language. Chatting was difficult and rather strained with Yu san translating my long, carefully chosen sentences into short stubby ones. Goodness knows what she was saying.

After ten minutes or so, we were told that we would be going upstairs. As we climbed the curving staircase, I felt a little bit like Scarlet in *Gone with the Wind*. I marvelled at the decor, avoided the artfully placed orchid plants and entered a large room. It was full of people. Around forty I would guess. What was going on? Were there forty of us for dinner? On the left hand side of the room was a fully stocked professional bar surrounded by bar stools. The room opened up into a large round area with glass walls and the whole of the city was laid out below us in twinkling darkness. It was a night-time spectacular as the house was situated half way up a mountain. I realised that we were seeing the view at its best because daytime reality would expose it as the world of unremitting concrete that it really was.

We were asked to sit opposite the bar together with Miyuki san and some other guests, away from all the other people, and we were instantly plied with food and drink.

Although we had been in Japan for several months by this time, this was the first time Jan and I had experienced having lots of unasked for food placed in front of us and being urged to eat it. All sorts of little dishes appeared and we started to feel panicky. Culture differences were beginning to get razor sharp. We assumed that we had to eat all the food put before us, as it would be rude not to, but Miyuki san's mother, being Japanese, was only offering us the food, we didn't have to eat it. Her culture gave food and drink and never asked if it was wanted. It was up to us whether we ate it or not.

We didn't know this and Miyuki san's mother didn't know of our different cultural traditions. We were reading from different scripts. Therefore, we were eating everything she put before us, getting fuller and more fractious, and the more we ate, the more she put before us. Finally, I said that I really couldn't eat any more, but she still insisted on leaving dishes of food before us. Bother! My stomach would explode if I ate any more. A dish of salad sat before me and wilted. I felt I was being so rude as Miyuki san's mother passed by once more and bade me eat up. What to do? Eat up and be sick or risk offending her? Finally, after discussions with Jan and the help of a Japanese lady who was sitting at our table, we grasped the concept that we didn't have to eat it all. Just a bite from each dish, an utterance of 'Ah delicious', was sufficient to placate everybody and save everyone's face. Oh dear. I wished I had known that six dishes ago!

After all this food and wine, I had to bow to the inevitable, and seek out the loo and like the rest of the house, it was state of the art, luxury personified. Unfortunately, that meant a toilet with lots of electrical buttons on it, for the Japanese passion for all things electrical does not stop at the toilet door. Entering, I passed the wash hand place, full of marble and other exotic things and entered the inner sanctum itself, and found four images of myself looking back. Mirrored walls, how I hate them. Two-way mirrors always go through my mind ever since I read, as an impressionable adolescent, about a two-way mirror that a famous actress said was in a toilet of a house where she attended a party. They told her afterwards! But here, in Miyuki san's house? Surely not. Well, if they were two-way, then they were in for a surprise, because bodily function attended to, I then turned to find the flush. Where was it? Nothing that looked vaguely like a flush was present. What to do? I remembered that Jan had told me a few days before, in another electrical loo she had used, that she found the flush amongst the electrical buttons. I studied them, they all had Japanese writing on them which of course, I couldn't read. I pondered, and finally, cock sure in my choice, I pressed the button with an image of a shower printed onto it. Well, in my experience, whenever you are cock sure, you get your comeuppance. I was amazed to see a little white plastic stick start a slow journey from under the rim of the toilet pan and stop right in the middle of it. Fascinated and puzzled, I looked at this white stick, looking rather obscene and ridiculous when suddenly, it shot out a thick jet of water straight into my face. It went up into my hair, down my clothes as I jumped back, and finally cascaded down the mirrored wall behind me. Soaked, and in a panic with no time to think, I tried to stop it by putting my hands over it. Big mistake, the water just jetted out in different directions. All four mirrored walls were now soaked. I was bordering on the drenched.

Finally, it stopped and the little white lever retreated back into its hole and calm was restored. But not really, because now I had a soaking wet loo and a soaking wet me. I pondered on what I should do now. You have to remember that I wanted to make a good impression here. I wanted this sweet young takarajienne and her mother to feel some form of respect and interest in me. I wanted them to think of me favourably as I think most people would who are interested in something and then meet someone who is very much involved in that interest. This wasn't the way to do it.

I walked into the hand washing area and looked around. As everything was upmarket there were no paper towels, oh, for a paper towel. There were only incredibly white, soft, small cotton hand towels, all neatly folded up in two little baskets. Oh dear, well nothing for it then. Taking a handful of pristine white towels, I proceeded to mop up. Some towels later, I gave up. I'd done my best. I mopped myself down as best I could and took a deep breath and garnered my courage and left the loo, hoping that no one would see me – oh, please don't let them know it was me! But alas, sod's law was at work again and as I exited there was someone waiting to go in. My secret was out.

Jan said, "What have you been doing? Are you OK? You were a long time."

"Don't press any electrical buttons," I told her, "I've just been mauled by a white water lever and believe me, it's an experience I never want to repeat."

She looked puzzled and finally said, "You look wet. What happened?"

So, the whole sorry saga came out, Jan, bless her, didn't laugh and looked suitably horrified. The lady sat near us was listening intently, her English ability limited but she managed to get the drift. She looked stricken and rushed off to tell Miyuki san's mother. Bother! Never let a foreigner get away with anything. When she returned with Miyuki san's mother, I asked her to tell her that I was very sorry, it was an accident and I felt very bad about it. Again, this was translated into a stubby sentence and I resolved for the umpteenth time that I must master Japanese and be able to explain for myself.

Well, that was the one and only time we went to Miyuki san's place. We never did discover what the other forty people were doing there. Yu san's reaction to our question was "Oh, just people I know, friends." It was pointless, I didn't walk on water and find out any information from her, I just got drowned instead.

By the way, the little white stick turned out to be the Japanese version of a bidet. As there is not enough space in normal Japanese homes for a full bidet, they have invented a moving bidet stick housed within the loo itself. You just have to remember to be sitting on the toilet awaiting its services before you press the button. And when you do press the button, make sure it says spray and not jet, unless you are a masochist or have a hide like a rhinoceros!

CHAPTER SEVEN

My School Starts

By now, Jan had returned to England and I was adjusting to life alone. I was apprehensive but determined to succeed. I was building a life for myself. I was making friends, I was enjoying myself. I still wanted to teach English to adults, desperately searching for a way of starting. I had just received my visa, there was nothing to stop me except my ignorance of how to start and how to do it in a professional manner acceptable in Japan. Ryoko kept telling me that I could do it from my front room, like our kids' class. "Is that possible?" I asked her rather forlornly, "I know that Yamamoto san and Fumi san were happy with my flat, but that was a personal thing, not business, do you think that people I don't know will want to come to my little flat in Nigawa?"

"Yes," she said emphatically, "to come to a foreigners flat and see how they live is very interesting to a Japanese person."

"But I have nothing in my flat," I was puzzled, "it's not interesting."

"It is to a Japanese, remember that we have very little contact with foreigners, especially from England. We are hungry to know you, anxious to meet you, but at the same time, feeling very shy and insecure. So many people will want to meet you and will be willing to pay for your lessons, you just have to present the right image." That image thing again.

"What sort of image?" I asked anxiously.

Ryoko smiled a knowing smile. "Elegance," she gently said. "Elegance is the key word. We Japanese think that English people are so elegant and live such elegant lifestyles that we want a little bit of the gloss, a taste of the flavour of Englishness." (By English, Japanese people mean all the countries that make up the UK, as they have little concept, or none at all, of Britishness; therefore I was always referred to as an English woman and adopted the practice myself. Having tried many times to explain the difference, I finally gave up.)

"You must advertise yourself as an English woman teacher and invite people to come to your flat." It took a while to get used to this kind of idea, I had thought of renting a room somewhere, but Ryoko was adamant, "If you want people to come, then it must be your flat. That's your easiest way and it is what people really want." I was reluctant to have lots of strangers traipsing into my home and couldn't quite believe that they would want to, or that it could be that simple. It took some adjusting to, but I rallied and put my trust in Ryoko.

Between us, we composed a suitable advertisement and we found a publication to put it in. Ryoko suggested the Kansai Flea Market to start with. A small free advertising newspaper, written in English for foreigners, but read widely by Japanese aspiring to get a flavour of foreign life.

In due course, in went the advert with my mobile phone number attached and I got my first call. I was so nervous I almost lost the caller in a terrible babble of English that she couldn't follow at all. Calm down Jill, keep it simple, I told myself.

"Meet me at Nigawa station tomorrow at 2.00pm," I

said very slowly and clearly. Repeating it patiently several times.

"OK," the timid sounding voice answered, "see you." That was it. My first appointment made.

Next day, Nigawa station was as busy as a hungry bee hive, but I was the only foreigner waiting there, so she found me easily. She took the initiative and shook my hand although I had bowed to her in the Japanese manner. Many Japanese like to shake hands with foreigners, thinking that it is the correct way of behaving, and although it was correct in this instance, unfortunately, many people do it inappropriately, shaking hands several times with the same person and offering a limp handshake that flops about disconcertingly for the recipient. I finally found out that lots of people got the idea of shaking hands so frequently by watching news clips on television of the then President George W. Bush at summit meetings!

Having sorted ourselves out, we made our way back to my flat. I made some tea and we chatted in a very simple way. "What's your name?" I asked her slowly.

"Hanashi Asako," she timidly replied.

"Where do you live?"

"Nishinomiya."

"Do you have a family?"

"Yes."

"Do you have children?"

"Yes."

"Do you like movies?"

"Yes."

"What kind of movies?"

"Happy."

I was beginning to get an idea of where we would have to start. She was too shy to elaborate and to unsure in her English to risk making a mistake in grammar or meaning. I would have my work cut out.

I was up for the challenge. I had studied several books on how to teach English as a foreign language. I realised later that they were far too academic and of no use in teaching students like Japanese housewives, who didn't want the lessons to be like school and wanted to have a good time in as far from an academic setting as they could. They wanted to meet a British woman, understand more about Britain and improve their English along the way. It was a whole new ballgame. No books could help me in this, I had to develop things for myself.

Ryoko helped of course. We got together many times and spent hours discussing strategy, cultural differences, possible lesson plans. I would go home and try and devise some interesting lessons for the students from our discussions. Some worked, some didn't. Trial and error. Trouble was, if I got it too wrong then I lost the student and students were hard to come by. After about three months I had around eleven students. But finding students was becoming 'very bothersome' in Ryoko's apt phrase.

I was starting to feel frustrated and inadequate and a little bit desperate. Every time my phone rang and a prospective student said the first tentative and nervous words into my phone, I was not able to put them at their ease because of my lack of Japanese speaking ability and their lack of English speaking ability. Japanese people, especially the women, tend to be shy and reserved and many have little confidence when meeting a foreigner. Either that, or some go to the other extreme and get very bolshie and rude, thinking, mistakenly, that this is imitating western society.

I did get the occasional odd ball and that was scary and extremely unpleasant. I remember one instance when I went on an outing with a sightseeing group. We were a mixed bunch of foreigners and Japanese of various ages although I don't remember much about the day except for a young Japanese woman in her mid twenties. She was on her own and I felt sorry for her as no one else was talking to her and half way through the day I decided to offer the hand of friendship and started chatting to her. She had enough English to understand me, and she told me that she was a student studying criminal psychology. I spoke to her for a while, but then I realised that she had a difficult personality, so I gave up, but I did give her my business card just in case she wanted to study English. Like a boy scout, I was always prepared and giving out my business card to anyone I thought suitable.

A few weeks later, I started getting strange phone calls, the person on the other end speaking in a weird voice and without preamble asking me personal questions like, "What part of England do you come from? What do you like about Japan? Where do you shop? Do you have any friends in Japan?" Strange questions like that. I was unnerved by this and hung up, but the calls continued to come once or twice a week, with the voices changing tone or pitch. It could have been the same person. One day, another strained voice asked to come to my flat for an English lesson. Not being able to tell whether this was the same person or persons, I agreed to meet her at the station in my usual fashion as this is where I met all my new students. It was neutral territory and if I felt they were not the kind of person I could trust, I would not take them back to my place. Fortunately, during the years I did this, I met no one that I didn't feel comfortable to take to my home – except for my feelings about this one.

I went to the station at the appointed time but no one turned up. This happened on three different occasions. Each appointment was made by a strange but somewhat different sounding voice, until finally, after another no show, I got a call an hour later. She said that she was still waiting at the station and that I hadn't turned up. My suspicions were aroused further when she demanded that I go back to the station now and meet her. I refused politely, but refused nonetheless. I was feeling unnerved and apprehensive and very stressed by all this. In my experience, bullying people such as these do not give up. Once they scent blood they start getting their kicks and feeling ever more powerful, and, as expected, another call came through a few days later. Another strange and strained voice, but the same atmosphere. Was this woman a clever impersonator or was it a group of women? Anyway, I was getting savvy as well as nervous. I changed the place where we would meet. This time, I arranged to meet her outside the station on the street, just opposite the supermarket. A very precise spot.

As I approached the supermarket, it was very sunny and I was using my sun umbrella to shield my face from the sun. I lifted it up to pass someone and we caught sight of each other at the same moment. My young student of criminal psychology was sitting astride a bicycle just to the side of the small supermarket. She immediately ducked her head and hid her face in the book she was holding and let her hair fall over her face until it completely covered it. A strange stance.

I took up my place and stood there for 15 minutes, and of course, no prospective student turned up. I kept watching the psychology student from under my umbrella, we were only a few yards away from each other. She didn't move a muscle and I'm sure she watched me from under her hair. Oh dear! What to do now? I decided that the best course of action was to ignore her, as I had no proof it was anything to do with her. So I left my spot and went into the station, but stopped by a window where she couldn't see me, and watched her again. After a minute or so, she put her book down and cycled off without looking around, or even checking her watch as if she had been waiting for someone.

It was a weird way to depart and after this, I felt sure that she was behind it all. What was she playing at? Putting her study of criminal psychology into practice? Trying out a mild form of psychological terror tactics to see how they worked? How far would she take it? What would she do next? What could I do about it? What should I do about it? It was a problem that had to be solved one way or another. I didn't want to make a formal complaint, and I had no proof.

I had worked out that Japanese people can sometimes take advantage of vulnerable foreigners, which is not unusual, the same thing happens throughout the world, although in Japan, it is not so common, and it was my bad luck to be singled out. I had also worked out that Japanese people rarely do this kind of thing to other Japanese people for the simple reason that if they are found out, then there is hell to pay. Not only would the wrath come down on the perpetrators head, but on the heads of his or her family too. The family is responsible for the good behaviour of its members and all will suffer if one lashes out. It is safer to exploit a foreigner because mostly, other people don't find out about it.

With this thinking in mind, I decided that I had to do something radical. I needed an assistant. A Japanese person who could front my calls for me and offer me some protection. But this left me with a bit of a quandary because I didn't earn enough money to employ someone, so it would have to be on a part time, casual basis.

As I was pondering this, trying to think of a suitable person, Maki san joined my classes. Of similar ages, we got on together really well. She was bouncy, intelligent, full of life and interested in many things. Small and spare of build, with an impish hair style and I could tell that she didn't suffer fools gladly. The perfect assistant for me.

I approached the subject at the end of a lesson and she

looked at me in total disbelief but with an encouragingly distinct glint of excitement in her eye.

"No," she said, "I couldn't."

I cajoled.

"No, it's impossible," she batted back.

"You are so suitable," I persuaded. "You can do it."

Finally, it came out, "Noooo," Maki san wailed, but with that glint in her eye now diamond like, "I have never had a job in my life."

"Never had a job?" I expressed surprise, "What do you mean, never?"

"I went straight from school to university and then I married my husband directly after I graduated and had two children. I have never had a job! I couldn't possibly do this." She looked at me coyly, "Could I?" she almost whispered.

I smiled, "Yes, you could, most definitely. You love chatting and you chat so easily and are naturally very friendly, you have such a nice way with you, I know that you can use this skill to find suitable students. After that, it will be up to me."

We looked at each other, pondering; rubbing chins so to speak. Maki san wavering, weighing up the possibilities. This was so important to me, I desperately needed Maki san and she was so suitable but seemed to lack the confidence to say yes. What could I do to persuade her?

In the end, she took a long shuddering breath, said in halting English, "I am so shocked. This is a chance in a lifetime for me. To work for a foreigner, and an English woman! It is a dream come true. Oh, I'd love to do it."

I felt exultant, "Then that's fixed then, you will be my assistant?"

"I'll ask my husband," she said.

Fortunately, he said yes and all strange 'phone calls stopped the instant Maki san started fronting my calls. Maki san remained my assistant until the end, doing a valiant job of weeding out the unsuitable, strange and downright odd ball, which fortunately weren't many, and giving confidence to the remainder, reassuring them that I was a "good woman, good teacher and very safe." *Kanpeki* – perfect!

I learned later that Maki san was being very Japanese during our conversation. It became obvious to me that she was a supremely confident and able person, and one who would have been a great asset to any employer. I was so lucky to have her support; and it came out slowly over the next few years with my increasing knowledge of Japanese culture, that Maki san only agreed to become my assistant because she liked me and wanted to help me; not because she wanted a job. It was pure altruism on her part. For a Japanese lady, especially one who is rich enough not to have to work, then sentences like, 'Oh, I have no confidence to work', really mean, I am rich enough not to have to work. Modesty must be preserved and directness avoided at all costs. For my part, she was an assistant par excellence and was pivotal to my success and I thank my lucky stars that she came my way. Maki san and her husband are people I treasure very much. They helped me from their hearts, like so many Japanese people I met. But I never told them how much I admired them and they never told me how much they admired me. I was learning and becoming more Japanese by the day.

Although there were many problems to resolve and I was living alone in a strange country, I was not lonely as I didn't have the time to be although I continued to feel apprehensive. I was not ready to go home, not ready to give up my Japanese life, such as it was. It wasn't much of a life really, struggling hard to build up my little school, my personal and rather unique school, and it took me some time to accept the fact that it was unique in its own way. I was catering to women like me, mostly older women, housewives or working women, who had a hankering to learn the ways of England as I had a hankering to learn the ways of Japan. They were struggling to master the English language as I was struggling with learning the Japanese language. Ryoko always used to say that I was unique, that was my selling point.

Most English teachers are young people working for large, impersonal schools and the older women feel the generation gap acutely. I was unusual in that I was a mature English woman, 'elegant, kind and trustworthy'. I was endorsed by Maki san. I was 'safe'.

Now that Maki san had joined me, my classes started to take off and we got together and composed a suitable advertisement and then she took me around various newspaper offices to insert it. The personal touch is very important. To meet the foreigner who is advertising in your local newspaper, to suss them out, judge their character is very important in the area I was living in. After all, it was their newspaper, with a reputation to uphold, they wanted to look me over. Nothing like this was said out loud of course, but I came to realise that is what was happening. Fortunately, with Maki san's help, I passed muster once again and my advertisements for students started to appear in the local newspapers every week.

I was continually learning my craft, studying books on teaching, lesson plans and the like. My life consisted of finding new students and improving my classes. I had little social life outside, in fact, I had no energy left for a social life. I was now concentrating on building my classes and developing my school and, because I had the flat to myself, Jan having left by now, I was able to turn the two-roomed flat into a one-room abode for me and the other room, I turned into my new school room. I spent very little of the money I earned and I used most of it to buy the new classroom furniture. Ryoko had instilled in me the concept of English elegance coupled with fun and interesting English lessons. Consequently an English Laura Ashley style room started to emerge, with an elegant hardwood table and chairs; a tall bookshelf which I used to start a free library of special books for the English learner; and many second hand videos of Hollywood films from the local rental shop which the students could take home as they wanted, to practice listening to English. Jan also sent me many English knick knacks to dot around the room.

Carpets are rather exotic to the Japanese, who tend to stick with lino in different hues, or tatami mats as the floor covering of choice. Therefore, a carpet was paramount to the English look of the room, but they were expensive. After much searching, I managed to find a basic light blue ribbed carpet, and lay it down to cover the tatami mats and then cover the middle of it with an elegant and expensive pastel blue and green rug. The finishing touches were the pretty flowered Laura Ashley curtains and chair cushions with their pink and green hues complementing the stylish prints of English gardens dotted around the room. A television and video set which sat in the corner and the crowning glory, a Royal Doulton teapot, jug and sugar bowl, coupled with a set of pretty and elegant bone china cups and saucers.

Teapots are of enormous importance in Japan and tea is given the reverence of a god. Most students just refused to believe me when I told them that teapots are not so important now in Britain, many people preferring to use the dunking tea bag method for everyday use. The Japanese have images in their minds of tea rooms in the Cotswolds, Harrods, luxury hotels and the like, thinking that most of us live like that every day, at least as far as teapots and teacups are concerned. Because of tea being seen as so quintessentially English, every lesson I made my students tea in the teapot and we enjoyed a cup together during the lesson. I poured the tea for them and asked them if they wanted milk and sugar. My students quaintly called it, 'The Tea Ceremony', which is a very grand name for what I was supplying. But I was immensely pleased by it.

By British standards, the room was tiny, the furniture leaving just enough room for us all to squeeze in comfortably to our chairs. But it was mine! I had arrived! I was making progress. I felt terribly proud of my little school room because I'd achieved it by my own efforts and hard work and established it in a strange country when everyone else told me I couldn't. I thanked my lucky stars for Ryoko, because without her, I couldn't have done it. Her patient advice and unstinting assistance of how to do things 'Japan style' was as necessary to me as my own determination to succeed. It just goes to show what two determined women can do when they set their minds to it. We both changed each other's lives for the better. Between us, we developed our dreams into realities. Everyone needs a mentor, she was most definitely mine.

However, I did have problems. I'd been developing my lessons, making them more academic, bringing in more grammar and grammar practice, things I thought were necessary to improve the appalling English of my students. They murdered the language, even though they had studied hard in the past. The understanding of the language was just not there. While I was developing my curriculum Maki san was doing her bit extraordinarily well. I was getting around seven or eight trial lesson appointments every month. I always offered students a trial lesson to encourage them to come along and see for themselves. I gave them what I thought was a good English grammar lesson. Most of them didn't join.

"Why?" I asked Maki san in desperation one day. "I've got this new room, English style no less, and I give them a great grammar lesson, but only about 10% are joining me. Why? Why? Why?" I was at the end of my tether, stressed, weary and disheartened. Trooping off to the station, two or three times a week to meet prospective students, taking them back to my flat, making them tea and chatting and then giving them a trial lesson, all of this taking about two hours of my time, was wearing me down. I didn't mind the hard work and would have been ecstatic if they had joined, but alas, there was something wrong. Continual failure was creating anxiety in me and I didn't know how to fix it.

I chatted this over separately with Maki san and Ryoko. We pulled it apart and analysed as much as we could. Both came to the same conclusion, one I found hard to fathom.

"They don't like the grammar lesson," both concluded.

"But these are really useful grammar lessons for them. I'm concentrating on their weak spots."

"Yes," replied Ryoko, "that's the point. They don't want you to show them how bad their English is, and they don't want to study too hard to correct it. They don't want it to be like school. Most Japanese people have bad memories about school and the system of teaching in Japan, which is all about memorising long lists of facts, words or dates, and then being tested on them. By the time the next test comes, they have forgotten all the things they learnt from the previous one. Therefore, they were always having to revise everything. It was such hard work for them. To know a subject by understanding it is not the Japanese way. We learn by rote, not understanding. It was often not a happy time for them and they were not able to learn with dignity and deep understanding of subjects."

"Why do they teach like that?" I asked her.

"Because it's always been like that as far as I know. It's our way. Many Japanese people think it is a bad way and needs to be changed, but the Government do not want to change things – maybe! Or the teachers do not want to change things – maybe! It's too hard for them to change – maybe! They don't know how to change, or they are not being allowed to change – maybe! I think it's very complicated and I hate our way of education, but it's what we have got to work with for now." Ryoko had obviously been giving this a lot of thought.

To me, it seemed a strange way to educate your children. To give lessons especially designed to make it difficult to understand the subject and just concentrate on memorising dates, facts etc. But when I thought about it and Japan's history of feudal domination I began to see a pattern. Some people may disagree with my assessment, but I offer it here as food for thought.

Japan was a feudal society until 1853. Not only that, but for the preceding two hundred years, the Shogun had decided to close the country in self-imposed isolation. No foreigner was allowed on its soil, except for some Jesuit priests and a few traders who were confined to an island off Nagasaki. The aristocracy of the time and the samurai, had total authority over the rest of the Japanese, who were basically peasants. The people in charge could do what they liked, including slicing off peoples' heads as they passed by if they thought the wayside peasants didn't bow to them deferentially enough. Suddenly, all this changed in 1853 when an American, Captain Perry, and his 'Black ships' lined themselves up off the shoreline near Tokyo, (then known as Edo) and gave an ultimatum. Open up your country and let us in, or we will turn our guns on you and kill you all – or words to that effect. They were let in and thereafter the Shogunate started to crumble and within fourteen years, the Shogun and samurai were gone and their dictatorial society ended. Absolute power turned into impotency in the blink of an eye (historically speaking). It must have been a terrible shock for the survivors, for many of the aristocracy and the samurai were still alive and had to make their way in this new society. Many embraced it and became part of the new leadership and hierarchy.

I'm not saying that all the new leaders in Japan were such people, there were plenty of genuine reformers who did valiant work to improve human rights, and to bring Japan out of its feudal ways of thinking and doing things; but what I am saying, is that deeply embedded in that new government were the old guard, the old bureaucrats and samurai families, who had enjoyed such power before. Now, the new concept of human rights and the birth of modern Japan was being forced onto them, but they were desperate to keep the status quo. So they did what Japan is so adept at doing. They went through the motions of modernising, but deep down, in the bowels of their souls, the old guard was still fighting its corner and hanging on to power and the old ways of doing things, seeming to adapt to modern ways, whilst not really changing at all. If they had to give human rights and education to the people, then so be it, but let's make it as hard as possible for them to learn. With education comes power. How to keep political power and keep the traditional stranglehold of power over the people? Why, educate them poorly of course. Make it so difficult to learn; put so much pressure on children and students to achieve academic success under difficult circumstances that they will have no time to think of much else. Make every decent job attainable only with copious academic qualifications, and keep the traditional and highly regarded concept of dedication and loyalty shown to the Shogunate of old, by replacing the Shogunate with one's company. Therefore, dedication and loyalty to one's company takes precedence over everything else, even one's family. This is shown by the amount of time one puts in at one's place of work, with unpaid overtime the norm. Many people work fourteen to sixteen hour days, six days a week as a matter of course. It is also common to spend a lot of the spare time one has with one's workmates, and work trips to spas or similar are encouraged, keeping outside influence to a minimum. The people are too tired to revolt and you have a malleable populace which has been educated this way from its first tentative steps as babies and accept it as normal.

Many of the descendants of those aristocratic and samurai families are still in charge today, still in the government and the backbone of the bureaucracy. The old ruling party, The LDP (The Liberal Democratic Party, but nothing to do with liberalism, they are deep Tories), had been in power since the end of the second world war. The secondary parties struggled to get votes and have only twice managed to oust them, even though they have free elections. That in itself should tell you a lot about the apathy and malleability of the population at large. Many people I spoke to would tell me that they never voted in elections because, 'All politicians are tarred with the same brush, they have no interest in us and are only interested in their own power, and that of their cronies. I hate them'. I would point out that if they didn't vote against them, then nothing would change, but that never seemed to go down well.

You are left with the classic Japanese syndrome. A modern, stylish, rich society on the surface, a veneer to fool, because just underneath, the real Japan, the Japan of the Shogunate and the samurai is still there, plying its trade, refusing to modernise its thinking. Keeping the masses as under achievers, making it very difficult for them to change the society in which they live. Making change, or even the thought of radical thinking, a crime of greatest proportions in the imagination of the population.

If the Government are pushed hard enough and have to do something to change whatever it is, they say things like, 'Yes, we must change. Let's get this country up and moving again. Let's improve life for everyone. Yes, yes, yes'. Then, they do nothing. Or they go through convoluted machinations, tying everyone up in knots of frustration and confusion, until, in the end, when a compromise is reached, they pick up the old strings and start knitting themselves back into the pattern of the past and the old ways.

Of course, nothing is quite as simple and lots of other factors come into play, which are far beyond the scope of this book. But these are my thoughts and observations, for what they are worth, on a complex subject.

*

I was becoming more and more like a true teacher, more academic with every passing week, and my students were wanting to pull away from all that, screaming silently. A big lesson learnt for me. A lesson I would have to think about deeply. A lesson that I either learned and put into practice or paid the price. You have to give the people what they want; otherwise, they go somewhere else.

It was a steep learning curve for me. How to find this balance. Ryoko had advised me to keep everything light hearted and enjoyable whilst at the same time offering methods of improving the students' English and expanding their understanding of British culture.

I worked so hard on this. My every available minute, when I was not with my students, was spent on this problem. I experimented with all sorts of lessons, lesson styles, subject matter. You name it I bet I tried it somewhere along the line. In the end, I took the Japanese fondness of childlike things and invested in a video lesson. I had learned about video lessons and discovered several for helping students with their English. The one I chose was *Wallace & Gromit: The Wrong Trousers!* This animation using the characters of *Wallace & Gromit* traversed the gap between children and adult entertainment in Britain and became an award winner. The same applied in Japan. My students loved it. The version I bought had been especially produced for beginners of English. I had learned that mostly, whatever their level, a Japanese woman will always say that her English is only at the level of a beginner. It is their innate modesty and the instilled culture of not blowing your own trumpet. Therefore, everyone, even my more advanced students, were very happy with a beginners version of *Wallace & Gromit*.

It saved me. I had a happy band of students who came week after week to discover the adventures of *Wallace & Gromit*. We laughed, we listened, we talked, it was my lifesaver. Of course, there were some students who did not wish to study in this way, and for these students, I continued to try and find the right medium for them.

As time progressed, my student base grew and I was feeling less stressed, and I totally revamped my trial lesson. Now most of the students who came for a trial lesson joined up. I was so happy and grateful to Ryoko and Maki san for their invaluable advice.

I've met a lot of foreigners, who came to Japan after university eager to get a job or just for the adventure of living in such a foreign place, but many were so condescending about the profession, saying disparagingly, 'Oh, yes, I'm an English conversation teacher, but it's only for a short time. It's a laugh really, I hate the job and I hope to get something much better soon'. It made me so mad because I wanted to be an English conversation teacher in Japan. It was my ideal; my goal; my heartfelt desire; but I had the greatest difficulty in getting a visa to do the job I loved. The fact that these unenthusiastic people were able to come to teach in Japan, get a working visa with ease, simply because they had a degree, while their hearts and minds were not in it and they felt it was beneath them, was always a sore point with me. I go back to my bone of contention. You don't need a university degree to teach English conversation. All you need is a good understanding of English grammar, the ability to speak English without a heavy regional accent, and the love of the job and your students. Because if you love the job and your students you will do it much better than the disgruntled or unenthusiastic degree holder.

I remember sitting in on an English lesson once, with an experienced teacher. It was a training session for me which I had arranged with the owner of a large, private school with students who paid a lot of money for their lessons. The teacher, an American, entered the room, sat down without greeting or looking at his three students gathered around the table. Without any preamble he said, 'Page 34', and asked what the rules of English were on this page. He corrected the students in a gruff, uninterested voice bordering on the disrespectful. Forty five minutes later, he concluded the lesson having not once looked at any of the students, or made any connection to them whatsoever. Robot like, he corrected their mistakes like a piston. His eyes straight ahead, unseeing, and his face impassive. I felt so sorry for them. I expect he had a degree!

CHAPTER EIGHT

Mothers and Babies

While I was developing my adult classes, and Ryoko and I continued with our once weekly kid's class in her front room, we continued to discuss and develop our ideas, until finally, we were ready to start our Mothers and Babies English Class. Babies and toddlers between the ages of one and three years could come, together with their mothers, and learn English with a native English speaker using songs and eurhythmics and have a jolly good time. Ryoko had been building towards this moment for a long time. She had been studying eurhythmics for years and was a great believer in the rhythm of language. Every language has its own rhythm and if you can find this rhythm you can progress in the language much more easily. Of course, language is absorbed by babies and toddlers before they are actually able to string sentences together. They are listening to the rhythm and sound of the language at first and then going on to more complexities like words later on. Their brains are working nonstop from birth on the language issue. If we could get these babies used to the different sounds and rhythm of English early on, then the theory goes that they should find the learning of it later on much easier. That was our goal anyway and what we tried to achieve in these lessons.

One of the highlights of the lessons for the mothers was

the last twenty minutes, when, with Ryoko keeping the babies engaged in playing with crayons, colouring in English words or numbers, I took the mothers to the other end of the room and we would have an English lesson together. They enjoyed this very much as it gave them the chance to take a lesson even though they were chained to their little ones.

During lessons for small children, research has indicated that you can have a lesson lasting forty minutes and the only time you gain access into the active learning curve would be for possibly five minutes, or less, of that time. You have to be there when that hole appears, it's different for each child. So, we were all working hard for forty minutes not to miss that five minute slot. That window of opportunity for the child. Mothers and teachers, working together. I learned so much from this class, about the psychology of children, having no kids myself, I really needed that knowledge and the art of teaching babies in an active and entertaining environment. How to keep them interested with a learning aim in view. It was great stuff and Ryoko proved to be a master of it – but we hadn't been accepted by the community centre yet.

Ryoko made the first advances, we had an application form. Spending agonies of time getting the application just right, we submitted it and were called in for an interview. Ryoko and I went along together. Her savvy and ability passed the first hurdle, with me helping only by my presence as a respectable and trustworthy foreigner. Quite frankly, foreigners have a bit of a bad name in Japan. So many foreigners go for the wrong reasons. To escape from their problems, or because they are not up to scratch at home and think they can cut it in an Asian country. Or for a laugh, or to get the girls and 'show those Japanese how to live' kind of mentality. They have no idea of the culture they are entering or of how damaging their big feet can be. Also, of course, this kind of person doesn't last long in Japan for, at the risk of saying the obvious, it is a very foreign country. It takes a long time to adapt to the differences, which really are a conundrum at first. Even in the other Asian cultures, Japan is looked at as an oddity. It is a unique culture and it takes a lot of work and a desire to understand it. As a simple example for the newly arrived foreigner, you cannot read any signs because they are all in Kanji (pictograms), so you cannot even check your dictionary. Nowadays, in large towns and cities, more public signs have an English translation underneath, but at the time we went in 2000 there were virtually no English signs. Also, most Japanese people cannot speak English and many are afraid of foreigners. Therefore, if you go to Japan in an emotional turmoil, as an escape route from your problems, you soon find that they have increased profoundly. Frustration and confusion will follow you everywhere, and from that, your ability to cope gets sorely tested. Ergo, many foreigners don't last. I was talking to the personnel officer, an American woman, of a large national English language school, who told me that they had so many people coming to work for them from America, Australia, Britain etc. and probably 50% of them wouldn't last out their yearly contract. They just up sticks and go back home. The record she said, was one man who stayed for only twenty four hours.

I don't want to lump all foreign people into this category, I met many 'good people' as the Japanese say. But the unthinking foreigners who go to Japan for the wrong reasons really do provide a problem for the rest of us who love the country. I always felt that I had to let people know that I was a 'good foreigner' and that of course, only comes with time. Trust cannot be bought or expressed. You have

123

to prove it.

I started this process by smartening myself up. British ways of sloppy dressing and casual clothes went out. Replaced by smart, formal clothes, always impeccably ironed and as clean as a new pin. Personal grooming is paramount in this country that breeds women who go to the supermarket looking like they're are all dressed up for their favourite child's wedding, and men habitually wear dark, formal suits, even in the heat of high summer.

I took great care that everything about my personal appearance was as good as I could make it. No, 'Oh, it will do', for this country. Therefore, on our first meeting with the pukka community centre's management, I passed muster. So did Ryoko. However, this was just the start of many meetings we had with them. Nothing happens quickly, everything takes lots of talk and procrastination. It's like a fine wine, make the basic brew, let it settle for a while, come back to it, taste it and spit it out, stir it awhile, taste it again, add more to the brew, taste it again, until, finally, you have an agreement.

This is what we did, although Ryoko got the full burden as I was really an impotent bystander, not being able to take part in the discussions. Ryoko translated for me as and when questions were directed at me, but really, in the end, we were two women. We needed a man. They wanted a man. They could rely on a man. They could trust a man. Women are fickle creatures, who could trust them? We needed a man to vouch for us. This was Japan. Ryoko's husband, Kenji san, came to the rescue again. Arriving on his white charger (actually, it was the local train) he entered the discussions.

Things moved quickly now that Kenji san was involved. Finally, agreement was reached and we were accepted into the community centre as a Mothers and Babies class. Four lessons a week, one hour each lesson.

Ryoko is a highly talented musician with a glorious soprano voice and can play any tune on the piano, either by ear or sight reading the music. She never fails to amaze me. She used all her musical skills on our Mothers and Babies class. Using a portable electric keyboard, she would play traditional English children's songs as we all sang and danced along. She got everybody moving and in a happy mood, and under her tutelage, I became a champion exponent of *The Little Teapot* song; *Incey Wincey Spider*; *Ring a Ring a Roses* and the like. I pranced around the room, singing the songs and doing the actions, with the kids and mothers in tow.

We had begun.

Unfortunately, I am not a fan of babies, or toddlers and I sometimes found the screaming, temper tantrums and crying that occasionally happened as the kids got tired and fractious, very trying. Although as I got to know the kids and their budding personalities, I really got quite fond of them.

I especially liked a cheeky, smiley little boy, aged around twelve months, who had just started to walk when he began his classes with us. He was a real charmer and was always smiling and happy, never crying. He was a joy. He was the opposite of another little boy who was always in a bad mood and uncooperative. Aged about two and a half, he was the oldest in the class by far, most of the others being aged twelve to eighteen months, so I think his miserable face reflected his thoughts that he was above all this baby stuff; but his mother loved the class and brought him along every week without fail.

We had all been in this class for about six months when at the start of one particular lesson, my smiling little boy came in and smiled in his usual fashion and started to explore the room as he liked to do, but then he did something extraordinary. As each of the kiddies came in, smiley baby went up to them and hugged them and gave each one a kiss. We all laughed and of course he did it all the more. He was in high good humour. Then, in came the miserable toddler, face downturned as usual, and smiley baby looked over and saw him enter, toddled over to him as he had done to the others, and without any warning smashed him hard on the nose with his fist. Everything stopped. Total silence ensued as everybody ceased all movement, lost in the incredulity of the moment, and most of all, poor miserable child sat on the floor with a look of total astonishment and disbelief. It was a tableau of open mouths and popping eyes. And then, suddenly, uproar. As if a starting pistol had gone off, all the kids began screaming, including smiley baby, and Ryoko and I rushed up to see if the miserable toddler was compos mentis. Fortunately, smiley baby was not strong enough to do any serious damage, and although miserable toddler was by now prone and screaming, he was not hurt. It was shock more than anything that made him cry with such gusto.

It was at this point I turned to Ryoko and said, "Do we have any insurance?"

Neither of us had thought of that!

But it was the worst thing that happened to us in these classes, for which I am eternally grateful.

CHAPTER NINE

It Could Only Happen in Japan

Things had been going well for me and I was getting established and feeling more confident. Eight months had gone by since Jan had returned to Britain and I had spent that time on non-stop work, building up my small school and studying 'How to Teach' books, picking up the tricks and tips of teaching Japanese students from my own experiences and from anyone else I could bore into sharing their knowledge with me. So it was with relief that during one of our regular telephone calls, Jan told me that she would like to return to Japan and was in a position to do so. A few weeks later, she joined me again and was able to take a lot of the strain of everyday living. For example, a simple thing like food shopping was still a major challenge for me. I couldn't read any labels, and, apart from fruit and vegetables, the food was a mystery. Was I buying soup or something quite different? Being vegetarian, it was important for me to find out whether pre-cooked food contained meat, but almost impossible to discover. I would sometimes go to supermarkets with Japanese friends and we would stroll the aisles together, researching, reading the small print and finding suitable food. But I was always floored by the Japanese habit of changing packaging – new is king - so by the time a few months had elapsed, most of the packaging had changed and I had to start all over again. This applied to everything, cleaning materials, toothpaste, soap, absolutely everything. It made shopping a time consuming and very tiring necessity. Of course, Jan was faced with these same problems, but at least she had the luxury of spending an inordinate time in the supermarket trying to puzzle it all out. Incongruously, our favourite supermarket was the Co-op! The Japanese Co-op is based on the British version and was for us, besides being totally unexpected, a life saver. It was large with a great range of goods, very near our flat, and it sold French bread. Japanese bread is a cross between cake and bread; very soft, very white and very sweet. For me, it was inedible; who wants toasted cake? Or cheese and tomato cake? Or egg and cress cake? As I always made sandwiches for my lunch, it was vital for me to have European style bread and the Co-op came up trumps.

I made enquiries with my ikebana teacher, Sato san, and she agreed to take Jan on as a student and sponsor her for a visa. Fortunately for us, both Jan and I found ikebana very enjoyable and studying it was not hard work, although, much to my chagrin, Jan was much better at it than I was. Sato san always said I was a 'good European flower arranger', but not so hot in the ikebana stakes. I found it hard to make the transition from lots of flowers make a good arrangement to, just a few flowers, or even just one, will offer contentment for the soul.

During this time, while we were sorting ourselves out we met a Canadian woman at FEW. She told us about a Japanese society which promotes friendship between countries. Unfortunately, there was a dearth of British people in the society and they were desperately looking for new British members. "I was persuaded to go to a meeting," she told us with raised eyebrows, "they told me that being a

Canadian gave me connections to Britain and therefore, would I please come along to make up the numbers." She told us that she was put off by the people there, her allegiance not being very strong in the first place, and so never repeated the experience.

"What happened, what do you mean?" I asked her.

"Well, a Japanese woman asked me what part of Britain I came from, and I replied that I was actually a Canadian. She looked at me with undisguised disdain and after a pause said, 'At least you're from the colonies', and swanned off."

I suppose I should have been forewarned by this, but it seemed like the loyal thing to do, so Jan and I decided to join up, ever eager for new experiences. Little did we know just what gems awaited us and I wouldn't have missed it for the world. This is where I first met a diplomat's wife, whom I shall call Jane Smith, and who was for me, the saving grace of the society. Her distinctive carriage and aura of county hiding a wicked sense of humour and a love of life and a healthy disrespect of form.

Our first get together with the society was to celebrate the Queen's birthday and I thought, what could be more incongruous than attending a birthday party for our Queen, a thing I had never done before, in a foreign land with foreigners. It was held at the Foreigners Club in Kobe, a monolith of a building over a hundred years old, sitting on top of a hill overlooking Kobe like an overseer. It looks like a Victorian gentleman's club, which is exactly what it is. An attractive British style building, standing in its own grounds with large, beautiful gardens. An anachronism. Inside, it is grand and imposing, the walls faced with high quality polished wood which fight for attention with the impressive mouldings. Victorian to the core, it was here, that we were to experience the unique flavour of our first meeting with the society.

There were around sixty people gathered to honour the Queen, most of them Japanese. Jan and I entered the reception room and this is where I made my first faux pas of the evening. Having been to many official functions in my time, I did know the form, but sometimes, one just has a bad day and one social gaff leads to another and then they start to unravel in front of you, like a ball of string thrown across a room. Were they that bad? Well, probably to the Japanese they were, as I was sure that the people gathered there were watching our every move out the corner of their eyes, but no one being so un-Japanese as to openly stare.

My ball of string started to unravel instantly as I failed to see the reception committee, standing there for the precise reason of welcoming all guests. How I missed them is a mystery even to me, but I just didn't see them. Perhaps it was because there was too much to take in. The large, high ceilinged room laid out with long tables just crammed with silver platters of beautifully presented food, interspersed with several inviting silver cauldrons. It was impressive. I was hungry. Then a waitress homed in on me offering a tray full of beer and soft drinks. I was so busy trying to find the Japanese for, "Have you any wine?" that I continued not to see the three person reception committee standing on my left. Jan touched my arm and steered me around and nodded at the reception committee, who were very stiff and formal, like cardboard cut-outs, with huge rosettes pinned to their lapels, and said, "I think we are supposed to shake hands before we enter." Never one to shirk my duties, I abandoned the waitress, but unfortunately, not with style. I bowed to her and said, "No thank you." A fatal mistake. A superior being, like a guest or customer, never bows to the servant or shop assistant. This is fundamental to Japanese society and a huge faux pas. Oh dear!

Regardless, realising my mistake, I pushed it under my

'things best forgotten, otherwise there lies the way to stress and anxiety belt', and approached the first man in the reception committee with what I hoped was aplomb. He was a Japanese of astounding tallness for one so old, so much so, that he was bent over, like a letter f. His shoulders were rounded to a fine hone, and his head jutted out just above them. Aged anywhere between sixty and seventy although he could have been older as the Japanese hold their age very well. He was a very quiet and shy man, keeping himself to himself and rather uncomfortable here I thought. For I had recognised him immediately. He was the big boss of the Takarazuka theatre, the grandson of the founder of the Hankyu railway and the Takarazuka Revue company.

Oh dear, what a bad introduction to a man I would truly like to impress. We shook hands and I fully expected him to speak English, as he is also a very important man in the business world, so I said, in my best voice, "How do you do? It's very nice to meet you." However, he just looked at me, said nothing, and looked a bit puzzled. Third mistake, I should have spoken to him in Japanese. When I realised that he was not going to say anything at all, not even hello, I moved on to the next man in the row whilst still looking at the stooped figure by my side, wondering about him, so much so that I didn't pay attention to the next hand that was being thrust in my direction. I was trying to get my mind into a Japanese mode, thinking, in my confusion, "I can't remember the Japanese for how do you do," when the second man shook my hand and said, "How do you do?" in perfect English.

I was so surprised I said, "Oh, you speak English, how nice." Then I looked at him and realised that he was English. Fourth mistake. But I had enough sense to realise that I should keep my mouth shut now, and moved on to the next person, a woman. We shook hands and I looked at her name badge, Mrs. Jane Smith. "Ah," I said, (some people never learn) "I've seen your name in the Society newsletter." She smiled a Japanese style smile, a faint, almost imperceptible movement of the lips, and turned her attention to Jan. Fifth mistake!

Well, life goes on. I finally got my wine and pondered on how strange life is. What was I doing here? In this English Gentleman's Club deep in the heart of Japan. I was wondering what kind of people gather together to celebrate the Queen's birthday. I suppose ex-pats do. But I had noticed a distinct reluctance of the Japanese people here to talk to us. We had gone out and mingled, but we were not getting a response. The Japanese people were ignoring us even though we were the only British people there apart from a few diplomats doing their duty. And they were ignoring us too! It was behaviour I didn't understand, but I wanted to find out more. Was it my social gaffs that had alerted them to someone who was 'not one of us,' or was it our attire? The Japanese men were all decked out in black suits and the women were all in expensive dresses. Jan and I were wearing trousers suits, albeit smart and expensive ones.

However, we were not to be ostracised so easily and we made a concerted effort to get into conversation with someone. Anyone would do at this stage. We got talking to a Japanese man and his wife who seemed quite friendly after an initial reluctance. He turned out to be a high level diplomat and we talked for fifteen minutes or so, about the Nordic lumber industry and the role of Japan in that part of the world. As a bit of light relief, we had an in depth discussion on Japanese history over the past two hundred years. It was hard work.

After this, with a great deal of effort from us, several people got into conversation, but not the British diplomats. There were about eight of them with their names engraved on their badges, but they spoke only to each other and didn't mix with the Japanese or us. As an experiment, I tried making eye contact with each one of them as I walked past, but no one returned it.

I went to get some more food and arrived at the silver platter containing the mashed potato, or creamed potato as it said on the label in English. You could put on weight just by looking at it. I was hungry and vegetarian, and as there was virtually nothing that a vegetarian could eat out of the vast expanse of food there, that creamed potato was looking more and more attractive. It's a strange phenomena in Japan, but this Buddhist country, where vegetarianism is part of the religion, nowadays looks upon the vegetarian as an alien being, as one of the strangest concepts ever invented.

I remember going into one small restaurant, very busy on a Saturday evening. It was typically Japanese, the size of a pea, with 4 tables along one wall and a counter opposite, with stools for customers to sit down. Behind the counter at one end was the chef, who did all his cooking in a wok on two small gas rings. The waiter housed himself at the other end and made up the salads and drinks. Small, homely, intimate, the chef joining in the conversations around him, it was a feel-good kind of a place, so typical of small, everyday, Japanese restaurants. But when I asked him if he could cook something vegetarian he said, in very simple Japanese,

"*Hai, yasai to hamu, dai joobu desu ka?*"

Yes, vegetables with ham, OK?

"*Iie, yasai dake onegai shimasu.*"

No, vegetables only please.

"*Oh, yasai to bacon dai joobu desu ka?*"

Oh, vegetables with bacon, OK?

"*Iie, yasai dake onegai shimasu.*" I repeated, I'm ashamed to say, louder.

"Ah, yasai to sausagee, dai joobu desu ka?"
Ah, vegetables and sausage, OK?
"Iie, yasai dake onegai shimasu."
No, vegetables only please.

I was getting worn out and unable to tell him any more in my inadequate Japanese. All those textbook pages I had studied hadn't prepared me for the inability of the Japanese to understand my Japanese; and my inability to understand their Japanese; or the ability of both of us to refuse to accept the intended meaning. Different pages on different scripts.

Finally, he understood, comprehension dawning on his face, *"YASAI DAKE?"* He shouted in bewilderment and burst out laughing. He couldn't stop himself and thought it was a great joke. Then he said that he could give us a salad. We accepted with gratitude as we were so hungry by this time we would almost have eaten his ham, bacon and sausage. He just couldn't understand the concept of cooking vegetables without some sort of meat, it was something that wasn't in his ken.

Also, meat means beef or pork and occasionally lamb. It does not mean ham, bacon or sausage and they are not classed as meat. So, if we went into a restaurant and asked for a salad with no meat, it would often come with bacon or ham bits scattered over the top. When asked why they had done this, as we asked for no meat, they would proudly say, "It's not meat, it's bacon and it's service." In other words, it's done as something special for you - without their asking you if you want it. Very Japanese.

We did go back to the small friendly restaurant, but with a Japanese friend, who explained to the chef that we were in fact, that strange thing, a vegetarian and it did mean that we didn't eat meat, which included bacon, ham and sausage. Astounded, but ready to please, he thought about it for a while and said, *"Spaghetti to tomato to broccoli to kinoko,*

134

dai joobu desu ka?" Spaghetti with tomato and broccoli and mushrooms, OK? We went back there regularly and he always did us proud, even if he did have a laugh about it each time. He wanted to please and I think we brightened up his day.

But back at the Kobe club my evening was not brightened by the lure of the creamed potato which was now paramount in my mind as it was the only thing that I could eat, apart from a few bits of salad (minus the bacon). Unfortunately, I arrived at the creamed potato at the same time as a British diplomat. We reached for the silver spoon together and being polite, I said, "Please," and indicated that he go first. He scooped up a small spoonful and offered it to me, being equally polite. I said that I had planned on having two scoops, so please help himself first. He was just too polite and he gave me another miniscule scoop, so I had to make do with that. Two small scoops of mashed, sorry creamed, potato, a lettuce leaf and a few cherry tomatoes was to be my lot I feared.

Even though we had 'broken the ice' over the potato, the diplomat made no attempt to make conversation with me as he poodled off back to his pals. By this time, I was getting battle fatigue, and was past caring. No wonder there are so few British people in the Society, I thought. But then, two ladies came over to me and started to chat, preventing me from finishing my paltry supper, but I didn't mind as they were delightful, a mother and daughter, full of bonhomie. Then Jane Smith came over, all in a rush, and joined us. She said to Jan and me, "I just *have* to talk to you two, you look so interesting. What are you *doing* here?" She didn't pause for breath, "Please call me Jane, I'm sooo curious about you two." Attractive, middle aged but filling out a little in the waistline, she was immaculate, in a homely way. Her voice was a rich plummy English of rounded vowels and precisely pronounced words. She was great fun, full of enthusiasm now she was 'off duty'. She was a gentle expert in eliciting information from one and we ended up telling her about our passion for Takarazuka. Expecting shock and horror from her, she surprised us by exclaiming and laughing, "Oh, me too, I love Takarazuka. How wonderful."

We talked about Takarazuka for a long time and went through all our respective memories and exciting moments and she roped three Japanese ladies into our conversation, who were on the elderly side and very stuck-up, but she told us that they were all Takarazuka fans. One of the ladies, probably the oldest of them, told us, in passable English, that her husband hated her watching Takarazuka's version of *Guys 'n' Dolls,* because he like to gamble and didn't want her reminded of it. She told us that her husband was like Sky Masterson in character and she thought that was very funny as she almost choked over her own mirth. Takarazuka fans get very passionate, even the stuck-up ones.

We were starting to enjoy ourselves now that we had been accepted by Jane and were getting on so well with her, the Arctic ice had been broken, at least a chink, but now it was time to go home. The reception was finished, but before we left, Jane invited us to a ladies only afternoon tea party at her home the following month. We accepted the invitation gladly, unaware of the strange things that would happen there, but for now, we were pleased to depart.

Maybe the problem was that Jan and I were mashed potato people and they were all creamed potato people. But mashed does not necessarily mean inferior, although I doubt that the creamed people would agree with that. Basic and unadulterated can be much healthier than refined adulterated versions. This applies to people as well as to potatoes. (As you can tell, I was a bit miffed!)

*

As promised Jane Smith wrote and invited Jan and me to the society's afternoon tea party to be held at the Smith's house. She enclosed a little map with the security code listed to enable us to get in through the gate. It was obvious from the map that she lived in some sort of compound.

'The tea party starts at 2.00pm but come at 1.00pm if you can', wrote Jane across the bottom of the invitation. I assumed that she liked us so much she wanted to spend some time getting to know us and I pictured us sitting in plush armchairs, chatting pleasantly until the others arrived. I was looking forward to it.

The compound was in a place called Mikage, only about ten minutes as the crow flies, from our flat in Nigawa. The train took a little longer, and half an hour after leaving home, we arrived at Mikage station and walked up the hill and found the compound immediately, but as we were a little early we backtracked to visit a small shopping area nearby. Mikage is an upmarket and snobbish place and the shops were no exception. They were the kind of shops that don't display prices, if you had to ask you couldn't afford it, type of place. Killing time, we were on our second circuit of window shopping and I said to Jan, "Have you noticed that there are no customers in the shops?"

"Yes I have, but look, there's one in that boutique over there, she must have gone in when we were over the other side."

I looked over and saw a woman in an expensive designer trouser suit, aged well over retirement, but so obviously wanting to be thirty again, or at least fifty anyway. Slim and straight backed and wearing a ridiculous little hat, like a

137

small, round box with a feather flying from the top, which was perched sideways on her obviously dyed black hair. She had about her a superior air of majestic proportions, seldom had I seen such a person before. This was the queen of stuck-up, no doubt about that. As we approached the shop she was condescending to patronise, both she and the assistant walked out of it, the assistant gently carrying a pair of trousers draped over both her arms. Or more accurately, the assistant walked out, but our lady customer sauntered out as if she were imitating a young, nubile model on a catwalk. She had one hand partially in her trouser pocket with the thumb hooked over the top, and her shoulders were swaying rhythmically as she walked at half speed, nose up, hips out, Marlene Dietrich without the humanity or style. The assistant turned to her and displayed the trousers in the light of day, explaining the qualities of them, while our lady stood there with insolence and superiority sewn into the seams of her being. She was so stuck up, she was almost fly paper. She ignored us completely, of course.

Oh well, that's Mikage for you, I thought as we made our way up the hill again to the compound. We stopped at the gates and tapped in the security code Jane had sent us. I felt like I was taking part in some kind of espionage rather than making a social call. The high iron fence signalling to all that this was a special place, set apart from the rest of the town, but part of it nonetheless. Inside the compound we found about a dozen detached and expensive modern houses, and finding the right one, we put on our 'we're wealthy today' hats and rang the bell. Fortunately, both Jan and I can hold our own in most society, so we were looking forward to our afternoon.

Jane answered the door in her pinny. "Oh, hello you two, come in, don't stand on ceremony," she bellowed in her deep, resonant, crisp tones. She had a voice that could sooth you, inspire confidence, but also could put the fear of god into you if she so chose. I liked her immensely.

She beckoned us in, "Leave your (sun) umbrellas outside but that's all, bring everything else in," she said.

"Oh, don't you take your shoes off here?" I asked very surprised. I had soon got used to taking my shoes off before I entered anyone's house, and not doing so had become almost as shocking as shopping naked in Marks and Spencer's underwear section.

"No," boomed Jane, "this is a British house, we don't do that sort of thing here! Come in, come in," she encouraged.

We entered a large hallway and then into the house proper, my feet sinking into the deep cream carpet. The house itself was like something out of *House and Garden* magazine displaying luxury and elegance only serious money can provide. The antique furniture was all genuine as I assumed the oil paintings were. It was like a traditional English country mansion in miniature.

I'd noticed a cool, sleek, low sports car, one that turns heads, in the garage. I wondered who it belonged to, Jane or her husband? I knew one thing for certain, she had enough aplomb to pull it off.

As we made our way through the house, I looked towards the living room, already picturing myself lounging in a comfortable armchair and sipping my Earl Grey tea, whilst chatting to Jane. "Not that way," she said, her beautiful voice and perfectly rounded vowels making me feel a bit homesick, "this way." She led us into a large, elegant room with a long table dominating the middle, filled up with cakes and sandwiches and through there into the kitchen, where we found two British women who were busy stuffing dozens of scones with jam and cream.

"Would you like to roll up your sleeves and help out?" asked Jane, her voice now authoritarian, shattering my cosy little dream of tea and relaxed conversation in the living room.

I rallied, "Of course, I'd love to!"

I'm not too domesticated and not used to such W.I. activities and upon saying so, was given the simple job of dolloping bits of cream onto the scones. "Too much cream," said the tall thin woman wearing glasses. She was English, but from a different class to Jane. Jane's voice said class, this woman's voice said money. She had the slightly insipid look of the typical English Rose and was also very pleasant and a great cook I found out later. Her fruit cake was tremendous and 'would keep for years', she informed me with a grin. She was also a kindly soul as she told me gently that, "It was not enough cream now."

She 'promoted' me to arranging the cakes onto plates but I think I must have failed this too because Jane suddenly said, "Let's get you two settled in before the others arrive. Follow me." She took us upstairs: "to leave our bags if we wanted to." I was surprised when she showed us into her and her husband's bedroom, rather than a guest room as she rushed to pick up a suit her husband had discarded across a chair. "Oh, I haven't put this away yet," she muttered, a little dismayed that she had forgotten about it. I thought, Why can't he put it away himself?

"Here's the bathroom," she said, still clutching his suit, now scrunched up to her bosom and trying to untangle the shirt. "Please use it, but if it's engaged there's another bathroom down the end of the hall in one of the guest bedrooms, and another one half way down the hall."

We headed down the wide, circular staircase bordered by oil paintings, and I was feeling very grand – but this was before my fall from grace and major faux pas. We were shown into the main reception room, which ran almost the full length of the house, laid out with many round and square tables, all with dazzlingly white table cloths and a posy of flowers livening up each one. Japanese waitresses employed for the day were hovering around, dressed in black uniforms, all of them middle aged, greying and ferociously efficient.

A few more British women and other foreigners had arrived to add support and we chatted to them in a rather desultory manner whilst we awaited the arrival of our main guests, the Japanese ladies who had been invited. A few started to arrive and to my surprise, the two charming Japanese women (mother and daughter), whom we met at the Queen's birthday party walked in and waved to me. They obviously wanted to chat, so I walked over to speak to them. They were very gentle souls, like sleepy puppies, pliable and eager to please, their tails always wagging. But unfortunately, like puppies, they didn't have a lot of interesting things to say, so I was scraping around for another topic of mutual interest to chat about when many more Japanese ladies started to arrive. And then, in true Japanese unfathomable fashion, a really bizarre thing happened.

We were standing about twelve feet from the doorway and it was rather cramped because of all the extra tables, therefore, I was forced to stand in a small space between tables while the two ladies I was chatting to stood in the space left for a walkway. The guests arriving couldn't get passed them, so the two delightful ladies moved away to make room and I was left squashed in between the tables unable to move because of all the women entering and several women who were chatting behind me. I tried to make the best of it and said, "Hello," and smiled my best smile to the lady in front of me who had just come in and was looking around, rather uncertainly. Unfortunately, she misinterpreted my friendliness and picked up my unoffered hand and took it in hers, shaking it ceremoniously. She said, "How do you do, pleased to meet you," in passable English. Shook my hand a few times more and moved on.

The next guest came in and followed her lead. She took my unoffered hand, shook it, bowed and said, "How do you do, pleased to meet you." And so did the next guest, and the next, and the next and suddenly, there was a queue through the door of twenty of so Japanese ladies all waiting their turn to shake my hand. I assumed they thought I was the reception committee and someone important. I was still stuck between the tables and unable to move and many of the women who had ignored me at the Queen's birthday celebration party were now waiting patiently to shake my hand, unquestioningly. I thought, This is bizarre, but what can I do about it? All the Japanese ladies waiting in the queue were looking at me with blank fish like eyes, I was unsure whether to feign a faint and struggle out of range by crawling under the tables, or whether to brave it out. If I did manage to extricate myself I wondered whether the ladies who I hadn't shaken hands with would have been grossly offended if I didn't stay to shake theirs. It was a bizarre quandary. Pure Japanese.

But I had little time to think because the ladies were coming up to me thick and fast, all politely stopping to shake my hand and in perfect English all said, "How do you do, pleased to meet you," in identical cadence. I was stuck in a mistake and I just had to see it through. Then to my surprise, 'my lady' from the boutique was standing in front of me. Box hat and feather still stuck sideways on her head. "How do you do, pleased to meet you," she said in excellent English. I said, "Ah, I've just seen you in the boutique," feeling sure that she must have noticed the two foreigners. However, I was obviously made of glass because she looked straight through me, not even a reflection to interest her,

142

and she walked silently away, as if I hadn't spoken.

Finally, my ordeal was over, the last hand had been shaken and greeted and I was free to move out of the way. I have been told many times that Japanese people do not question anything. They just accept. That is the way people have been educated and brought up, therefore, no one questioned who I was and what I was doing there. Everyone queued up and waited their turn because that was what the others were doing. The fact that I was inelegantly wedged between tables, not wearing a name badge or any official identification didn't seem to sway anyone.

People are not encouraged to ask questions, or to think for themselves, or even to be curious. For instance, at school, the children do not ask questions of the teacher. The teacher is there to teach, not to encourage free thinking and analysis. If you do not understand anything, you ask the teacher after class or ask your friends. As a student asked me once, "You don't do this in your country do you? You can ask questions and discussions emerge between the teachers and the students?"

"Yes," I answered simply. She looked wistfully and longingly into the distance. Some people do want to know and to understand more. But it was too late for our elderly ladies of the society I felt.

After the party, I apologised to Jane for it and explained how it happened. She was very gracious and said, "Not at all, you go ahead. I've done enough of them in my time." So she had seen the strange turn of events. Oh well, I didn't suppose I would hear from her again after all that.

During the tea party, I noticed that the same formula was adopted as at the Queen's birthday party. The Japanese ladies did not attempt to speak to any of the foreigners and congregated in the furthest corner of the room and crammed themselves in as closely as they could on a few tables, where they stayed throughout the afternoon, apart from several visits to the food table. I did try to chat to a few over the food table and met again the lady whose husband didn't like her watching *Guys 'n' Dolls*. I asked her if she was going to see the latest Takarazuka show? She looked at me aghast that I should be speaking to her, but I persisted and then, when she realised that she had no choice but to speak to me, she told me once more, quite out of context, that her husband didn't like her watching *Guys 'n' Dolls* and that he was like Sky Masterson in character.

"Isn't he?" she said to her friend who was passing by with a plate of cakes, who looked, but decided to ignore us and walked away.

Why did these women come? Why were they members of this society? It exists to promote friendship between the people of different countries, but the Japanese people who belong to it, ignore the foreign people who are there. Which presumably, is why there are so few British people or other foreigners bothering to attend the functions. I have my own theory about this.

Japanese society is one of the most snobbish in the world. I liken it to times gone by in Britain, when human rights were not valued and a person 'below' you was made to feel 'their place'. There is a certain 'high' social class in Japan, who treat other people they think are below them with astonishing rudeness. In this so polite society, they are obnoxious to everyone but the people they think of as their peers. They are rude to the point of coarseness of manner.

Why do these women want to be in this society? I think it is for the snob value. To be able to say to their friends that they went to the Queen's Birthday Party reception at the Kobe Foreigners' Club. That they went to tea at a diplomat's house. Or something like that. One-upmanship. But of course, they don't actually want to meet any foreigners.

144

That spoils it. They just want to boast about being there. They don't want to work for it. Or maybe they're just painfully shy and will only do what everyone else does. If no one will break the mould and take the initiative to speak with the foreign women, then neither will anyone else in their social group. But one thing is very clear, if the Japanese women don't make the effort and get to know the foreign women, then we will never know.

Japanese society has its own unique style and has distanced itself from other countries and cultures throughout its history. China and Korea, their near neighbours, were always important, if only because of invasion worries, but Japan did its usual trick of only taking the parts of the other cultures they liked and then bending and shaping them to fit their own unique style and ignoring the rest, while they clutched their own culture protectively tight into their hearts and refused to change it.

At first, I thought that my culture and thought processes were superior, but the more I got to know Japan and the people, I began to have my doubts. Once I started to understand the way of thinking, which is totally at odds with ours, I started to see merit in it. If this sounds very patronising, it's not meant to be, I have the greatest respect for the Japanese and their way of doing things. Even if they do infuriate one on a regular basis. Vivre la difference!

Not all Japanese people are like this of course. The people we were friendly with and our students did not act in this way, but this 'superior' social class is alive and kicking and passing it along to their children. Through the years I met young women who were pretenders to the thrones of the women at the society, being trained in the art of superiority by their families and peers. As an instance, I remember dear, delightful, full of life and fun, Kelly, my African American friend. She told me about a dour incident that had just happened to her.

She had recently accepted a job at a pukka university, and was very pleased with herself, having progressed through her own efforts and abilities to get this position. It was a women's university, one of those really snobby places so admired by the Japanese. She hadn't been teaching there long when she was called in to see the principal, who told her that one of her students had accused her of being disrespectful to her in class. That Kelly had asked the name of the student in a disrespectful manner and when told had ridiculed the name by poking fun at it. Kelly was astounded and could not fathom this at all. She expressed her shock and innocence to any such misdemeanour, but the principal told her that she should apologise to the student in front of the whole class.

Now Kelly was a proud woman, but she was also a woman who had underlying inferiority feelings and that made her even more determined to be up there and stand proud. Proud of being black, proud of being a woman and proud of her own achievements. Therefore, this request didn't sit well with her, especially as she didn't think she was guilty as charged. She decided to ignore it.

The students, with no apology forthcoming, started to withdraw their cooperation in class – en masse. Then they became verbally abusive towards her. It got so bad that Kelly felt she must complain to the principal, but he backed the students up and said that Kelly had to apologise otherwise she would be sacked. She had no choice and was faced with having to go into class and grovel in apology. Grovel was necessary, nothing less would be acceptable now.

I could tell that she was terribly upset by it all, so much so that she couldn't speak of it anymore or accept my sympathy. Her eyes filled up with tears and she told me to stop and talk of something else. She was devastated by the cruelty, unfairness and cold blooded nastiness of the students towards her.

Kelly had a great sense of humour and was always joking around, but in an adult and responsible way. She was not an immature woman. I think what happened was a classic case of reading from different scripts. In Kelly's mind, she was having a bit of fun with the students, making them feel more relaxed and also hoping that they might unbend and become a little more human and less stuck up.

The students, on the other hand, were in their straight laced jackets and were flexing their fledgling muscles by trying it on in the attempted control of a foreigner and to make her kowtow to them and their power over her. However, having said that, I have learned that the Japanese also treat their own people this way. It's their culture's way of controlling people, of making them behave as everyone else does. Typical bullying tactics in fact. Bullying is a major problem throughout society, both in childhood and in adult life. It's built into everyday life and is accepted by many as a good way to behave. People who have a propensity towards bullying will use this tactic throughout their lives, whilst other poor souls will suffer from them. Kelly was one.

She died eighteen months later, very bravely and stoically, of cancer. Attending her last FEW dinner at the Hilton Hotel in a wheelchair. Still feisty, watching *Sex and The City* videos with her friends right up until the last week. She worked hard at life and lived it right up to the end, her spirit intact and fighting. Atta girl!

*

Among many Japanese, the fear of foreigners is strong and ingrained. One is accepted on the surface, offered the hand of friendship, but it remains on the surface, deep friendships with foreigners are rare among the ordinary Japanese and one finds after a while that one is ostracised. Instead of a budding friendship developing and improving with each meeting, the meetings stop and you never see them again. It's very strange and I thought at first that it was me, that I had done something unacceptable in their society by mistake, or that they simply didn't like me, but it happened too often for that and I learned with experience that this is the way of the Japanese. To accept a foreigner into your inner life, for them to become important to you, is not acceptable to the majority. Foreigners don't understand the Japanese psyche and many want to change them into their own way of thinking. The Japanese are too polite, frightened or incensed to have open discussions about this and therefore just withdraw into their shells and slam them shut. That's why the people who develop friendships with foreigners are unusual in that they are more open-minded and ready to expand their thinking and experiences. They are willing to let you into their group. If you find one, treasure them.

Japanese peoples' lives are lived in groups. Each group is separate and does not integrate. It starts at school where you have your classroom group and other people are not allowed into it. It belongs only to the people within that classroom. This philosophy continues throughout society, family, university, work, sports, politics, or whatever else you do in your life. Everything is compartmentalised.

People talk of their 'tennis friends', or 'English class friends', etc. and loyalty to that group is expected and demanded. Therefore, for people to let you into their family or social group is very rare and a great privilege. Ryoko let us into her family group.

Needless to say, I would never be allowed into the group of the society's Japanese members.

Ryoko, Kenji san and children with Jill and Jan

Jan at Nigawa with a Hankyu Railway train on its way to Takarazuka

Maki san and Jill in her school room

Jill's school room

Jan's school room

The Hana no Michi & the Takarazuka theatre

The Hana no Michi during cherry blossom time

The outside foyer of the Takarazuka theatre

The inside foyer of the Takarazuka theatre

The Maiko san serving us beer

Chatting to the students

Entertaining us with a traditional Japanese dance

Jan and Jill with the Maiko san

The outside of the Funny House restaurant

The inside of the Funny House restaurant

The Yadarigi cafe and the bags of the fan club bosses

The Yadarigi cafe

Masayo san wearing her 'devil's hood' wedding clothes

Masayo san and Shinji in their Edo period costumes

In their western wedding clothes with the gas poker

2005.10.23

Chatting to Masayo san's grandmother

Naoko san at the Funny House restaurant

Sawa chan

CHAPTER TEN

A Truly Extraordinary Event

Life was exciting in a businesslike way, as Jan and I were working very hard to build-up our student base. She had now joined me as a teacher in my school to keep pace with the increasing student numbers. We did lots of training sessions on the lessons, on which she, of course, put her own personal stamp and after some initial reluctance by Jan to get involved in the teaching side of things, she soon found that 'her' students became very loyal to her and enjoyed her lessons enormously. All the money earned was ploughed back into the business or saved. Since Jan had returned, we had increased our student numbers even more and were using both the rooms in the flat for teaching. But building numbers also caused problems and one of them was that students wanted to come at the most convenient time for them, and for many of them, that was at the same time as everyone else. If we couldn't accommodate them at the time they wanted then we lost that student. Which was why we were using two teachers and both rooms. The smaller room was full of furniture and could only be used for teaching, but the larger room had enough space for Jan to use it for teaching, and we could live there too. After pulling our futons out of the cupboard, and moving the furniture aside, we could also sleep, Japanese fashion, on the floor. This is the traditional Japanese way of living, still practiced today, although as you can imagine, this was not ideal for us. Trouble loomed and tempers frayed, it was too much to bear, and the strain of working and living in such confined quarters was at breaking point. So we scrabbled together as much spare cash as we could and set off in our quest to find a new flat to live in, after which we intended to turn our existing flat into two dedicated school rooms. This decision heralded the worst time of my life in Japan, but, in the way of this country, it also exposed me to one of the most extraordinary events of my entire life.

The decision to move is not to be taken lightly. The reason is what is euphemistically called, key money. It is paid to the landlord by the tenant, before being allowed to move in, i.e. get possession of the key. This amount is considerable, anything from one thousand pounds upwards, depending on the quality of the property. And not only that, you only get a part of it back if you have been a good tenant and nothing if you caused some damage. We had paid key money on our present flat of three thousand pounds, and would only get two thousand pounds back if all was well. Also, we would have to pay key money again on any new flat we rented. This system was made illegal in Britain in the 1960s, but it lives and thrives in Japan today. Even though we knew we would be throwing money away by moving, we had to; we had no choice by this stage as there was also another problem with our flat besides the lack of space.

Unbeknown to us when we had moved into the flat, about two and a half years previously, our area was to become the most re-built I have ever known without a redevelopment order. Within a two minute walk of the flat, 42 detached houses were knocked down and rebuilt. I counted them all. One by one and one after the other. No sooner would there be the demise of one house, and the consequent rise from the rubble of a brand new house or houses, than another one would be knocked down and the process repeated, ad nauseam. The noise of constant major building work was intrusive, like Chinese torture, drip, drip, until you felt defeated.

People who had large houses were selling them to developers, who would then knock them down and put up several smaller houses on the space, all cheek by jowl, without gardens. Also, people with 'older' houses were knocking them down and rebuilding. You can imagine the noise and pollution of all that building work. The crowning glory was when a fairly modern block of twenty six flats opposite us was knocked down, and its lovely Japanese garden uprooted and destroyed. In its place went twelve, very plain and uninteresting detached houses, again with no gardens, cheek by jowl. This was another reason why we decided to move, we couldn't stand the noise any longer.

The Japanese almost never repair houses. They just knock them down and rebuild. I had at first thought this was because of earthquakes making them unsafe, but I discovered that it is more to do with society, fashion and a government keen on encouraging people to spend their money. About ten percent of the workforce is employed in the building trade, and they are kept in constant employment. Tax deductions are given if you rebuild, none if you just repair.

Since the end of the last war, when Japan had to rebuild its towns and cities, it started the fad for rebuilding, it's now a fashionable necessity to rebuild your home every twenty or thirty years. It has become a 'consumer durable' and a must do kind of thing, rather than a rational decision. A friend told me that she was going to buy her own house. She was so happy, but she said, "Of course, we're not rich, so we have to buy an old house and rebuild it. We've found one in a suitable position."

"How old is it?" I asked.

"Oh, very old, at least thirty years."

"But why do you have to re-build? Has it been damaged in earthquakes?"

My friend looked at me with astonishment. "No, I don't think so, but we always re-build houses when they get to twenty or thirty years old."

"But why?" I asked again.

"Mmmm," some time elapsed while she gave this serious thought. She laughed a little nervously, put her hand to her mouth and said in a quiet voice, "I don't know."

Being the brash, know-it-all foreigner, I said, "But why don't you know? Do you mean that you will spend all that money and not know why?"

"Yes," she replied, "that's what we do. We have no choice."

'We have no choice', that's the crux of it. People do what's expected of them, not because they have thought things out and made a rational decision. The power of the 'group', in this case, society, which forces people to toe the rigid line of expectation coupled with an educational system that discourages independent thought. What you are left with is a passive society that doesn't think deeply about things – or if they do, they don't talk about it. This is Mr and Mrs Average Japanese.

I watched so many houses being rebuilt, I became an armchair expert. The thing that astonished me most was their frailty. Modern houses are built on shallow foundations with wooden frames and ply board walls. The ply is then covered on the outside with a purpose made rigid plastic sheet made to look like bricks, or cement, to give it waterproofing, while inside, the walls are given a thin layer of insulation and another sheet of ply is applied over that, papered and painted. That's a basic Japanese new house. It's like living in a caravan, very hot in summer and very cold in winter. The money needed for rebuilding keeps many people in perpetual debt. There is also the other question of the waste of resources. I understand that steps are now being taken to try and change this, but in the meantime, it continues and Jan and I were just a small part of the victims of such unnecessary excess.

New is king, for this attitude goes for every other thing you can imagine. Televisions, computers, cars, bikes, anything and everything in fact, is thrown away once it's deemed old (maybe a couple of years) and dumped for a newer and 'better' model. There is no such thing as recycle. Most cars more than a few years old, get sent abroad for resale, as there is no market in Japan for them. No one wants to shame themselves with an 'old' car. Since the economic bubble burst in 2008 things are getting better as far as recycling is concerned, people are not buying new so often, and attitudes are slowly changing, but it took a world collapse of the banking system to make a change in this respect .

One Friday afternoon, about 1.00 o'clock, I had just returned home from a two hour Japanese lesson when I saw seven men standing on the flat roof of the house opposite. All were wearing hard hats and goggles and each one was clutching a pneumatic drill. I could see the whites of their eyes as they were only about fifteen feet away from my balcony. In the time it took me to shut my open mouth, blink and absorb what I was looking at, the drills started. All seven of them at the same instant. You don't need me to tell you about the noise and dust this caused. Damage to eardrums was guaranteed. Suffice it to say, that the house was old (for Japan) and therefore so strongly built that it took them three days to finally destroy the flat roof and dispose of the rubble. How they didn't fall through I have no idea.

It took three weeks altogether to knock that house down completely. Three weeks of drills, machinery, dust and distress (mine). They erected a typical modern style, flimsy house in its place, which will only take a day or two to knock down next time they rebuild.

So we moved. It wasn't far from our existing flat, about four miles, and we paid our key money four thousand pounds in this case, and felt it was our good fortune to find a riverside flat in Takarazuka, only a five minute walk from the theatre. We were very pleased and I thought – You just try and redevelop the river! I was full of confidence and gloated at my good fortune as I looked out over the peaceful river, with the road in the far distance. It was lovely, no car noise, no building noise, perfect. For two weeks it was perfect. Then the lorries started arriving, dropping off large, suspicious looking bags at the side of the riverbank. Then the men arrived with heavy equipment. What on earth?

I got my culture shock early one morning a few days later as the drills started and the lorries trundled and workmen proceeded to dig up the riverbed. For the next four months, immediately outside our block of flats, the riverbed was dug up using huge drills and carted away in a series of nonstop lorries. From dawn to dusk, six days a week, they dug up the bedrock. On checking how long this work would take, I was advised that it was 'indefinite, probably years, as they would be rebuilding the banks with concrete and making the river deeper'.

I'd heard about the Japanese Government's mania for concreting over beautiful countryside and their desire to turn all rivers into concrete channels; to make dams, ruining peoples' villages and livelihoods; when a lot of the time, the work was not necessary. New roads, wide and fast were built into the countryside and then abruptly stopped in the middle of nowhere. All of this destroying the natural habitats of countless birds, insects and other wildlife. It was jobs for the boys and companies made huge profits. But I never imagined that I would be on the receiving end of such a policy. You never know what's waiting around the corner, and that's certainly true in Japan.

My stress levels started to rise dangerously. Although we now had enough space with a nice large flat, we also had to keep all the windows and doors closed because of the noise and dust, coupled with the intense irritation of not being able to have peace and quiet in one's own home. Double this with our neighbours above, who together with their toddler, seemed to be descended from elephants from the amount of noise their footsteps made above us. And they never slept. The thumping feet went on for most of the night, every night. We could never make out just what it was they were doing, walking around until 2.00am and starting again at 5.00am. We couldn't sleep, we couldn't enjoy any peace at any time, as when the riverbed was quiet, our neighbours thundered above us, when they finally stopped or went out, the riverbed thundered. It was hell.

On top of all this, I was having serious visa worries again. My two-year cultural visa was due to end shortly and I was told that I couldn't have an extension to it. I searched around for other cultural activities to join up to, but alas I could not find any that would sponsor me for a visa. I was in a turmoil of frustration and aggravation. What to do? I was desperate to stay and work in Japan. I loved the life and the people and my school. I didn't want to leave because I couldn't get a visa. I couldn't give up. I wouldn't give up.

I met an American man who ran his own large English Conversation school who had shown me some kindness and expressed a desire to help me as he said I was just the kind of English Conversation teacher Japan should be encouraging because, "I was sincere and had the best interests of the students at heart. I also looked like a university professor – even though you don't have a degree." He added, "You look the part, and that's one of the most important things here. I understand your predicament and I'm sympathetic, I know what it's like when Japan gets under your skin." Out of the blue he added, "I'll sponsor you for a visa, I want to help you." I was flabbergasted and asked him if he would shake hands on it. He did. Thank goodness. But I was naive and disappointed and also very angry as six weeks later, there was still no sign of him producing the paperwork necessary to apply for my visa. Procrastination after procrastination ensued and, finally, he was always 'out', when I rang and didn't return my phone calls.

I never did find out why. Whether he changed his mind and didn't have the courage to say so, or whether he was a strange person and loved to mess with people, I couldn't say, but it was my misfortune to have met him right at this vitally important time for me. I had wasted six weeks waiting for him, and that left me with only four weeks before my visa ran out and I would have to leave the country. Whether they would allow me back in, I didn't know, but even if they did, it would not be on the kind of visa that allowed me to stay and to work. I loved my school. It was my life. I was desperate.

I answered one of the many advertisements in the English language press from a 'Visa Specialist'. A Japanese lawyer who specialised in getting foreigners visas and I went to see him with three weeks left on my visa. A seismic culture shock awaited me. I began to realise that getting information out of this man was akin to prizing open a mollusc with one's fingernails. He wouldn't answer a simple direct question with a direct answer. I suppose he was just being Japanese, but it doesn't help in situations of this kind and was a culture shock that sent my stress levels into the stratosphere. I knew that in normal life directness was discouraged, but I didn't expect it in the law.

Frankly, I don't think I was the ideal client either; my case was difficult and I was typically British in my attitude, expecting a straightforward, simple answer and getting angry with the continual round-the-houses-style of the typical Japanese. The Japanese language is structured so that the most important point of the conversation comes at the end of an often tortured verbal route, and then it's usually vague. Therefore, although we were speaking English, the lawyer was still using this pattern of communication.

It was my first real experience of this in a situation that mattered enormously and I couldn't cope with it. After a five-hour meeting, I reeled away from his office with the advice that my best choice was to apply for a business visa and for this, I needed at least three million yen in my bank account. I didn't have anything like that kind of money and no way to borrow such a sum (at that time, about £18,000 in British sterling). I was at my wits end. Finally, I decided to confide in my friend Suzanne. She's a feisty New Yorker, who calls a spade a spade and has a big spirited and generous heart. Jan and I met her for lunch, which turned into one of the most amazing experiences of my life. A one off.

I told Suzanne of my dilemma with the earnestness and desperation I felt. "Gee, that's a tough one Jill, I can't think of anything you can try. I'm so sorry." It was a subdued lunch, with Jan doing her best to keep the atmosphere jolly, but Suzanne and I were deep in our independent thoughts. Suddenly, she shot up out of her seat as if bitten by a scorpion. "I know," she shouted, "I'll ask Shimada san." With that, she disappeared into the ladies loo, clutching her mobile phone.

We waited for her to come back, bemused and thinking

that she had been in Japan for too long as she had done the classic Japanese thing of shooting off without explanation, leaving us puzzled and anxious. But I remembered my giant leap of faith and hoped for the best. Eventually, Suzanne reappeared in tears, her eyes streaming as she sobbed into her hankie. "Oh, Suzanne," I asked, "what's the matter, what's happened? Are you OK?"

"Oooohhh," she managed to blurt out through her hankie, and all in a rush said, "Shimada san said yes. We are going to her house now to get the money."

"What do you mean, she said yes and we are going to get the money? What's happened? Please sit down and tell us what's going on and if you are OK or not?"

"Yes, I'm OK, I'm crying because I'm so happy because when I explained the situation to Shimada san, she said that if I said that Jill was OK, then that was good enough for her and I could have the money right now. Coincidentally, she had that very amount in the house she said."

"That's unbelievable. Are you sure?"

"Yes, yes, yes," bellowed an excited Suzanne, "let's go now, I can't stay here a minute longer." Bouncing and hyper, she rushed to the cash register, urging us to hurry up and follow her. "Lunch is on me," she yelled, as we rushed behind her through the restaurant's door to her car.

On the way to Shimada san's house, Suzanne told us about her and about how she had been able to help Shimada san with some personal problems, and because of this Shimada san was able to overcome her troubles. Therefore, as far as Shimada san was concerned, if Suzanne said she wanted her to lend me three million yen then she would do so. That was enough for her. No guarantees, no receipts, nothing was required. Just Suzanne's say so. I was bowled over and started to shake with emotion, and as we got to Shimada san's house, I was in a daze. We got out of the car and approached the house, Suzanne leading the way and opening the sliding front door without knocking. Inside, waiting in the genkan was Ikuko Shimada san, an elegant middle-aged woman, very smart and sophisticated, of medium height, and with a very pleasant disposition. She bowed to us earnestly and smiled and welcomed Suzanne who introduced us. Shimada san, who had been clutching a brown envelope, elegantly offered it to me and bowing said, "Here you are, three million yen." Just like that.

"Well, aren't you going to invite us in?" asked Suzanne her voice rising in amazement.

"No need," said Shimada san, "I don't need any guarantees, the money is here, it's yours," she said looking at me.

"Well, I want to tell you all about it, so let's go in for a short while, you can't just hand over all that money without any communication at all," said Suzanne. "We're all in a state of shock even if you're not." Shimada san bowed acquiescence and invited us in to her visitors' room. She has a visitors' room because she has an unusual hobby, one that is very Japanese and very special. She is a matchmaker. She introduces men and women who are looking for a wife or husband. It may be a hobby, but Shimada san is top quality, recommendation only, so one cannot just approach her to say that you are looking for a spouse, it's not a commercial enterprise. Someone she trusts has to recommend you to her and then you are interviewed before you are accepted. No money changes hands, she doesn't make a profit. As her family is grown up and she has no husband now, she has no restrictions on her time, or what she decides to do with that time. Her father was a matchmaker before her, again as a hobby and in his spare time. He was successful in his business and personal life and he felt that he wanted to help people to find happiness in a good marriage and family, just as he had. It is still very important in Japan today, to find yourself with a good quality spouse. Again, this is where Japan and the West part company. In Japan, many people today still do not marry for love. It is a business contract, of the kind where the husband will support the wife and any children, work for them as hard as he can, and in return, the wife will do all in her power to give him children to be proud of. The fact that the parents may lead totally separate lives apart from when they are with the children, is not spoken about openly.

Also, it is very difficult to meet a suitable partner, for although there are social places like discos, bars etc. where young people can meet, the ethos of business contract rather than love still prevails for many people. Therefore, to find a partner in such social chaos and in a drunken or excitable state is not looked at as desirable. People still want to do background checks on future spouses, hence the service of a matchmaker is still necessary in today's modern society. Of course, some meet their spouses through work or friends, where their background is already known and the service of a matchmaker is not necessary.

Although arranged marriages are going out of fashion, one official figure I read recently, said that a third of Japan's marriages were still arranged through *omiai*, which is the name of an arranged meeting through a matchmaker. (The word *miai* is always given the honourific 'o' in front of it.) I'd met many older people who told me that their marriages were arranged through omiai and they had come to love and respect their partners and to treasure them greatly – and some who said the opposite with great gusto. There are few divorces, although I know that many of these couples lived their own lives and were not in each other's pockets.

We were sitting in Shimada san's omiai visitors' room, drinking tea and talking of other things than omiai. I insisted on giving Shimada san a receipt for the money, although she said it wasn't necessary, and my heartfelt thanks. The money was in cash, but of course I didn't count it, which would have been too rude. The system is that when money changes hands in such a situation, as well as always being in cash, nobody checks it by counting it. If it turns out that there has been a mistake when it's checked later, it will be pointed out and put right without question (or they'll say nothing and never do business with you again). It's a matter of mutual trust. Of course, banks, shops etc. will count any money they are given, but in circumstances like this, on such a personal basis, it is a matter of trust.

For me, this was taking trust to its ultimate level. It was like a dream. An unexpected, incredible, fantastic dream. Shimada san was all graciousness, and good humour and dismissed my thanks. "Not necessary," she said in her excellent English, "it is my great pleasure to help you out. You give me happiness by accepting my generosity. It is enough."

We left her then, as she was busy with other things and, with Suzanne, we drove to the nearest branch of my bank and deposited the money. There are no cheques, it is a cash society and because everyone is so honest, people walk around with enormous amounts of money tucked into their bags or pockets. As my business grew, I regularly walked around with the equivalent of several thousand pounds in my bag because I couldn't get to the bank during the daytime to pay in my students' monthly fees. At first, it gave me an insecure feeling, but after I got used to it, it became second nature. You can pull out your purse stuffed with money, no one will try to steal it from you. I've seen people take out huge wads of money from the cash machines in the banks and casually put it in their bags, never worrying that someone will see them walking away with it and try and steal it from them. It just doesn't happen. This is Japan.

But I was not that blasé with this money, I wanted it safely secure in the bank, but unfortunately, the bank was closed and I had to deposit it into the ATM machine. With my whole body shaking, Suzanne helped me with the unbelievably difficult task of putting all that money, into a hole in a machine, trusting that nothing would go wrong. Of course, it didn't, this is Japan. The three million yen was counted by the machine and recorded on my passbook.

Jan and I went out that night to our favourite restaurant at the Washington Hotel in Takarazuka town and raised a celebratory glass of wine to Shimada san and Suzanne. We both agreed that this was one of the most incredible things that had happened to either of us. This is indeed Japan. Where unbelievable things happen and fairy tales do come true.

Several years later, Shimada san confided in me that her father was also her teacher and mentor through life, saying to her often, "Ikuko, we have to think about what we can do for others first and we shouldn't expect anything from other people. Keep in mind that we say give-and-take, but *give* should come first."

On the day that Suzanne rang her to ask her to help me out, by an extraordinary coincidence, she and her elderly father had just come back from the bank with that exact amount of money. They were sat together on the sofa when Shimada san took the call. She explained the situation to her father, and asked him whether she should help me? He replied, "Sure, why don't you lend this money to her?" He repeated an old Japanese saying, which was his motto, "*Kurumono, kobamazu, sarumono owazu,*" which translates into English as; we should accept what happens and not worry about the consequences. If the other person does not honour their obligations to you, then let them go, don't chase them or chastise them to get your property back, as it was obviously necessary for them to do what they did. On hearing this, I felt humbled.

I was on such a high with Shimada san's generosity and friendship and I was full of hope and confidence as I made another appointment with the lawyer. But culture shocks continued to bounce around and another seismic one was quivering with anticipation as it waited for me to walk, unsuspecting, into its iron hard grip. As I joyfully told the lawyer to go ahead with the paperwork to apply for my business visa, that I had the required money, he looked shocked, surprised, and not a little dismayed. He managed to tell me, in a roundabout, long protracted way of course, that I could not apply for a business visa as he felt it would be rejected. "Why?" I'm ashamed to say, I yelled. My stress level was overflowing and in danger of engulfing me. I was drowning in stress. He explained that my case was very unusual, because, normally, people without the requisite qualifications do not apply for visas to be English conversation teachers. As this was very rare, he didn't really know how to help me. He thought that the business visa was best, but he didn't expect me to raise the money and therefore, didn't tell me the full story. For now, he told me, I had to employ two people full time at a liveable wage, and employ and pay them before I put in my application. The employees had to provide lots of information about themselves too. Of course, I had to keep that precious three million yen in my bank account, as it was not my money to use. I had gone through the trauma of getting it thinking, falsely, that all I had to do was show the immigration people that I had enough money to support the start of the business and myself.

It was an impossible situation, and after another meeting lasting three hours, I finally had to admit defeat and left the lawyer in as much of a state as I was in. I left his office in a condition of shock and disbelief. He had not given me best advice and had told me that he had not given me the full details of all that was required as he, "thought I would not like to hear about them, as I had already had too much bad news!" *Shinjirarenai*. Unbelievable. That was a bumper culture shock.

A few days later, I spoke to an Australian woman I knew who was a law professor at one of the universities. I told her my tale of woe and she confirmed that lawyers are not required by law to give best advice. At least they weren't at that time, and it was a case of buyer beware. She recommended a top class lawyer to me and I went to visit him and he agreed to see me because I was a friend of hers. He confirmed that I was scuppered, and could only get a working visa if a company sponsored me, and even then, in that unlikely scenario, because of my lack of university degree, it would, most likely be denied. He explained that the law about English-language teachers needing a degree had been changed about ten years previously. Prior to that date, one didn't need a degree to get such a visa. He was very sorry, but he couldn't help me now that the law had changed.

I didn't know where to turn. My life in Japan was crumbling under me. I tried everything I could think of to help me get that vital and precious visa, but I had failed. I was depressed and devastated and only had one week left to run on my visa. I was still teaching and, in the way of sod's law, I was getting more and more new students. It was an impossible situation that I didn't know how to fix, or had the power to fix.

But this is Japan, the land of fairy tales and unbelievable

happenings. Exactly one week before I had to leave, dear Suzanne phoned me. "I've had another thought," she said. "His name is Ken, and he was in a similar situation to you some years ago. I know he joined a franchise system and it enabled him to open his own English school, but I don't know how it all works."

We talked some more and I said, "Yes, I know about that franchise system, I spoke to them before I moved to Japan, but they told me that they could not get me a visa without a university degree. So I haven't contacted them as there was no point. Does this Ken have a degree?" I asked.

"Yes, I think so, but try him anyway, what have you to lose?"

What indeed!

I phoned Ken, who was startled, but helpful. He advised me that the owner of the franchise school was a smart cookie and very approachable. "Try him, you never know what may come out of the hat. Here's his number, give him a ring."

With a sinking heart, and in pure desperation for I had no faith in this direction, I did indeed give him a ring. He was out of town and not due back for three days! My spirit was deflating with each passing blow and I had hit rock bottom. The next day, a puff of hope was inserted into it, when he phoned me from his mobile. He apologised for being unavailable the day before and wanted to talk to me. His first question was, "How many students do you have in your school now?"

"Forty two," I replied.

"Mmm," he said, "that tells me that you can cut it, but you are a challenge. I've never attempted to get a visa for someone without a degree. I tell you what, I'm back in town the day after tomorrow. Come and see me and we'll discuss it. Bring all your official documents, CV, certificates etc. and we'll go through everything together." Talk about my future hanging by a thread.

I duly went to meet him, shaking with nervousness, because this was my last chance. At the end of the long meeting, we got to talking about the nitty gritty of a franchise system and, after a bit of bartering, we agreed on a possible price for me to buy my little piece of franchise heaven. If I could get the visa. He said that he would get together with his associates and have a brain storming session and see what they could come up with. "There must be a way," he reiterated. "What a challenge, I love challenges like this, I'll work my socks off on this one, because I'd love to have you on board. I think you'd be an asset to my company, I'll do my best for you because obviously, that's good for my business too."

We signed an agreement and I paid a deposit with the proviso to pay the rest if I got the visa. If not, he would refund my not inconsiderable deposit. We were working against time as I had to leave the country in three days. He was true to his word and worked very hard and put together a package for the visa people.

I went back to his office to collect it, and he said, "Don't worry so much, give a good impression when you go to the visa office, don't answer any of their questions, just tell them all the information they need is in the file. The file is sealed, so you can't read it, but it's in Japanese anyway. Keep positive and make sure that you get your passport stamped that you have applied for a new visa. That allows you to stay in the country until the decision is made by the visa authorities." I left his office and went directly to the visa office, shaking with fear but trying not to show it, and put in my application. They stamped my passport, it said, 'Visa applied for 30th March'. My current visa said, 'Expires 30th March'.

I waited three weeks before I got the news. I had been granted my new working visa and was now able to work in Japan for another year. It helped I think, that I was British, for there was a dearth of British teachers in Japan, but whatever swung it my way, I'm eternally grateful to all the people at the franchise system and their confidence in me.

I now started life as a School of English franchisee. I explained to them that I would like to get a dedicated school and stop teaching from my old apartment. I wanted to move out of the traumatic flat in Takarazuka, leave the drills, lorries and thumping feet of my dream gone wrong, and return to my little flat in Nigawa. It may have been small, but it was quiet compared to the flat in Takarazuka, for there was rarely a sound in that building, and even the house building noise around us was of no consequence compared to the noise of the river bed being dug up; and the neighbours were all as quiet as the proverbial church mice. Jan and I couldn't wait to go back to living in our old flat. This meant that I had to find a new place for the school as we couldn't teach and live in the same small place any longer. Part of the agreement with the franchise company was that they would help me find a suitable flat to run my school from and gain the agreement of the landlord to run a school from it. True to their word, one of their staff was out instantly, searching the area for a suitable place. "It has to have a decent person as a landlord and an agent who is reliable," they advised. "But that's our business, yours is to go and view the places we choose for you and find a suitable one."

Within a week, I was looking at flats with an efficient young woman from the franchise company. It took us a couple of days, but without too much trauma, I found a place that was just perfect. It was within my budget (with the ubiquitous key money of course), close enough to the station (a five minute walk) and in a nice area. I didn't even mind that it was almost under the Shinkansen line, whose trains thundered above us on a flyover. It seemed friendly and comforting to have the wonderful bullet trains passing by in such close proximity, and the soundproofing of the line was so good, it was hardly noticeable once inside. I was so happy I glowed.

From here, I was able to progress in my business and pay back Shimada san the money which had been left, untouched, in my bank account. Jan and I invited her and Suzanne out to lunch in a nice restaurant and gave her back her three million yen. In cash of course, the money sitting tightly in its envelope and securely lodged in my handbag. Over lunch, we gave Shimada san and Suzanne some Wedgewood pottery as a thank you for all their help. As I handed the envelope to Shimada san with profuse thanks, she just smiled a confirming smile, as if to say, 'There, I told you everything would be fine. Don't worry, this is Japan'. Of course, she didn't count it!

Jan and I went out again that evening to our favourite restaurant at the Washington Hotel and thanked our lucky stars for great friends like Suzanne and Shimada san. The lesson here is that although Japan is a country with huge possibilities for a foreigner, and that a foreigner, on his or her own can achieve many things, we are all, in reality, reliant on the goodwill of Japanese friends and acquaintances, who are willing to help us achieve our dreams. People really do go the extra mile for you if they trust you and believe in you.

CHAPTER ELEVEN

Tea Schools and Arranged Marriages

It was about two years later that I came in contact with Shimada san again, although this time it was on a more personal basis, connected to her omiai business. It came about because of a student of mine. Sometimes, one just hits it off with a particular student, and Naoko san was one of them. In her late twenties, tall, elegant and fashionable, she was good looking with unusually big round eyes for a Japanese and long black hair tied back in a pony tail. She had a great sense of humour and was always laughing and relaxed. She was like a sunflower and brightened up my day. She also had a determination to succeed that matched my own. We got on like the proverbial house on fire.

When she joined my classes I asked her what she did for a living, she said, "I'm a tea teacher."

"A what?"

"A tea teacher. I teach Japanese people how to make the perfect English cup of tea!" She laughed, so did I.

"What do you mean by a tea teacher exactly? Do you make tea and show them how to do it?" I was intrigued and also rather incredulous.

"Yes, that's exactly what I do. I hire a room, advertise, and people join up for a course of lessons. We make tea in a teapot and I show them how to pour the milk, explain about milk first or last, and about sugar or lemon. They are very interested in this because everyone thinks that English tea is very elegant and worthwhile."

I was amazed. I'd never heard of such a thing. "Do you have many students?"

"No, I don't," she laughed (I think she was laughing at my expression), "I'm only just starting up, so I have to work hard and hope for the best. I do have some classes over the next three months and all being well, I'll grow from there. I have lots of plans in my head."

"How did you get started? Did you have to have training to make a first class cup of English tea?" I asked tongue in cheek.

She surprised me by saying, "Yes, of course, I went to England to study tea."

"But there are no tea schools in England. Are there?" My voice rising as I was getting more amazed by the second.

"No, it was a big shock for me, because when I went to England to study my English, I also wanted to study about tea. Unfortunately, I couldn't find a single tea school." She looked suitably shocked, but her face brightened instantly as she added, "But I didn't give up and after serious thought, I decided to pay a visit to the director of the Bramah Tea and Coffee museum in London. I'd been there before and asked them if they had their own school, but alas, they didn't. One day, in desperation, I decided to go back and ask the owner of the museum if he could help me."

"What happened, did he help?"

"Yes, fortunately. He was a very nice man who took pity on me and said that although he had no school, he would be willing for me to visit the museum regularly and he would teach me all he knew about tea, the mixtures and the varieties." She looked wistful as she remembered. "I went there regularly and he let me serve in his gift shop, and between customers, we talked about tea. We both shared a passion for tea and it was a wonderful time for me. He was like a mentor." She looked even more wistful.

"What was he like?"

"He was in his sixties and very well dressed. He taught me in a very kind and relaxed way. I felt very happy and safe with him." (To feel safe is very important to Japanese people.)

I brought her down to earth with a bump as I said, "You know that most British people don't use a tea pot anymore don't you? We just use a teabag in a mug."

"Oh, no, please don't tell my students that, they would never believe it. Is it true?" Her smile gone.

"Yes, it's true, we've lost our elegance with tea." Naoko san was looking confused, so I explained more fully, "I think that Japanese people think of the old days, the pre-teabag days, and they think of afternoon tea at a posh hotel, or comfy, cosy tea rooms for tourists in the Cotswolds. They think that British people follow this tradition every day, but it's not what really happens. Now, everything has to be quick and easy, convenience is the master, and therefore, most people use tea bags in a mug for everyday use."

Poor Naoko san's face was thoughtful. "Yes, I see, but you serve us tea every lesson from an elegant tea pot and pretty bone china cups and saucers."

"Yes, that's right, I do, but that's because it's what my students think is typically English and what they enjoy. But generally, I haven't used a teapot for thirty years or so."

Naoko san said, "Well, I'm surprised, but I think it's a pity. Making a cup of tea with a lovely pot and pretty cups is so enjoyable."

"Yes, I agree with you," I nodded, remembering my grandmother and her teapot and pretty cups. "It's a pity."

After this soul searching and frank exchange about tea,

Naoko san and I became good friends and were always able to talk honestly to each other. Therefore, I was very disappointed, when six months later, she had to leave my class. The tea business was taking a while to get started and she had decided to take a temporary full-time job for six months. It was some time before I was to see her again.

*

My new school was in a small dormitory town called Koutouen. It was a fifteen minute walk from my flat in Nigawa and an upmarket place, completely developed since the war, with a good mix of professional people living there. Just the right sort of place for my school. Lots of expensive and middle class houses squashed in with many small, intimate blocks of flats, not an inch of space wasted, but whether it was through planning or through the people that lived there, it had a very relaxed, comfortable and community feel to it.

One of the things which I hated, but had to do regularly, was to stand on Koutouen's railway station's concourse handing out flyers about my school. I remember one particular day doing this when it was cold, wet and windy, three simple adjectives that were guaranteed to depress me. There were hordes of people coming and going and I could see that I was not alone in my feeling as a sea of miserable looking faces approached me. It was past rush hour and the travellers were housewives, pensioners, students, travelling business people etc. The Japanese are great travellers; weather is ignored, the activity being the important thing.

As the train services are so efficient and numerous, the majority of people travel by train, especially in the built-up areas. That's why I stood on the concourse of this small, ultra-clean station in the middle of February. The cold was cruel and unrelenting, the kind that gets into your bones and freezes you from within. The rain blew in through the open walls and made everything damp, including me. It was miserable and disheartening.

I had stood there for about an hour, trying to give out flyers to chosen people, the ones I thought would make good students, but no one was interested, as they fussed with their umbrellas, wiped their dripping faces, everyone looking tense and miserable. Grumpy faces with frowns embedded.

It was at times like these that I used to think, Why am I here? What am I doing? You're a foreigner for goodness sake, and not so young at that. What are you doing trying to solicit business on a railway concourse in the middle of February in a foreign country, with the weather doing its damnedest to carry you off with pneumonia? Why are you putting yourself through this torture? The reason was quite simple. It's the Japanese way of doing things. One soon realises that few things change in Japan except in April, and every April brings about every major change of life and lifestyle. People change jobs, get sacked, made redundant, kids change their schools, shops and restaurants start up and close down. April is the magic month. Therefore, for my school, most of the changes to student numbers came in April. Students left and new ones joined. People started thinking about new schools in January, February and March and so, to be out in the world, handing out your school's flyers, trying to attract new students is an important part of an English conversation teacher's working life in the first three months of any year. Hate it you may, but do it you have to as it's probably the most effective way of telling people about the school, especially if it's the teachers themselves who are handing them out, giving the passers-by the chance to size you up. As the teacher has to do this in his or her spare time, one doesn't have the luxury of waiting for perfect weather.

As I stood there trying to ignore the weather, keeping my smile genuine as I chose my target passers-by, my mind wandered to the railways and pondered on why they are the best in the world. There are various private railway companies throughout the country. Cities are awash in them as they criss-cross each other, with several companies vying for business. Invariably, they are all extremely efficient, clean, comfortable, on time, frequent, cheap and a pleasure to travel on. Most towns and small communities have their own railway station. For example, my local railway, which is called the Hankyu railway, runs a line up and down an eight mile strip, from Nishinomiya Kitaguchi to Takarazuka. It has seven stations and trains run every five minutes in rush hours and every seven minutes thereafter, between 5.00am – 12.30am. With its attractive maroon carriages, without exception as clean as a freshly scrubbed morning face, it is also safe, fast and cheap. I loved that railway line because it never let me down; the staff were always kind and helpful and made me feel like I mattered. Trains arrived on time and took me in comfort to wherever I wanted to go. I didn't need a car, all I needed was a railway ticket as I could go anywhere on the train with an occasional bus journey thrown in for the more remote areas. I could live in Japan just for the railways.

In the towns and cities, every station, regardless of size, has its own community of shops, restaurants and businesses gathered snugly around it, ensuring that whoever gets off there will not need to walk more than a few steps to be catered to for most needs. Even though the larger stations have the best and most diverse shops, you don't need to venture outside your local station area unless the thirst for variety and difference overtakes you. It's a system that I found very strange at first, but as I got used to it, I appreciated its convenience and availability. Many of the stations have a modern, upmarket, purpose built shopping building, that houses many of the shops, cafes and restaurants under one roof, which means you can walk from your train station directly into the building. Therefore, one can walk into the shops without having to suffer the heat of summer, or cold of winter. It's especially useful in the rainy season. Trains and all public buildings are air conditioned and, if one tried really hard, I think one could live almost exclusively in a man-made environment, hardly ever seeing the outside world.

These stations are the best places to distribute information about your business. The only trouble is trying not to fall over everyone else who is trying to do the same for their own business. Hairdressers were the worst as they seemed to get everywhere and always got the best spots. They were unrelenting in the amount of time and effort they put in – there are an awful lot of hairdressers in Japan. But if Jan could strike lucky and commandeer the best spot, she was the best distributor of flyers I have ever known. The official figures were that you had to give out one thousand flyers to get one student (or customer); a ratio of 1000-1 but Jan could do a ratio of 100-1. I don't know how she managed it, but I am eternally grateful. Being so good at this was not so good for Jan, as she became the chief distributor, and this is really a horrible job, boring, repetitive, hard on the feet, back and morale. You have to keep that smile going for, if it slips, so will your acceptance rate, people will ignore you and pass by without a further glance. Interestingly, I noticed that if a lot of people were coming towards me, for example, when a train had just emptied, they always saw me straight away being the only foreigner there, and if I offered a flyer to someone in the front of that mass and they refused, all the people who had seen this refusal would refuse too. But if that first person accepted it, then everyone else did too, especially if I was picky who I offered them to. Psychology is all.

The whole idea of this tortuous advertising was to entice a prospective student to book a trial lesson. The phone number of my assistant, Maki san, was printed on each flyer and she worked her magic as she encouraged suitable people to take a trial lesson and discouraged anyone she thought unsuitable. The skill involved in turning a trial lesson student into a member of the school is one that has to be learned from trial and error. One of the great secrets of it for me was the discovery that one's qualifications and experience as a teacher play only a small part in whether a student joins or not. Your experience comes out in the way you conduct yourself and the overall impression you make, but what is really important is to make the student feel safe, welcome and to give the impression that you can help them without being threatening to their self-esteem or personal safety. A soft, gentle, powder puff approach is what works best.

I employed a young man on a part-time basis, his name was Bill and he was an Australian student. Big, rugby player physique, a he man, a hunk. All the women loved him because he was confident enough to project himself in a different way with his women students. He understood Japanese psychology, in fact, he was a psychology student and he always spoke to his women students in a soft, gentle voice, like velvet on cotton wool. It can take a while to adopt this approach comfortably and naturally, but once you have it, it becomes second nature and is really good for one's stress levels as it sooths and softens everything and the students respond in kind. I rarely experienced any aggression, and if I lost my temper a little through stress and frustration (outside the school I hasten to add), the Japanese person on the receiving end invariably refused to respond in kind, but returned my anger with gentle and genteel magnanimity.

It made me feel a heel.

My school started life as a ladies only school as I thought it safer not to have men coming into my home. If I was unfortunate enough to encounter a weirdo, at least I would have a reasonable chance of defending myself if it was a woman. I continued this practice when I opened up my dedicated school in Koutouen. By this time, I had realised that Japanese women always deferred to men and that would apply in the classroom too. The whole atmosphere of the lessons would change if I mixed men and women together. The women would not feel free to express themselves as they wanted and I knew that many of them would clam up altogether. One of the unique aspects of my school was that women could come there and relax and be themselves.

Classes were a maximum of three students, with some taking private one-to-one lessons. A year or so after opening the school in Koutouen we got so busy we had to employ a part-time teacher. We chose Bill because not only was he eminently suitable, but because I really needed to open up the school to men, as some were making enquiries about joining us. A lot of men preferred to be taught by another man, therefore, Bill got most of the male students to teach. This was the only time I ever had any trouble at the school, although it was not a student who caused it, all our male students always behaved impeccably. Bill was teaching one of his favourite male students, an economist by profession, and Bill was able to let his more macho side come out during his lessons, but one evening, when everyone else had gone home, they were just finishing up when they heard a terrible commotion at the front door. I had always instilled in Bill the necessity of not just closing the front door, but of locking it too. This held him in good stead here because someone was trying to get in, shouting at the top of his voice, "Give me your money," in Japanese. "Open up, give me your money," over and over and shaking and thumping the front door and window, which had reinforced glass thank goodness. Bill and his student tried to reason with him through the locked door, but that only made him more violent and deciding that passivity was the better part of valour, they agreed to make an emergency call to the police. Bill told me, "I was really scared; he was drunk out of his mind." They waited about forty minutes and finally the police arrived, five of them, on bicycles, one behind the other, at a leisurely pace and parked their bikes carefully before approaching the school. They timed it perfectly, because by this time the strange man had gone on to pastures new, or suffered a loss of consciousness, either way, he was nowhere in sight. The police went away again without further ado.

"Well," said Bill the next day, "I wouldn't want to be in serious need of police protection."

*

Once I had perfected my trial lesson I am pleased to say that most prospective students joined the school, giving us an average of seventy students at this time. All students, who came for a trial lesson told me that they were only 'beginners' in speaking English, even if their English was quite advanced, keeping to the tradition of showing modesty in all things. This made it hard to gauge their language ability at first, and I would spend several minutes chatting to them over a cup of tea, getting them to relax, so that I could tease out their English. To make a mistake on the level of the student during a trial lesson meant that the student didn't join, so this was very important.

This word 'beginner' is a misnomer because, as I said before, all Japanese people have six years of English study at school and many have ten years or more. What they do suffer from is that strange way of teaching that Japan employs. All through their education, children will be taught by rote, not understanding. A strange system, but one that has given work to many thousands of native English speakers. Our job was to give them the confidence to speak and not worry about making mistakes, and to increase their listening ability. As I went through the trial lesson with them, I could see lights going on inside their heads as they understood where I was gently leading them. By the end of the lesson (about half an hour later), they were speaking grammatically correct English and could tell me their name, job, hobbies and where they lived in perfect English. The more advanced students could tell me how often they did things and where and when they did them. But they knew this anyway, they just couldn't get it out without guidance. We call them 'false beginners'. Japan was, and is, full of them.

It was in this manner, we found two delightful new students. They were both young working women and therefore only able to come on Saturdays. Fortunately, they both had a similar level of English – false beginners! Therefore, I put them in the same class and they became friends. They were unmarried, aged around thirty and, after about a year, as they grew more confident in their English ability and their friendship with themselves and with Jan, their teacher, they confided to each other that they were looking for a husband. They were attractive women, smart, intelligent, great fashion sense, good personalities, they had everything going for them, but they were having trouble finding a 'good' husband. As a general rule, young Japanese men don't have a very good reputation amongst their women folk, they are seen as boring, with many of them being stigmatised as being a 'Mama's boy'. Young women tend to look upon many young men as being spoilt to the core by their mothers, who do everything for them, as if they are their son's personal slave. They wait on them with devotion any time of the day, even in the middle of the night if that's what the precious son wants. I remember a student of mine telling me that her twenty-year-old son woke her up at 3.00am the morning of her lesson with me. He was playing computer games with his friend and they wanted a cup of coffee. He went into her bedroom and woke her up and told her to make some coffee. I was astounded and very innocent at that stage of Japanese mothers' devotion, and said, "Did you tell him off?" She looked a mixture of shame and pride, but the pride won out and she answered, "Well, I'm a good mother, I got up and made them coffee, but I was very annoyed!" So, I hope you can understand a little why these two attractive women were having trouble finding a 'suitable man'.

*

Although Jan had been promoted to chief flyer distributor, I did make the occasional efforts at flyering and it was during one of these efforts that I met Naoko san again. I was handing out flyers with great rapidity as a train had just emptied and everyone was coming towards me at a fast clip, in a mass. I handed a flyer to one young lady as she passed by my peripheral vision and suddenly, we both did a double take. It was Naoko san. We laughed and stopped to chat for a while and she told me that she had opened up a new tea school. "It's not far from here. Do you want to see it?"

I felt guilty abandoning my post, but not much, and we made our way out of the station. Shortly afterwards we stood outside her new school. Naoko san explained that she and her father had this school specially built for them as her father, a teacher, had recently retired and wanted to continue teaching privately, and Naoko san wanted a permanent place for her tea school, therefore, they would share it. "I know this school," I said, "I pass it every day on the way to my school. I had no idea it was yours."

The building is small and wedged shaped, like a piece of cheese, about twenty feet long by ten feet wide at its widest point. It is right on the road and opposite the Hankyu railway. I think of it as a magic building, because when I went inside, it seemed much bigger inside than out. The architect had cleverly designed it in light Swedish wood and together with many large windows and a high ceiling gave it the impression of space. It is a great little building and although it rattles and rolls a little to the tunes of the trains and large vehicles passing, surprisingly, it is all tranquillity inside. Naoko san had succeeded. She now had her own elegant and purpose-built school in which to teach her students about tea and was hard at work developing her lessons and attracting students.

One of the things she had done was to go to Sri Lanka and continue her study of tea. Ceylon tea being world famous, it was the logical place to start. She brought all this new knowledge back to Japan and started her business in earnest. There are now many women, for most of her students are women, who, thanks to Naoko san, have a deeper understanding of the joy of tea, especially when made in the Spode or Royal Doulton teapots she always uses.

Naoko san and I took up our friendship again and decided to meet once a week in a restaurant to practice our language skills. Over a leisurely dinner, we would speak half in English and half in Japanese. We did this every week for three years in my favourite restaurant, The Funny House in Takarazuka. One such evening, Naoko san confided in me that her sister, Sawa chan, was looking for a husband. I'd known Sawa chan for some time as after Naoko san and I met up again, she had joined us several times for our weekly dinners and some time before, had decided to join my school. As she could only come on a Saturday, I'd put her into the class of the two young women who were 'husband hunting'. They all got on very well together and this class soon became affectionately known as the 'omiai class' by Jan and I.

Naoko san said, "Sawa chan wants to get married, but she cannot find a suitable husband. She wants to meet someone who has a different work ethic to the normal salary man because they work very long hours, six days a week and are slaves to their company. They, in turn, expect their wives to be a slave to them, but it's very hard to meet someone who is not a typical salary man. She wants to have a life together with her husband, but if she rarely sees him, because he's always at work, then that's not satisfactory for her."

Normally, a woman is expected to give up work when she gets married and to devote herself to her husband and family. She has to be at home when her husband returns from work at 10.00pm, 11.00pm or even midnight. She then gives him his dinner and makes sure he has everything he needs for a restful few hours before leaving again next morning at about 7.00 o'clock. If there are any children, the wife takes care of them and the husband sees very little of them. Therefore, I could understand Sawa chan's reluctance to marry a normal salary man. She wanted something better and more satisfying.

I looked at Naoko san, and knowing that I would

surprise her, said very quietly, "I know a matchmaker."

Her eyes widened in surprise, her mouth dropped a little, "*HONTO*," (really), she said in a loud, disbelieving voice. "How do you know such a person? Are you sure?" Her voice had risen and the Mama san looked over questioningly, wondering what was going on. I laughed to reassure her that nothing was wrong.

"Yes, I'm sure, I met her some time ago when she did me a great favour [the three million yen] and I have never forgotten her. Her name is Shimada san. Would you like me to contact her and ask her if she is willing to take Sawa chan onto her books?"

"I'll ask Sawa chan if she wants to use a matchmaker," Naoko san said and added, "unbelievable Jill *sensei*, (she always called me Jill sensei; Jill teacher). Unbelievable!"

I knew Sawa chan well and was fond of her and cared about her feelings, and as this was a very delicate and personal subject where people exposed themselves to personal rejection, I was concerned that she understood the risks of damaged feelings she was putting herself forward for. I wanted to make sure she understood that Shimada san may say no, sorry, she couldn't help her. I explained that Shimada san had a high reputation within her community and was a very pukka lady and consequently, was very particular who she acted for in this connection. There was a risk that Sawa chan may experience the shock of rejection if Shimada san, for some reason, felt she couldn't accept her.

"*Hai, wakarimashita.*" (Yes, understood), Naoko san said, nodding continuously. "Unbelievable!"

The following week, as Naoko san and I settled to our Funny House dinner again, she told me that Sawa chan had considered this very carefully, once she got over the shock of a foreigner introducing her to a Japanese matchmaker, and had decided that she would like to join Shimada san's service and take her chances.

"I'll send an e-mail to Shimada san and recommend Sawa chan," I said, feeling very important. I had no problem in recommending Sawa chan very highly. She's a beautiful young woman, tall and elegant like her sister, and with a personality as good as her looks. Her humour is apparent from a first meeting and as you get to know her, and she relaxes a little, it comes out in lots of super little ways. If you say something to her that she hasn't heard before, or that she finds hard to believe, she will move her head to the side slightly, look directly at you with smiling eyes and say with exaggerated inflection and mischief, something like, "Eh, Jill sensei is that *true*?" It never failed to make me laugh as she was so genuine in her incredulity and expressed it so mildly and engagingly.

Shimada san responded immediately, in a very positive light, but warned me that she may not be able to help. She would have to do an interview with Sawa chan, together with her mother and Naoko san too. This way, she would see all the family together. She explained, "Know the mother and you will know the daughter, so I am very interested in the mother." She also explained that she didn't need to see the father. "Know the wife and you will know the husband, the mother of the family is the key."

Consequently, a couple of weeks later, all three of them visited Shimada san's house for their interview. I, for one, was very nervous and greatly intrigued. I suppose I was nervous because I wanted this to succeed, to see where it would lead and I was fascinated by this little bit of old Japan, still vibrant and useful in today's society.

Naoko san told me later that, after the interview, Shimada san told them that she had many women on her books, but not so many men, and therefore, didn't really need any more women. Oh dear! But she was willing to accept Sawa chan as being a very suitable person and family for her, and she would do her very best to help, although she also warned them that they shouldn't expect lots of introductions. Sawa chan would have to go elsewhere if she wanted that. Sawa chan was delighted and didn't want to go elsewhere. Image is all in Japan and Shimada san had a good reputation; therefore, Sawa chan was satisfied. So she settled back to wait for the call however long it took.

I remember many of my older students telling me that they had many omiai meetings, several of them saying that they had over fifty and one had over seventy!

I know that Sawa chan had some meetings with men who were deemed suitable but they didn't result in marriage. However, she is now married – but she didn't meet her husband through an omiai!

A matchmaker is called a *nakoudo* in Japanese and traditionally, they were someone like an aunt or uncle who took an interest in their family and tried to help to get their family members a good wife or husband. Good in this instance meaning as well educated as possible, prosperous and from as good a family as the nakoudo's family, or even a little step up, if at all possible. It was not a love match, it was a business proposition, and this concept still holds true today. Mothers of sons especially want them to marry because it is still the daughter or daughter-in-law who is the main carer of the elderly and infirm.

Men and women lead separate social lives and after marriage, the husbands and wives will keep those separate lives intact as a matter of course. Men will be invited to parties, social gatherings etc without their wives and vice versa. Japan is very much a separatist society.

Once a marriage is arranged and agreed to, you don't have to get married immediately. I remember one elderly man, who told me a story, in the presence of his wife that when he and his wife got engaged in their early twenties, he was posted to France by his company. They decided to wait until he returned before getting married. It was six years before he came back and when he arrived at the airport, his family and his fiancé's family were there to meet him. He went up to his fiancé and took her hand, gave her a kiss and said, "You have grown more beautiful with the passing years." She replied, "That's your fiancé over there, I'm her sister." Both husband and wife thought this very funny, or at least he did, but his wife had the long-suffering look of a woman who lives to support her husband in all things. A good Japanese wife in other words.

*

Whether people decide to get married through a love match or an omiai meeting, either way, they have to legally get married. I will talk more about the legal side of marriage in another chapter, but there are a large number of couples who chose to go through a mock western-style Christian marriage ceremony as well as the legal marriage in city hall. They have a big, white wedding with all the trimmings of a plush western marriage ceremony and the reception afterwards. The ceremony does not take place in a church and is not legal, the reason being that the wedding vows and service is officiated by a moonlighting English teacher. Male English teachers, (not female, much to my chagrin) could earn a tidy sum by going off on weekends to various parts of Japan officiating as a priest in sham Christian wedding ceremonies. One Australian man I met used to do this every weekend. He'd signed on with an agency and he travelled around to various locations and put on his 'vestments' and performed 'marriages' in hotels. He told me that he was very popular because he did it very conscientiously and earnestly, and although everyone present knew he wasn't really a priest, they didn't care because they didn't want him to be, they didn't really want to get married legally in a Christian service, they just wanted the experience of a foreigner 'marrying' them and all the pomp and circumstance of a western-style wedding ceremony. The fun of it. It wasn't thought about deeply. The surface was the thing, what it looked like was more important than the underlying meaning. Many people say that Japanese society is 'all form and no substance'. That's a bit harsh I think, but it's certainly true in this case.

I remember doing a school trip to a posh hotel in Kobe, where we had booked afternoon tea for our students, and as Jan and I were looking for the tea room, we noticed a wedding ceremony going on in a room with glass doors. We could see the bride and groom standing in front of the 'priest' and all the guests seated behind them. It was all very serious and the 'priest' made the sign of the cross over them, his collar and tie showing beneath his cassock. He looked like he'd made a good job of it and as we were looking in, the bride and groom turned and started to walk up the 'aisle' towards us. We stepped back to the far wall and were joined by some of our students and we made an informal reception committee as the doors opened and the bride and groom stepped out into the hotel's corridor. Both of them looked radiant, the bride in her exquisite white wedding dress, complete with veil and train, and the groom in his grey morning suit, waistcoat, cravat and gloves. Joining in the fun, we all said a heartfelt, "Ah," and broke into applause and continued applauding them as they walked in procession past us. By the time they had passed by our smiles were as big as theirs. I felt radiant myself and it boosted my spirits no end, and I thought, to hell with it, who cares that they were 'married' by a foreign English teacher if everyone was so happy. Japan does that to you.

CHAPTER TWELVE

Christmas Parties

Even though I now had my own school for adults, I was still teaching the kids' class with Ryoko and always kept some free spots in my schedule to help her with her various children's classes whenever she needed me. Ryoko had decided to spread her classes around, rather than use one dedicated schoolroom, and she had classes in various parts of the area. They were, and still are, very successful. She also had some special English classes at kindergartens as a guest teacher and I sometimes made guest appearances at these schools, especially at Christmas time.

Japan is not a Christian country, but they have taken to Christmas as a retail opportunity and an excuse to party. In the run up to Christmas, shops and shopping areas are festooned with Christmas decorations to equal any in the world. Expense is no object in many places. Traditional Christmas songs in English bombard one's ears everywhere. You can't get away from Christmas, even if you wanted to. That is, until Christmas Eve. When it all stops. After the shops close at about 8.00pm on December 24th, gangs of workmen arrive dressed in smart uniforms, clean and freshly pressed, and work all night to dismantle the decorations. In their place, they erect large and elaborate traditional Japanese New Year decorations. Therefore, come Christmas day, everything Christmassy is gone, as if it had never been. No Christmas goods in the shops, no decorations or music. It's a normal working day and everything has been changed for celebrating the New Year.

It was during the run up to one Christmas, while people were still having Christmas parties that Ryoko asked me to be a special Christmas guest at one of the schools where she was a guest teacher. We drove through deepest Osaka and arrived at a large kindergarten. Everyone was ready for us and the kids were very excited. This school was large enough to have a hall with a stage. It was on this stage that we would do our show.

But first, it had been a long drive, and I had to visit the loo before we started. Ryoko showed me where it was and apologised as she led me to the kids toilet area. "I'm sorry," she said, "this school only has one toilet for the teachers and it is situated in with the kids toilets." I followed Ryoko in and passed a row of about six small low urinals, just the right height for little boys, several of whom were taking the opportunity to empty their bladders before the show, same as me. They craned their necks to follow our progress as we passed and an excited hum started. Opposite the urinals was a row of cubicles without doors, equipped with tiny low toilets. Again, several of them were occupied by little girls doing their business in full public view. Oh, poor things, I thought. They don't get any privacy. I had looked at them because they were so unexpected, but immediately withdrew my gaze and followed Ryoko to the end of the room where, in glorious isolation, stood an adult size cubicle. The one for the teachers.

Ryoko left me there and I shut the door and locked it. Thank goodness, I thought, at least this has a door and some privacy. As I squatted over the toilet, I became aware that the hum of the kids had stopped, replaced by a silence interspersed by intakes of breath and slight shuffling sounds. I looked up and to my horror, saw that there was a gap between the door and the wall panel of about ten millimetres. Pressed up against this gap was a vertical line of single eyes, starting at the bottom and reaching up to the height of a five year old. The eyes didn't blink or move and all had an amazed look of seeing something new and exciting. A foreigner doing what comes naturally.

There was nothing for it. I just completed my own business with as much dignity as I could and opened the door. The kids stepped back and stared up at me. Amazement still in their eyes. I washed my hands and they followed me. I tried to make conversation with them, and look cool and confident, which was a little difficult after my shock. As I walked out of the toilet area, a little line of kids followed me, like the Pied Piper.

It was time for our show. Basically, it was an English lesson for small children, using the story of Christmas and Christmas items. I held up a large card with a picture of, for example, holly, and I would say, 'holly,' and they repeated it after me, and so on. Then, Ryoko told them the Christmas story in Japanese and I, when prompted by her, would say various English words. After that, Ryoko and I chatted in English about Christmas and I told them about Christmas in Britain and what the children did there. Santa filling Christmas stockings went down very well and all mouths were open by this stage as Ryoko translated back into Japanese. In fact, we'd never had such an attentive audience with a hundred pairs of eyes riveted on me.

When we finished and left the stage, dozens of the children came up to me, all trying to hold my hands, still looking up at me in wonder. In fact, several little kerfuffle's started as more of them wanted their turn at holding my hands. I said to Ryoko, "I must have done a superb lesson

191

today; I've never been so popular. I wonder what it was that made them like me so much."

Ryoko looked a little abashed and answered, "Well, it might be something to do with the fact that before you came, I told them you were Santa's sister."

*

I was always looking for ways of keeping my students happy and interested and one of the most enjoyable ways for me was the school trip and the Christmas party. With my assistant, Maki san's help, I arranged an annual Christmas party at a local university where we had a Christmas lunch of beef (or fish) and vegetables with chocolate cake to follow. This was the nearest I could get to a Christmas menu, with the chef refusing to cook chicken (turkeys are not known). I was told that his reaction to my request for chicken was, "Chicken, too ordinary, I cannot cook for my patrons." End of discussion.

As most Japanese only have images of a real Christmas from films and books, I tried to make everything as authentic as possible. Jan, Maki san and I would arrive early and decorate the room and tables. Lots of tinsel, crackers (sent from Britain by my parents), snow, trees, reindeers and one year, Maki san's husband volunteered to be Santa Claus. Jan and I would spend days buying presents and wrapping them, with everyone getting a present on entering. After lunch, we would play games or have a quiz with lots of mystery prizes and one year, Naoko san came and gave us a demonstration on how to make the perfect English cup of tea.

Firstly, we had to have a lesson on how to pull a cracker and when I asked everyone to wear their paper hats there was some reluctance at first until I told them that although they had images of elegant British people enjoying elegant dinners on Christmas day, most of us were sitting there with paper hats on our heads! They were astounded, but after some persuasion joined in the fun, and though it was hard work, I don't know who enjoyed it the most, the students or us.

The twice-yearly school trips were equally enjoyable and I'd look for places with a tenuous English connection. For example, an English-style garden or a trip to the Ritz Carlton's English style tea room. But one year, we did something very Japanese and it turned out to be the best school trip of all.

Every year for the month of April, the *geisha* and *maiko* of Kyoto perform a show to celebrate spring, held in the special geisha theatre in Kyoto. The show is called the *Miyako Odori* and the geisha and maiko perform traditional dances wearing beautiful kimono and other geisha or maiko provide the music. They are, in fact, performing artists, specialising in the traditional arts. They are not prostitutes, but available for hire, invariably by men, to entertain them whilst they eat and drink at prestigious tea houses (where they normally drink sake or beer rather than tea). They train for six years in the traditional arts of Japan, flower arranging, the tea ceremony, singing, dancing and playing musical instruments. They must be proficient in all these skills as well as being able to talk entertainingly to men whilst keeping their dignity and reputation intact. During their training, they are called maiko. They only become geisha at the successful end of their training, when they are considered sufficiently skilled to be able to command the very high fees for their time.

Interestingly, there has been a renewed interest by young girls of sixteen or so, especially from the countryside, in applying to train as geisha. The long economic recession making this life seem more attractive.

It is very difficult to get tickets to see the Miyako Odori, so it was something of a coup that I found a Canadian man, Peter, who had lived in the Gion area (which is an area in Kyoto famous for geisha) for many years and was well known in that world. He ran a small business arranging tours of the area and through his connections, he was also able to get us tickets to see the Miyako Odori and the icing on the cake, lunch with a maiko san. A geisha would have been cost prohibitive, but a maiko came a lot cheaper. I asked him to arrange such a lunch for us together with a tour and seats in the theatre.

Everyone was excited as Peter took us around Gion and told us many things we didn't know. He spoke fluent Japanese and it was the only time that Jan and I were totally ignored by our students as they were enthralled with all the stories and information Peter was entertaining them with. At one stage, we came to an unscheduled stop that forced everyone's mouth agape, as a maiko san suddenly appeared out of a doorway and glided in front of us on geta clogs and in full regalia. We all tried not to stare too outlandishly, but failed. She was an extraordinary sight, like a floating vision from another age. Dressed in a very colourful kimono, her hair arranged in the bygone style of the Edo period and bedecked with ornaments, her face and neck painted white, her lips crimson, she glided along as if on air. It was a tour stopper and Peter called out a greeting and they had a chat for a minute or two. It was at times like this that I really remembered that I was living in a very foreign culture, although our students were just as entranced and fascinated as I was.

Lunch was in a traditional restaurant, sitting on the floor on our knees. Very hard for me, impossible actually, as I sat there with my legs stretched inelegantly in front of me like irritating protuberances. Everyone was excited, this was the highlight of the trip, and the noise level was high as we awaited our maiko san. It stopped abruptly with her arrival. Everyone's eyes were on her as she entered the room very demurely. Slim and pretty, although it was difficult to judge because her face and neck were covered in the traditional white make-up of the maiko with her lips painted into a crimson rose bud. Wearing a delicate green kimono and large ornaments in her hair, she was an absolute delight as she made everyone feel comfortable and able to speak to her in a relaxed manner. This was important because none of our students had ever had such an experience before and I think several of them were nervous. They told me that it was impossible for them to do such a thing on their own. They were all so happy.

The maiko san told Peter that she had never had such an experience before either. Her party clients were all men, she told him, it was so enjoyable to have women for a change as the atmosphere was so different. She told him that the men often ignored her and were only interested in her filling up their glasses with beer or sake, but here, the women asked her many questions about her lifestyle; make-up; kimono; and, intriguingly, how she slept on her elaborate hairstyle without squashing it? When she answered, "On a high pillow made out of a block of wood," groans of sympathy enveloped her.

"It was so enjoyable for me," she said. "I was the centre of attention and everyone was so interested in my life and training." She wanted to thank us for giving her the opportunity for such an experience.

After lunch, she performed a traditional dance very elegantly and posed for photos with everyone with a grace and charm that cannot be learned. By the end of the afternoon, everyone liked her and felt a respect for her and her professional abilities. She was seventeen years old.

CHAPTER THIRTEEN

Passive Revolutions

All societies have unwritten rules governing the acceptable behaviour of its people. In Japan, these rules are extremely strict, complex and elaborate. If you ask an ordinary Japanese person what these rules are, usually they will not know because it's not something they would normally think about and analyse, they are not consciously aware of them.

Whereas today, the rules of society in many western countries have relaxed, for me, going to Japan was like stepping back into to an age similar to my childhood in 1950's Britain, where pre-war values were still strong and keeping their grip on the population at large, but at the same time, young people were feeling around for a new way of thinking, searching for a new age that they could identify with and would suit them better.

I feel the same push of the young is starting to happen in Japan, albeit in unique Japanese style – an indirect style that challenges from the bottom up. The people without power, the young women and men, are causing an un-orchestrated silent revolution by the simple policy of withdrawing their consent to take part in the society of their elders. For example, the young women who refuse to marry and have children, (it is unheard of to have a child out of wedlock, even for the young). The young men who have withdrawn into themselves and refuse to leave their bedrooms for

197

months or years on end and play no part in their society whatsoever.

I was able to understand a little of what this means on a personal level after a student of mine told me one day that her son hadn't left his room for two years. I'd known this student for over five years, but that was the first time she had mentioned it.

"Why not?" I asked, puzzled.

"I don't know, he just sits in his room at his computer all day and gets fat. I'm so angry with him because he's there all the time. I can't have my own time, I'm afraid to leave him too long."

"What does he do on his computer?"

"He told me he plays computer games, but I don't really know. In fact, he hardly ever speaks to me and he never speaks to his father. He eats in his room, and spends all day and night in there. He's thirty years old, but I feel like I still have a child, one I can't control. He hasn't been out of the house for two years. I don't know what to do."

I didn't quite know what to say to all that, but some time later, after reading articles in the (English language) newspapers, I realised that her son was the tip of an iceberg, and that another phenomenon was happening in the country.

To its great shock, the general population started to discover the secret world of the *hikikomori*. That's the name given to young men (it seems to be almost wholly young men) who hide themselves away from the world and from the people in it. Jobless, ambitionless, hopeless with their spirits broken. Across the country, unbeknown to the mass of the population, young men were and are turning into hermits in their own homes. Turning their backs on their society and their part in it.

At first, amongst their families, it was a shameful secret,

and still is to many, but news has leaked out of the scale of the problem. It is estimated that amongst Japanese youth, at least a million young men have become hermits in their homes and it is suspected that the figure is much higher. They have withdrawn from society and from their family and friends.

When this started to happen several years ago, there was no support from the medical profession, with the doctors seeming to prefer the ostrich approach, and mothers were left to fend for themselves, with, in the worst cases, sons who refused to leave their rooms, speak, wash, change their clothes and the only way they would eat would be if their mother left a tray outside their door. Some mothers hadn't actually seen their sons for a considerable amount of time having to feed them via the closed doors. The country is now waking up to this major problem of their youth, and is expressing concern and bafflement. Without any help for the victim and his family, it's a mighty burden to bear and has resulted in several hikikomoris cracking wide open and murdering their parents or family.

Nobody really knows the reason behind the appearance of hikikomoris, but it's been suggested that this phenomenon is taking place with young men who are different to their peers. Young men with vision and a quirky, or lateral way of thinking, as opposed to being a Japanese clone personality. In a country that abhors difference, and all square pegs are subjected to a ruthless forcing into submission from all sides of society, this is one way of silently challenging the bullying tactics of their society's efforts to make them conform. Instead of conforming, they have withdrawn totally. To my way of thinking, whether the young men realise it or not, it's a passive revolution.

Japan needs new minds, new ways of thinking and

achieving. Quirky minds applied to problems of technology, politics, and society's woes could be of great benefit for the future. It's a fascinating situation that has happened to over a million young men, but wholly in isolation to each other – or are they all sitting in their rooms talking to one another on their computers? At the time of writing, nobody seems to know.

Not to be outdone, the young women are having their own passive revolution too. Traditionally, they are expected to be married by the age of twenty five, and give up their jobs to devote themselves to their husband and children. However, a lot of young women are looking at their parents' lives of personal sacrifice to conformity and expectation, and deciding that it is not something they want to emulate. The young men have become hermits, but the young women have taken the opposite stance. They are out there, in society, playing the game. Saying to everyone, 'Oh, yes, I want to get married, but I can't find a husband'. Or, 'All the good husbands are already taken, there are no good one's left for me'. At the same time, they are enjoying life to the full, living at home with their parents, working full time and spending all their earnings on foreign holidays, dinners out with female friends, brand goods, and having a great time.

Look around any shopping area or fashionable district and you will find restaurants, cafes, shops, full of young women enjoying themselves with other young women. Reinforcing the separatist society.

Dubbed 'parasite singles' by the media, these young women have no intention of marrying and carrying on the family line whilst at the same time most of them are not admitting it. (Although recently, some braver souls are declaring their intention to remain single and childless for life.) It's another example of passive revolution. These young people are the brokers of this revolution and have become peripheral citizens. For what do you do if you live in a rigid, oppressive society, a free one on the outside, but with an invisible spider's web of unbreakable silk binding you to its traditions and a culture of cruel bullying on the inside?

The Japanese people are known for their kindness, especially to foreigners, and that is very true. But it's a personal kindness, a one-to-one thing. Japanese society en masse has a cruel streak running through it that seems to be accepted by the majority of the population.

In a country where its population is already falling with births plummeting and the longevity of its senior citizens continuing to increase, as a lover of this country, I find this very worrying. I feel that it's a revolution they cannot afford to let escalate without catastrophic results to their society.

CHAPTER FOURTEEN

Takarazuka Tour to Hiroshima

I'd like to take you back in time to our first year in Japan, when most things were still new for us. At 7.30 on a Saturday morning, Jan and I were hurrying along the narrow road from our flat to Nigawa railway station to catch the train to Takarazuka. This road is representative of a normal urban road, which means it is exceedingly narrow with just enough space for two cars to pass very slowly, or one car has to back up to a wider part. Also, on each side of the road, there is an open concrete channel measuring two feet deep, by two feet wide which takes the deluge of water that nature throws down in the rainy season when these channels run like rivers for days on end. So, if you are a car backing up, be careful! However, I only ever saw one car which suffered the ignominy of falling down a channel and the driver (a man) was looking very embarrassed as the van from the garage hauled him out.

Walking along this road, as always, we were mindful of the early morning cars that passed us from time to time. We were always out of step with the Japanese here, and got lots of odd furtive looks, because we were forever checking behind us for cars or bicycles before we changed our course and if one was looming, or we heard one coming, we would stand as far to the side of the road as we could to let it pass. The Japanese, on the other hand, would walk down roads heedless of vehicles of any kind, change course without the slightest look or warning, wander all over the road and even cross roads sometimes without a glance behind them. It was unsettling to us and unfathomable. "Don't they care about their safety?" I would ask Jan time after time (I can be a bit like that sometimes).

"Doesn't seem like it, unbelievable," was Jan's unvarying reply. This carelessness by the Japanese never failed to astound us, but one day, as I was walking along with a Japanese friend and making my strange dance of avoiding danger, while she, being Japanese, was blindly ignoring all traffic, a solution to the enigma popped out. (Solutions to the most baffling of culture shocks seem to pop out unbidden. You can analyse and ask all you like and get no insight into the puzzle, but a chance remark can illuminate and understanding will dawn. Unfortunately, sometimes this can take years.)

She said, puzzled, "What are you doing Jill? Are you afraid of the cars?"

"Well, not afraid exactly, but there is so little space and the cars pass so close to one, I want to make sure that none hit me."

"Oh, they won't hit you; it's their responsibility not to."

"It's their responsibility not to hit you?" I repeated, astounded. "But what if they do hit you? You can't guarantee that they won't."

"No, that's true," she mused, "but don't worry, it will be their fault, not yours."

"Their fault," my voice rose, "oh, that's OK then, if I'm knocked down by a car, killed or maimed for life, then it's OK, because it's not my fault?" I was incredulous.

"Yes, that's about it, we Japanese don't worry about things like that, the driver has to expect us to move into his path at any time, without warning. If he hits us, then it's his fault, even though we didn't check whether it was safe or not. That's the Japanese way; he will have to pay us compensation."

Now that's a culture shock! To let other people decide your fate for you without taking any responsibility for your own safety. Well, if I'm honest, it seemed to work, because I never saw a mishap of any sort in seven years of walking on such roads. (Although I heard about a few!)

We arrived at Takarazuka and popped ourselves in front of the Takarazuka hotel at 8.00am as arranged, to meet Yu san. We were going to Hiroshima together, to follow our favourite Takarazuka troupe, who were out on tour, and which we thought was a straightforward and unproblematic thing to do. But we had reckoned without Yu san's input.

First, let me take you to a little corner of the Takarazuka world, a world only the most ardent and enthusiastic fan will take the trouble to discover. A world of strangeness, obsession and very Japanese.

The ticket lottery. For without tickets, no one can go and see a show, and without that, there's no point to any of it, but to get a ticket for Takarazuka and understanding the system for selling them, is equivalent to obtaining a degree in quantum physics. At least, that's what Jan and I felt it to be. It took us several years to work out what was happening, how it was happening and why, because no one would explain, or they were unable to explain in English, or maybe they just like to keep it secret? Here's a crash course.

Firstly, one doesn't do the obvious and just go to the box office and buy a ticket. One can do that of course, the box office is there and it does sell tickets. But mostly, they are tickets for the nether regions of the theatre, the gods and standing room only. To get a ticket for a good seat is much more involved and could only be tolerated in a country like Japan, for it is convoluted, unfair, and complex. Let's start with the fan clubs. The way I see it, one of the reasons that tickets are so hard to come by is that the fan clubs buy up all the good ones. The convolution comes from the management trying to sell tickets to people outside the fan clubs, therefore, curbing the fan clubs' power and keeping some good tickets for themselves, resulting in a love hate relationship developing between them. Each relies on the other for their existence, but a subtle war has been waged in the past and now a truce has been established, albeit by degrees. Therefore, to buy a ticket for a good seat requires either a connection to high places within the organisation of the Takarazuka company, or within an organisation that has an arrangement with the Takarazuka management – or a trip to the lottery with the fan clubs. For many fans, it's a trip to the lottery. For every new show, each has a lottery weekend. A month before a new show opens and on the day that tickets for that show go on sale, the Takarazuka theatre opens up its doors to the thousands of ordinary fans who want the chance of a good seat to see their favourite stars. A trip to the lottery, for me, was fascinating and exciting to be a part of and left me with a mixed feeling of amazement, enjoyment and camaraderie. It was uplifting and strangely fulfilling.

On lottery day, if you turn up at the theatre at 6.00am or earlier, you will be first in the queue for the lottery and find yourself in the company of up to around five thousand other fans all queuing patiently in the rain, wind, cold or heat for the doors to open at 7.00am. It is organised like a military campaign, both by the management and the fan clubs. As the doors open, the fans are led quietly and at a steady pace, into the first foyer of the theatre complex. This foyer is large and is flanked by cafes, restaurants and gift shops (all closed at this hour). You could probably get a thousand people into it if they squashed up a bit.

The first lot of fans are led through to the edge of this foyer, where they are positioned four abreast, in a straight line, facing the main doorway they have just come through. The next line is then positioned next to them, but facing the other way, i.e. with their backs to the main doorway, then, the next line faces the doorway and the next faces away, etc until the foyer is full. This line up ensures that, when ready, the queue can move in the exact sequence that everybody arrived in and without interruption or argument. When this foyer is full, the line is taken into the separate foyer of the theatre itself, where it continues in the same manner until the downstairs area is full. It then snakes upstairs and, if the show is popular enough, the queue will continue up to the second floor, making a total of three floors of fans.

The atmosphere is so charged that it's like a gun waiting to go off, albeit a gun of blanks as everyone is in high good humour. You can almost reach out and grab the excitement floating in the air, it's so palpable. The high-pitched noise of the women talking is like a wail of sirens, naturally ebbing and flowing with their conversations. Women in Japan are encouraged to speak in a high pitched, thin voice, which en masse, can hit nerve endings in the ears of foreigners like me.

I can smell the theatre even now. It has a delicate, flowery perfume all of its own, and the walls and columns of the foyer are painted in soft pinks, greys and cream, with vibrant reds in the carpets and furnishings just to remind you that although this is a place of relaxation, it is also a place of great excitement.

There is never any trouble, everyone waits their turn patiently and finally, after a wait of many hours for some fans, at 8.00 o'clock on the dot, the lottery draw takes place. This consists of as many envelopes as there are people waiting, as, on entry, we have all been clocked in and counted by one of the employees. Inside every one of these envelopes is a docket to tell you how lucky you have been in the draw. The luckiest getting number 1 and the unluckiest getting number 5000 or so. That is the order you must keep to buy your ticket. The unluckiest having to come back tomorrow or the day after, to get what is left of the tickets, as it will take all that time for everyone to be served.

When the staff members carrying the boxes of lottery envelopes appear, the talking stops abruptly, it goes churchlike, as everyone's eyes are on the staff that walk from the office area, carrying the four boxes of lottery envelopes wherein our fate is held. There is a table situated at the front of the queue in both foyers, and two of the boxes are placed on each one of those tables, one for each side of the table. On the say so from the staff, the front of each queue in each foyer slowly and in an orderly manner, approaches the table. No one speaks, it's all very dramatic. I can feel everyone's thoughts willing themselves to pick up a number from one to a hundred, for that will mean they are first in the queue to buy tickets. As we all approach the table we choose which side of it we want to go to, and like the animals in the ark, we follow each other, two by two and without pausing (the fans are very well trained) we pick up an envelope out of the pile and walk on. One envelope to each person. And as this is Japan, no one tries to cheat and pick up two envelopes. It's all so civilised, yet there is a staff member standing near each box who watches everyone – just in case. It's been my experience that this country is one of the most honest countries in the world, but one reason for that, is that one is given little opportunity to be dishonest!

Many of the fans give their envelopes, unopened, to the fan club of the star they support. The fan club 'bosses' of the important stars then disperse to their favourite cafes around the theatre, ensconcing themselves for the duration of the run. There, with the permission of the owners, they conduct all their business with the fans throughout the run of the show. During the seven years I was living in Japan, and for many years before that, the 'bosses' of otokoyaku top stars always held court at the Yadarigi cafe which was directly in front of the theatre. Ordinary fans would know that this was out of bounds for them and they would not be welcome there. The cafe existed on the business of the fan clubs, special fans and out of towners who occasionally wandered in, not realising its special significance, for it was all hidden in a bubble of normality. But once inside, they would all be welcomed by the waitress with a smile. Business is business after all. Jan and I came under the umbrella of special fans and we always got a big welcome from the three staff. Our order for lunch went to Ko san, the chef of the Funny House restaurant, who cooked the lunches at the Yadarigi. For this cafe was also owned by the Mama san of the Funny House.

The Yadarigi cafe holds a special place in my heart akin to the Funny House restaurant. It was as quirky as the Funny House but in a totally different way. It had also been there for about forty years; steeped in the history of Takarazuka like a mulled wine, soft, spicy and satisfying. Not altering over time. Updating was not an option and so it should be because it would lose all the character it had developed naturally. This stood out instantly with its old bay windows crammed full of posters advertising forthcoming shows from 'old girls' as they are called, who had left the theatre but were still putting on dinner shows and appearing in musicals around the country. If a fan needed to know about upcoming shows, it could usually be found in the window of the Yadarigi. If you looked carefully through the posters, you could just make out various orchid plants lining the window sills inside. As you pushed the old chipped door open to enter, you felt that every chip had a history attached to it.

It was inside that the current and forthcoming theatre shows were advertised with giant posters brightening up the age encrusted walls. But even more than this, you could feel the history of the place as you cast your eyes upwards to the ceiling. There, black wooden beams were covered with hundreds of small name tags used by the performers over the decades. Names that were marvelled at even now for the fame of their namesake's performances. Scattered amongst them were some names few remembered any more, but if you asked the waitress, she could tell you what troupe each name belonged to. That was part of her job, to keep the fans happy and interested.

Jan and I were extremely fortunate in being accepted by both the Funny House and the Yadarigi cafe because it was they, with their many contacts, who always obtained our tickets to see the shows. Unselfishly going to the trouble to help us out. Of course, because of the stature of both the restaurant and cafe, we always got very good tickets for the best seats. We were very lucky and grateful.

Sitting amongst all this history, the present day's fan club hierarchy sort out the lottery tickets in number order and give them out to their waiting members. The docket tells them the exact time and day they have to attend the box office to get, and pay for the tickets. The theatre allows three sets of two tickets each, six in all. The fan clubs give the ticket money to the fans who are buying them and when they are bought, the fans return the tickets to the fan club personnel. If a fan decides to join a fan club, then she is expected to do her duty and become a loyal fan by turning up, whenever possible, at things like ticket lotteries, because the more fans that turn up, the more tickets that can be bought, and the more tickets bought, ensures the future of that star because that proves that she is popular. If a star is not popular, she can find that her yearly contract is not renewed. It's a hard life.

Later on, the fans advise the fan clubs of the dates they wish to come to see the show (for most fans will come to see the show several times). The fan clubs will then say yes or no for those dates, and also decide what kind of ticket they get, i.e. a good one or a not such a good one, or even a bad one. No one demurs; everyone accepts one's fate and does one's duty for the fan club. In practice, what usually happens is that each loyal fan is given one very good ticket, and thereafter, they will decrease downwards until the last ticket may be up in the gods. It all depends on circumstances, and your perceived loyalty to your star and fan club, how many good tickets you are given.

The fans collect their ticket on the day of the show, half an hour before it starts. On entering the main foyer of the theatre there are many lines of fan clubs stretching out before you with queues of patiently waiting fans standing in front of them. When your turn comes, you say your name to the fan club 'boss' who checks the box of envelopes she has before her and hands over the envelope upon which your name is written. Inside is the ticket allotted to you for that day's show. The amount of money needed is written on the front of the envelope and you hand over the requisite amount, already prepared in a very pretty envelope. Normally, a fan adds an extra one thousand yen to the envelope for what is euphemistically called, 'flower money'. It is all very polite, calm and organised, although there is a buzz of excitement throughout the foyer that never fails to thrill. It's a feeling like no other, as the strange way of doing things creates its own atmosphere that is unique and tantalising.

*

This long and exacting business of ticket sales is a vital part of the Takarazuka scene and is the reason why we didn't have any access to tickets for the show which was being taken out on tour. (Now we were living in Japan, we had stopped asking Suzuki san in the ticket office to get us tickets, much to his relief I'm sure). It was the reason that we were standing outside the Takarazuka Hotel waiting for Yu san because she had connections and was able to get us tickets and was kind enough to arrange them for us. Unfortunately, she was late. Half an hour later, a member of the hotel staff came out to us and invited us into the hotel to wait as it was cold outside. But we politely refused, afraid of missing Yu san. Twenty minutes later, she pulled up in her people carrier with a dour face and a perfunctory, "Hello, let's go," as if we had kept her waiting! We drove in silence, all attempts at chat ignored by her, but she finally said to us, "Karaoke, with Kei san," in a low energy voice. It was all she needed to say, we understood instantly that she had been out late the night before, drinking and singing karaoke with her friend Kei san. She had a hangover. (Yu san had told us of Kei san, but we had never met her. She was an ex-takarajienne, who had left the Takarazuka theatre many years before.)

We considered ourselves fortunate that Yu san had turned up at all in the circumstances, for without her, we would not be able to take our first sip of Takarazuka on tour. Yu san had told us that it was very different to Takarazuka in situ because both performers and fans let their hair down a bit and were able to relax more. "It's fun," she said. But we had to get there first and we were stuck in traffic jams galore and after an hour of stop and start we hadn't gone more than a few miles, when Yu san suddenly perked up at a particularly unattractive road junction and pointing over the concrete pillars, flyovers and traffic junctions said, "That's where Kei san lives and has her family business."

"Oh, what's that?" I asked.

"Dry ice," said Yu san, "let's stop here and you can meet her." Without waiting for an answer we swooped around the roads and pulled up at the back of some buildings. Yu san, being Yu san, tooted rather than go to the trouble of getting out, but no one appeared. After a few more toots, she got out of the car in a bit of a huff, still hung over, and slowly sauntered to one of the buildings. Out popped a very attractive smiling woman who had statuesque posture and wore her clothes like a model, but with the naturalness of a child. Tall, slim, but with a strong build, her face was full of life and vigour. She was a pleasure on this dull morning.

She was very pleased to meet us, but spoke no English and our Japanese, as always on these occasions, was a long time in being processed from brain to mouth. We managed a friendly and well pronounced, *"Konichi wa, hajimemashita, dozo yoroshiko onegai shimasu."* That translates as, hello, how do you do, but in fact, is much more than that. It is a very Japanese greeting and the nuance is, hello, pleased to meet you and please look upon me favourably. We shook hands with her and this threw her completely as she was obviously not used to shaking hands, but she was gracious as she giggled, if that's possible, although she seemed to have no trouble with the concept of combining the two. Japanese women often giggle like schoolgirls, even old Japanese women. It's a trait I still find disturbing and odd. For a woman to act in a childlike way is looked upon as a good thing in this society, but I could never accept it especially when over indulged in as some women did. Kei san was shy and gentle and she rejuvenated us as we waved goodbye after our brief stop.

Yu san drove skilfully and carefully. She's a good driver, but because of the gridlock on the roads it still took us another hour to get to Osaka. During this time, Yu san had several phone calls with her friend Akira san. She explained that he was coming with us to see the show. She also said that he was a Buddhist monk and was 'very famous' in Takarazuka as he had been on television several times because he was a fan of a Takarazuka star and had been for the past fifteen years. I asked Yu san why that made him famous and she said it was because there are so few men who are fans of Takarazuka, and as he had been a fan for so long, that was unusual in a man. Also, of course, because he was a Buddhist monk, that made him even more unusual. Ergo, Akira san was a celebrity.

We finally arrived in Osaka and in true Yu san fashion, without explanation or preamble, she dropped us in a car park and pointed to a set of stairs. "You go upstairs here and Akira san is waiting for you. He has a bald head, so you can't miss him. I'll go and park the car." With that, she was driving off into the distance.

Unsure of ourselves, we approached the escalator in front of us and were surprised to find that it was the side entrance of a luxury hotel. As we entered, we spotted a man sitting on a plush red sofa surrounded by bags of shopping. No, that's can't be him, I thought, looking for his bald head, this man was wearing a woolly hat. But no sooner was I thinking this than up he popped, a big, warm, engaging grin on his face and said, "*Jill san to Janeto san*" (Jill and Janet) which is all I caught in a swirl of Japanese that followed. He was a delight. His woolly hat pulled down over his eyebrows, (he didn't like people to see his bald head, he told us), aged around 30, tall and slim, and with a face so happy and animated, that one took to him straight away. He had a soft, gentle manner and, 'Just adored Takarazuka'. He was totally relaxed dressed in skin tight, black and white striped leather trousers, topped with a brown Regency style jacket be-sparkled with eight extra large silver buttons securing the front and two more on the back, marking the start of the tails. He was great fun. I felt at home with him straight away.

Yu san appeared in a flurry and greeted Akira san with a grin and a pat on the shoulder, and without further ado, we all made a scramble to catch our train. On this particular journey, Akira san kept us company as Yu san slept. As he had absolutely no English whatsoever we communicated with the odd word here and there, a dictionary and sign language. The speedy Shinkansen (bullet train) only took about fifty minutes to get to Hiroshima and during this time, Akira san told us all about his favourite Takarazuka star and all the shows she had appeared in. We 'ood' and 'aad' in the appropriate places, for that was all that was necessary and we all had a jolly good time. He showed us the present that he had bought for his star, which was a thick white fleecy jacket, and he told us that Yu san had bought her favourite stars some sushi to eat, hence all the phone calls to Akira san as we drove to Osaka – he was on the other end, rushing around buying the presents. As we drew into Hiroshima, Yu san rallied and we asked her whether we should have bought presents for our favourite stars. "It depends on your heart." she told us.

We ascertained that it is usual for fans to buy their favourite stars presents and to give them to the fan club boss before the show. The boss then keeps all the presents to give to her star after the show. Presents range from small ones like

Akira san's and Yu san's to more expensive ones like large, and very expensive, displays of flowers. There are also some fans, who are well heeled (probably with rich husbands) who give things like new cars and I've even heard of one star who had a house bought for her by one of her big fans. The world can open up for you when you become a top Takarazuka star. As the stars are women and the fans are also women, this is viewed by many Japanese husbands as a nice little hobby for the wife, and is seen as non-threatening to him. The fact that their wife may be 'in love' with another woman (i.e. a Takarazuka otokoyaku) is regarded as unimportant and not taken seriously. To reiterate, many of these women fans see the otokoyakus as men when they are on stage, not women. When Takarazuka came to London, the British papers were full of 'lesbian' this and that, making unsubstantiated assumptions and seemingly unable to see anything else; but in Japan, this concept, on the whole, doesn't exist regarding Takarazuka. Ask an ordinary fan why they like the otokoyakus and they will tell you it's because it's like a dreamland where the 'men' are handsome, kind and talented, and always do the right thing. Probably, most fans don't know or analyse why they are fans, they just are and it's an OK thing to be. It's perfectly respectable and there's nothing wrong with being a Takarazuka fan in the eyes of Japanese society as a whole.

My own opinion is that Takarazuka is all things to all people. You make of it what you want, and take from it what you need. The Japanese attitude towards it has allowed it to prosper in the mainstream. It is regarded as legitimate family theatre, albeit a little unusual, but the Japanese like to be unusual. Granted, it's not treated with such reverence as the all-male Kabuki theatre, but I think that's because Takarazuka is modern light entertainment performed by women. It's also a new phenomenon, being only just under a hundred years old, whereas Kabuki has been going for three hundred and some years and although it too was light entertainment in its day, it has had chance to mature and gain stature. By the way, Kabuki was started by a woman; and Takarazuka was started by a man.

As Jan and I had no time to shop, in desperation, we decided to buy our two favourite stars a bag of cooked chestnuts each, the luxurious chestnut stall being positioned at the exit of the station. Yu san told us that they would be pleased with that as they have no chance to go out and shop and buy food for themselves whilst on tour.

We were getting very short of time now and running two hours late. Jan and I were staying overnight in Hiroshima so that we could visit the Commemorative Peace Park the next day, so when we rushed out of the station we all had to take a taxi to our hotel so that we could drop off our bags. But then Akira san ran off at top speed, nobody knowing what he was up to. We registered fast and rushed out again to get another taxi. No Akira san. We stood outside the hotel, looking up and down the street anxiously, looking at our watches every few seconds until finally, in the distance, we could see him running towards us, grinning from ear to ear. The traffic was thundering around us on the main thoroughfare, people were everywhere. After the devastation of the atomic bomb, Hiroshima is now a pleasant, modern city with a friendly and relaxed feel to it. But we were feeling anything but relaxed as we watched him weave his way amongst the crowds towards us, his coat tails flapping behind him, his shiny buttons glinting in the dull sun. No one looked at him in his Regency clothes and woolly hat pulled down over his eyebrows, his grin and pure enjoyment telling everyone that he was harmless.

He reached our side, breathing heavily and clutching gift

bags and cards to his chest. We hailed a passing taxi and all piled in with Yu san and Akira san frantically stuffing their presents into the gift bags, writing out the cards and attaching them to the bags. Akira san, bless him, had bought us two small gift bags for our presents, but had forgotten to get us cards. He looked crestfallen when he realised, but the taxi was now drawing up to the theatre and as we only had fifteen minutes to get our tickets and find our seats, all was forgotten in our clamber to get into the theatre.

It was raining when we got out of the taxi and cold too. I looked up at a stark concrete building, which had a large concourse surrounding it, but I had no time to soak up any more details as Yu san, our natural leader, took off at a quick trot and of course, we all followed her, Akira san first with us trotting behind him in a sort of foolish snake dance. Yu san's white coat was flapping behind her as were Akira san's jacket tails. We were just flapping. Because of course, as foreigners, we stuck out like pears on a strawberry plant in this crowd of Japanese women. We were the only foreigners there and we were doing our best to look elegant under difficult circumstances, although I fear we were losing the battle decisively. We had no choice but to follow at a quick trot too, having no control over anything that was happening.

To get to the side of the theatre we had to pass across the concourse which was thronged with women, hundreds of them were mingling and chatting, arriving, sorting themselves out. Oh dear, I thought, we will never get through this lot. But I had figured without Yu san, who manoeuvred her way through the crowds with a ruthlessness that has to be admired, and we all followed behind, squeezing our way through the temporary and quickly closing gaps she made. "*Sumimasen, sumimasen,*" (excuse me, excuse me,) being the only words we spoke during this time, and finally we arrived at a door marked 'Private.' Not one to be intimidated by this sign, Yu san, without hesitation, pushed open the door and ran down the six or so steps that led into a small antechamber, which I guessed then led backstage. A young woman was standing guard over a small desk and Yu san, without preamble thrust her present towards the woman. We assumed from this gesture that this is where we had to give in our presents.

In a breathless voice, I managed to say, "But they won't know who our presents are from because we don't have any gift tags." Yu san looked at us with growing impatience, as she plunged into her bag and gave us one piece of paper from her notepad each. We then wrote our short message and stuck them to our bags of chestnuts. "*No*," said a resigned Yu san, "you don't stick it *on the present*, you stick it on the outside of the gift bag!" Her tone indicating we were a lost cause in etiquette. "Too late now," she shouted, "we must leave immediately." Akira san was more sympathetic, and he ignored Yu san's anxious shouts, as he helped us to un-stick our messages and to re-stick them onto the gift bags. We smiled sweetly at the woman behind the desk and gave her our presents. She smiled sweetly back and bowed. Goodness knows what she thought of us.

Yu san was trotting again, and again we all followed, albeit unwillingly. She trotted up to the fan club table of our favourite top star, and as we were waiting our turn Yu san thought it was a good idea for all of us to say *arigato* (thanks) in unison when we were handed our tickets. She said, "I will raise my right hand and when I lower it, we all say in a loud voice, arigato. "Make it loud and long," she told us. We always do what Yu san says, she's that kind of a person, and we thought that maybe this was some kind of a Japanese ritual that we hadn't come across before, so, rather reluctantly, but giving it our all, when Yu san's hand went up we all watched for the downward stroke like trained dogs. Down went her hand and we all shouted, "A-*ri-ga-toooo*," in loud voices to the staff of the fan club. They looked very startled and bemused and rather embarrassed. Not a Japanese ritual then!

But we were happy, we were there and we had our tickets and to our joy, we had good seats. During the interval, we bumped into Miyuki san's mother in the foyer. She had obviously forgiven me for soaking her toilet, and she told me that Miyuki san was appearing in the show and was very excited to be part of the tour as this was her first one. "She is only a 'little star'," she confided to me with great pride.

When a show goes out on tour, only half of the troupe goes with it, the other half stay in Takarazuka and put on another show in the small second Takarazuka theatre, called the Bow Hall, which specialises in shows starring 'little stars'. This gives them the experience of playing important roles which they cannot get within the large troupe. Also, this applies to the youngsters out on tour and this is vital not only for experience, but can also help them to pick up new fans, which is very important for a takarajienne. The revue we watched in Hiroshima was no exception and many little stars shone brightly that day, including Miyuki san.

As usual, the show left me spellbound and I was in a haze of sequins, feathers, colours and stomping music as the final curtain came down. The audience were on their feet applauding and shouting 'Bravo,' which is very unlike a Takarazuka audience, who are usually very reserved. The curtain went up again and all the performers were on such a high of adrenaline that they sparkled almost as much as their sequins, and obviously relished the enthusiasm of the audience. Everyone waved. The performers waved to the audience and the audience waved back, some performers gave themselves over to silly actions in their exuberance and excitement, like twisting around or jumping up and down. This sounds terribly tame, and so it is, this is family entertainment, but it's a big step up from the staid behaviour in the Takarazuka Grand Theatre, where no one oversteps the accepted norm. Yu san was right, stars and fans do let their hair down when out on tour. It may be only a little, as no one dares be more exuberant, or take too many liberties, or even want to, but that's what makes it all the more exciting, a little often says a lot.

We came out of the show on such a high that if you had observed us, you would have thought we had been drinking. Laughing, chatting, skipping even, we made our way out of the theatre to the taxi rank, amongst the thousand or so other people in the audience. All of us equally elated if the noise level was anything to go by. We left Yu san and Akira san at Hiroshima station and we all hugged each other enthusiastically, Yu san's hangover vanished and forgotten. Akira san said, with tears in his eyes, "Oh, it's like a dream. I'm so happy." We all agreed with him as we waved our goodbyes, all of us cocooned in our Takarazuka bubble.

There is a dark side to Takarazuka. If you're looking for political correctness, then Takarazuka is not for you. It is old-fashioned, reactionary and although women front the company, behind the scenes, it is predominantly middle aged and elderly men who make the decisions, write the shows and to whom everyone else kowtows. The whole ethos of nearly every Takarazuka show idolises men and undervalues women; the otokoyakus getting all the adulation and the performers who play female parts usually ignored with very small fan bases (if any). It's so sad, because some of the performers playing female parts are excellent and deserve a lot more recognition. But alas, it is not so. One of the

221

reasons being that fans think it unnatural to idolise a female performer because she is a woman. They forget, or choose to forget, that the otokoyaku is also a woman. The psychology of Takarazuka is very interesting and fascinating and there are several books published on the subject written by foreigners. I haven't read any of them. I prefer my own little cocooned world because Takarazuka is different for everyone and I have my own image and ideology, which I don't want shaped by someone else's opinions. I have made my own mind up about Takarazuka and for me, it is my escape from the world, my fantasy, my little bit of fairyland, and I choose to ignore the sexual politics. Although, being a staunch supporter of women's rights throughout my life, if you had told me before I discovered Takarazuka that I would say that, I would have been very angry and denied I could be such a turncoat. But call me what you will, that's the power of Takarazuka over me.

I remember talking to a very beautiful young French fan I happened to meet, who had excellent English. She told me that she had studied gender politics at University. I asked her what she thought of the gender politics of the Takarazuka theatre and she said it was a great advantage sometimes not to be able to understand all that was being said on stage. But she added in a rather low and confidential voice, "I know it's old-fashioned and not politically correct. I know that the performers who play the female parts are not given much recognition, if any. I know that the performers who play the male parts are revered as little gods. I know all this. But I just can't stop loving it. I just can't." Quite!

CHAPTER FIFTEEN

Hiroshima's Hope

At first, the contrast between our two days spent in Hiroshima was stinging. The joy of the day before and our visit to the Takarazuka show and then, our visit to the Hiroshima Peace Park and Museum, which commemorates the first atomic bomb dropped on Japan during World War two.

Hiroshima today, is a modern, bustling city. The people are friendly and strangely enough, I always felt cosy there. I revisited Hiroshima and this area several times and became very fond of it. But on this, our first visit, Jan and I were having trouble finding the right tram at the terminal. There were people everywhere and each tram that came in, emptied and filled up instantly with everyone calm and polite, queuing up for their turn. A few people looked at our puzzled expressions and a man said, "Where you go?"

"Peace Park," I answered simply.

"Ah, this one for you," he pointed. "Take twenty minute," he added helpfully, "you see, no miss. Byebye."

Travelling by tram is a great way to view a city, and as we travelled down one of the wide main roads, lined with upmarket shops and arcades, it was buzzing with enough people to make it interesting, but not enough to make it difficult to move, which can happen in Japan. Everything looked prosperous and well-kept; the skyscrapers attractive, the roads wide enough to take the volume of traffic and the people looked as if they had places to go and things to do. It gave out a feel good feeling. The tram dropped us off this main thoroughfare, right outside the Peace Park, our friendly man was right when he had said, 'You see, no miss'. I had no trouble identifying it because in the middle of all this prosperity and business as usual going on, one could clearly see the ruins of the only building now left of that other Hiroshima; the pre-atomic bomb one, with the eerie and fascinating ruins of the former Hiroshima Prefectural Industrial Exposition Hall, now thankfully, simply called the A-Bomb Dome. It stands in forlorn isolation, shored up with strengthening buttresses, as the people are determined that it will now never fall down. A lasting memorial of the destructive capabilities of the atomic bomb. The ruin stands proud and tall in the middle of life as it is now, representing all that remains of life as it had been. The Peace Park is now green, where it had been black, now peaceful where it had been the scene of unimaginable horror, now full of plants, where it had been full of rubble, dirt and mud, mixed up with what remained of countless people.

Even though it is situated in the middle of a very busy city, with a main highway close by and visible, the atmosphere in the Peace Park is calm, and a palpable aura of something that is just out of reach, hangs over everything. It is as if one has walked through a time barrier into another world, and although you can see the modern one going on nearby, it is not part of this one. I felt as if I had been plucked from one dimension, and put down in another.

The ruin of the Atomic Dome was part of that other world we had entered, and it separated us and took us back in time. As we walked around what was left of the building, reading the inscriptions, which were concise with only facts recorded, it was enough to give anyone with only the slightest imagination a grizzly picture of the horrors of this place. Wherever you go in the Peace Park, you encounter no preaching or moralising; there is no need for it, the facts say it all. The beauty of Hiroshima today is that there is no blame attached. It happened. It's reported. Nothing more needs to be said. I was deeply moved by it.

Hiroshima is a city of rivers; they dot the landscape like snakes of various sizes and indeed, are beautiful and peaceful today. But on that infamous day in August 1945, they were a scene of horror unimaginable. Huge numbers of people, unable to endure the pain of their injuries and burns, jumped into the rivers to kill themselves. 'Thousands of corpses were seen floating in all of Hiroshima's rivers', is a quote from the time. A survivor says that at 8.15 that morning, 'A white flash, at the same instant, searing heat and blast whirlwinds. Several hours later, black rain beat down on those people still running about trying to escape. Gradually, a circle of motionless death spread outward from the centre of the city'.

This searing heat caused horrendous burns to people and their skin literally hung from them like rags, exposing their raw flesh. The black rain brought back to earth all the debris that the massive explosion had caused and covered what was left of the city. Hiroshima was a charred plain for as far as the eye could see.

Here is a poem by Tamiki Hara san, (translated by Ichiro Kono san) which for me, sums up the hell of Hiroshima.

This is a human being,
Look how the Atom bomb has changed it,
Flesh swells fearfully,
All men and women take one shape,
The voice that trickles from swollen lips,
On the festering, charred black face,

Whispers the words,
"Please help me,"
This, this is a human being,
This is the face of a human being.

Besides the people who lost their lives to this bomb at detonation, many people were exposed to radiation fallout after the initial explosion, doctors, nurses, helpers who rushed into the area, many died years later from the after effects.

The damage to the people of Hiroshima was so cataclysmic, the conviction that humanity cannot co-exist with nuclear weapons and their use must not be allowed, became deeply rooted in their minds. In this spirit, the unwavering hope for the abolition of nuclear weapons and the realisation of a lasting world peace, the city of Hiroshima turned towards the world and began its journey on the path to peace. Successive Mayors of the city have sent telegrams protesting at every nuclear weapons test which has taken place in the world since 1968. They are sent to the countries responsible and each express fervent hope that it will be the last such telegram they will have to send.

The Peace Park is more than a place of remembrance; it is also a place of hope. There are bucketsful of it there. The day I visited, it was awash with schoolchildren, all dressed in their school uniforms, on trips to learn about the history of their country. They had assignments to complete and history lessons to absorb, but their youth protected them from the deep horrors embedded there. The facts ran off them like jelly down a throat, which was just as well because they were having a high old time, laughing with great enjoyment as they had their group photos taken in front of memorials, their camaraderie infectious, their joy in life uplifting. Which adds to the poignancy of the place.

We came across a small group of school children showing due respect to an old man. No laughing here as the kids sat in front of him on the grass, hanging on to his every word. He spoke in a soft, low, weak voice because he was a survivor of the atomic bomb, now very old and wizened, but like so many old Japanese people, spritely and surprisingly agile. His face was lined with the life he had lived, deep furrows divided up his features, his sparse hair combed carefully and his thin, spindly body sat on a low stool telling the children his story and the story of that fateful day. Someone told us later, that these few survivors come to the park in turns to tell the school children their stories. 'Lest we forget'.

As we walked through the park viewing the different memorials, the weather was beautiful, with the sun shining down like a low energy light bulb, slow and easy, comfortable and comforting. There are many memorials commemorating groups of people who died that day, but the most touching one for me was the Memorial to the Mobilised Students. During the Second World War, three million school children, over the age of twelve, were mobilised to help the country with labour services. They were taken from their schools and put to work. Ten thousand of them were killed doing that work, six thousand of them in Hiroshima on that fateful day.

The memorial itself is not beautiful. It's a tall concrete tower. Even the sun shining directly upon it was not able to improve it. Most of the memorials here are not beautiful, and why should they be? They are commemorating an ugly fact. Nevertheless, it stands proudly and the sentiment behind the tower cannot be faulted. The plaque says that, '...the tower was built to console their souls'. The Goddess of Peace stands majestic in the folds of the tower, with eight Doves of Peace scattered amongst the folds. The students' memorial prays for peace. Unattractive as it is, it is deeply moving, especially as it was covered in thousands of paper models of cranes. This bird has come to represent peace and prayer and one of the traditions of Japan is that when a loved one is ill, you make many paper cranes and thread them together to make long streamers. A thousand cranes means your loved one will recover. Here, there are many kinds of streamers, some of a single colour, others multicoloured, it doesn't matter, the effect is stunning. One of the most striking streamers I saw was made out of junk mail. Some cranes are small, about an inch long, others three or four inches long, but all are strung together into 'loving' streamers, size isn't important, it's a personal choice. I call them 'loving' streamers because the whole idea behind making these cranes and stringing them together is an act of love and a fervent wish for recovery. The park is full of these streamers and they come from school children all over the world, who, by making and sending them, extend their love to the people of Japan and pray for peace. This to me is the glory of the park. The joy and hope of all the children worldwide left a lump in my throat and tears in my eyes. I was, and am, deeply moved by this simple act and purity of thought.

We were slowly making our way to the museum itself, I could see it in the distance, a modern glass building, not unattractive, but we experienced some reluctance to go inside. We eyed it from the far end of the park, looking down a gentle vista of pools and fountains, which housed two large concrete half circles, one either end. The flame of peace burned in one of them, and as the sun ebbed and flowed, it caused the flame to alter its appearance, strong one minute and transparent the next. I was struck by the feeling of space and calmness. The elegance of this part of the park is in stark contrast to the unattractive memorials nearby.

Suddenly, we were accosted by six schoolchildren, who were so excited that we were startled by their sudden approach. There were three boys and three girls, young teenagers, and then I noticed that they had an adult with them. He was in his middle thirties I would guess, nice looking in a homely way, and he asked us, in extremely good English, if we minded if the students asked us some questions.

"What kind of questions?" I asked in a semi-suspicious voice, because I think they had startled me more than I admitted.

"Oh, I'm sorry," he said, realising that we were uneasy. "I'm the children's teacher and we are on a special trip here from Osaka, to research the history of Hiroshima and the atom bomb, and to ask other people who are here what their feelings are about the Peace Park, the museum and about nuclear war. It is a fact-finding exercise for the children, to help them assimilate what is around them and also, hopefully, to practice their English by talking to people like you."

I melted. "Yes, of course, I would be glad to talk to you," I said with a smile, and Jan nodded her agreement. "I live near Osaka, too." I added.

"No, really?" one girl said while the others looked confused. She explained to them what I had said. Everyone's face lit up and one brave boy, for the boys here tend to be more timid with foreigners than the girls, asked me, "Where you from in Osaka please?" I told him that I lived near Nishinomiya Kitaguchi. They all nodded and laughed saying, "Your Japanese is very good. You speak very well."

"You like Japan?" asked another of the boys, but he had trouble getting it out and went all red as he stammered, "Yooouuu likeee, ah, lika, ah, lika Nihon?" (Nihon is the

Japanese name for Japan.) His friends didn't laugh at him, as they all watched us closely, their pencils poised. But, unfortunately, we couldn't understand what he said, and had to ask him to repeat it. Now he really was in a tizzy and looked stricken. But one of the girls came to his aid and asked the question again for him. This time we understood and we said to him that, yes, we liked Japan very much. They all said "Oooohhh, aahhh, Honto?" (Really) "Why, you like?" asked the same girl. "Because everyone is very kind," I told her.

It's an interesting fact, that the men folk tend to be more nervous of westerners than the women are. If you want anything done, ask a Japanese woman. This goes for restaurants, government offices, anywhere in fact. As a general rule, the men seem to be more conscious of the restrictions of protocol and find it difficult to think laterally. They cannot unbend so easily.

Another one of the girls asked us what we thought of nuclear war? I hesitated, thinking of how to put it so that they could understand. "War very bad," I answered, feeling like a Sioux Indian chief. Jan looked at me sideways and nodded, "Yes, very bad," she repeated. It satisfied everyone, as all of them nodded their agreement.

We finished with the children, all of us bowing and thanking each other profusely, and went on our way. We heard the kids laughing behind us, not in a derogatory way, but in a happy way as if they were very pleased with themselves that they had spoken to some foreigners in English. There is a touching innocence amongst both adults and children. They take delight in the small things and keep innocent pleasures close to their hearts. It's very attractive and alluring once you get used to it and start to understand it. It changes your cynical attitude and brings back to you the simple joys of life. But it took me several years to get to this stage, to knock off the hardwood veneer of western life and to appreciate this more innocent view of the world.

At last, we finally entered the museum itself and there were two things that struck me instantly. The first was that there were many western people there, and the second was that it was silent. No-one was speaking; it was the most silent museum I have ever been inside. Actually, in reality, it was quite noisy because there were many TV screens placed within the walls, all telling us, in sequence, a different aspect of that awful day and the progress of the destruction and suffering, using photographs taken several days after the event and peoples' testimonies as well as the film the Americans took from the airplane at the time of the bomb's deployment. They run on a loop and the commentary was in English, or at least it was when we were visiting there. Maybe that was why it was so silent, with everyone struck mute by the images and commentary. It knocks you into shock when you realise that you can read about it all you like, but when confronted by more realism, you understand that you didn't appreciate just how awful it was. When the visitors in the museum did converse, it was in whispers. As if not to offend.

A lot of the realism came from reconstructions around the museum, as of course, because most people died, there was no one on the ground to film it. The museum was divided into different areas, all of them dark and each one showing the horrors of that day in a time progression, leading on from one abomination to another, until I was stopped dead in my tracks by a lifelike and life size model of a young teenager, the skin of her arms hanging down over her hands and fingers in long strips, her arms outstretched and a blank look upon her face. It was at this moment that, unconsciously, my mind started to switch off to protect itself from the overwhelming despair I was feeling.

Thank goodness for the school kids, who were busily being un-phased and showing bravado to their friends as they skittered from one exhibit to the next. They were not disrespectful or noisy; they were just kids with jelly in their throats.

CHAPTER SIXTEEN

Special Students Join My School

Maybe Japan should be re-named, Just Taking a Nap. Wherever you look, you will find people sleeping. Standing at bus stops, strap hanging in trains, drivers asleep at the wheel whilst they wait for traffic lights to change. Audiences in theatres and cinemas, hospital waiting rooms, queues in supermarkets, anywhere there are people, you will see people taking forty winks. Standing or sitting down, it doesn't make any difference. I've even seen people standing, first in the queue, inches from the edge of a very crowded platform, clutching their briefcases to them and taking a nap as the train thunders in only inches from their noses.

I think that this is mostly due to the length of time that people spend out of bed, they work too long and don't get enough sleep, ergo, they are always tired. So I wasn't surprised when we went to a ballet concert to find half the audience asleep. To be fair, the concert was yet to start and I felt that most of these men, because they were mostly men, would come fully awake once their protégés appeared on stage. This was no ordinary ballet concert, it was one put on by Mika chan's ballet school. My good friend, Ryoko and her husband, Kenji san, had invited us to their daughter's 'first stage'.

This was shortly after our trip to Hiroshima and she was six years old at this time. Kenji san and I were chatting

233

in our pigeon English and Japanese and he told me about his change of life. Together with the support of Ryoko, he had taken the risky step of quitting his job and starting his own design company. At this stage, he was the designer, accountant, salesman and general dogs-body of his company (and I had no idea beforehand that he was so talented in design). A big risk for a man with a young family, but Ryoko and Kenji san had wanted to live their dreams too, and decided that they could do it. So I was very pleased to see him looking so fit, well and happy at the concert and he told me that everything was going very well for him, although it was hard work. Kenji san is the kind of man who fits into different kinds of society and can talk to anyone at their level. Ryoko had told me that, 'Everyone loves Kenji, he has a special skill with people'.

I was feeling excited as the theatre filled up. It was plush and up market, hired for the day by Mika chan's ballet school and paid for by the doting families of the budding ballerinas. I assumed that many of the men who were asleep were grandfathers and uncles because I could see many excited-looking dads, including Kenji san, who were very much awake, setting up their video cameras in the aisles, adjusting tripods and doing technical things. Grandmothers, aunts and various family members were all looking extremely smart, everyone wearing their best formal clothes, while mothers were backstage with their offspring, getting them organized and calming them down.

The buzz of excitement should have been reaching its crescendo at one minute to curtain up, but most of the men were still asleep. Then, suddenly, the music started, jarring almost everyone awake in an instant as the curtain rose and 'the babies' came on. I call them 'the babies' because not one of them was over four years old and they were the sweetest poppets you ever saw, at least on stage. Moving around in graceless circles, their arms and legs out of synchronisation, tutus bouncing up and down, they did their best in what must have been a steep learning curve for them. Their first show.

Some were worse than others, and one little girl got lost and ended up the wrong end of the stage and was brought back in no uncertain terms by her friend, who grabbed her arm and marched her back to her place. Some looked at their friends as if to say, 'What do we do now'? And proceeded to jump, or kick their leg several beats after everyone else. They were shy, brazen, frozen with fright or just plain bewildered, but they were there, taking part, that was the main thing and they brought a lump to my throat. Great applause at the end seemed to confuse them even more as the curtain came down and hid them from our eager eyes.

Another group came on, slightly older, the five-year olds. This group was different because one of their members was a boy. The Billy Elliot of Japan. He was dressed in short tight trousers and jacket, like an Austrian mountain boy, and he danced his little heart out. As the girls were softly prancing, their tutus gently bouncing, he danced the same steps with confidence and vigor, already his male ego had given him the confidence to excel and expect the limelight. For, as with all males in Japan, the encouraging and confidence building reflections he got back from society, of his life and the efforts he made in it, reassured him to think of himself as being superior to girls; and were very different to the muted and confidence-sapping reflections most girls received. It was true in this instance too. For he had most of the applause. He got the solo spot and the girls danced around him. He was the Little Prince; the girls were hidden amongst each other. But I don't want to take anything away from him, he was good, he did his best, and he was incredibly sweet and charming. It wasn't his fault that society was on his side; he was just the lucky one. They took their bows, he was allowed to take a separate bow all of his own and he received thunderous applause, the girls had to make do with a group bow and were clapped politely as they followed him off stage, already embedded into their roles as subservient to males.

Japan is in the dark ages as far as gender equality is concerned. Men and boys still rule and women and girls are treated very much as second-class citizens. Women are encouraged to remain in the secondary role at every corner of life and in every situation. The traditional viewpoint is still predominant, which is that the women's role in life is to service their men folk and to breed children. The men will justify themselves and say that women are 'the boss' at home, that they rule the purse strings, but I have my doubts about that, it's illusionary, and I've seen so many examples of men asserting their authority over their wives that have left me cringing. A good example of this is the most obvious one to me and I have had experience of this so many times from many quarters. The husband will let his wife make social arrangements or arrange trips away and then, at the very last minute, the husband will feign an illness or 'have to work' or whatever. Either way, the wife's arrangements are cancelled instantly, sometimes just hours beforehand, or even during the social engagement. Her phone will ring and she is told to return home as the husband needs her for whatever reason. The women always comply although obviously upset. It's no wonder that many young women want to stay single and keep their independence.

Finally, it was time for Mika chan's spot. She was with the six year olds and as they danced their way onto the stage, I spotted her straight away. She looked confident and in total control and although I am biased, she danced beautifully. No looking around at the others for her, no getting lost or forgetting her steps, she danced like a star. A confident star. I thought, Yes, Mika chan, you've got it if you want to use it.

She loved to dance; in fact, it was a job to stop her from dancing. If you went out with her, she would walk very properly and behave beautifully, holding your hand, but stop for a chat, window shopping or for the pedestrian crossing, you would find her pulling your arm in one direction or the other as she practiced her toe points, or some other ballet step. She also loved music and was always watching a musical or an opera on video. She was an ardent fan of Takarazuka, and therefore, many of the musicals she watched were Takarazuka musicals. Ask her what she wanted to be when she grew up and she would quietly and a little shyly say, "A Takarazuka top star." Not a Takarazuka star, but a Takarazuka top star!

If she ever does become a takarajienne, she will find that life will change dramatically for her. The world can open up, make you an important person and give you chances to meet influential people you would normally never meet. Give you a status that you would not usually have as a woman. You can mingle and be accepted within a society not usually open to the ordinary woman. These are some of the reasons why I like Takarazuka.

Recently, there have been several women accepted as writers/directors into the company and one female conductor has been allowed to join. She has proved to be incredibly popular with the audiences. All of this gives me hope that the company will embrace the rights of women to be equal to men. (Or am I living in cloud cuckoo land?) After all, it is women to whom the Takarazuka Theatre Company owes its existence. Male dominance is a problem all over Japan, not just in the Takarazuka theatre. All major companies are male dominated. The glass ceiling is either not necessary because women are almost totally shut out of meaningful employment, or it is iceberg thick.

The mystery of the Takarazuka theatre is often talked about by fans and this is because everyone involved, especially the performers, are instructed not to talk or gossip about anything that happens within its hallowed walls. Talk on television, or in magazine interviews, all you like about your latest show or fashion accessory, new car etc. but don't gossip about company politics, in fighting, or whatever within the company. This would be the world that Mika chan would enter if she was accepted. This philosophy applies to all Japanese companies and there are almost no whistle blowers because it's quite possible that you would never work again, for that company or any other. You could be ruined professionally.

Therefore, fans who are interested in these things have to draw their own conclusions and rumour is rife. It's the natural way; keep things a secret and you invite speculation. One of the advantages of not speaking Japanese very well is that one is outside the loop of this kind of thing, because, for me, to be subjected to too much rumour and speculation would take the edge off everything. I love the mystery of Takarazuka. I prefer my performers to be mysterious, because when you get past the greasepaint and the glamour of the footlights, what do you get underneath? A human being with all the normal joys and worries that afflict us all.

I found this out one day at my school. We had been settled in the new school at Koutouen for about a year and with all our hard work, it was doing very well. I was getting many trial lessons but one has no idea who is coming for a trial, as all one has is a name and the appointment is always made over the telephone. One particularly busy day, as I was eating my lunch, the door bell rang. My trial lesson. Fifteen minutes early. I cleared away my lunch and went to the door as quickly as I could.

I opened the door and recognised her instantly. A takarajienne – a famous one! She had used her real name to book the trial lesson, not her stage name. Oh dear, my dream come true and my worst nightmare coupled together. My dream come true if she liked me, respected me and joined, my worst nightmare if she didn't.

I invited her in and she sat down, elegant, poised, tall – for she was an otokoyaku – well dressed, with her short hair dyed blond in the fashion of Takarazuka performers, with just a hint of immaculately applied make up. Her voice low and sonorous as befits an otokoyaku and a smile so genuine and engaging that you couldn't help falling into it.

I started to get nervous, and as it was obvious from the start that her English was not good, we had some difficulty in understanding each other. This always makes it difficult for a trial lesson, and for this to happen with a famous takarajienne put extra strain upon me, being a loyal Takarazuka fan. It was down to me, whether I could gather together my skills to make her want to join. All students who come for a trial lesson will have already sussed out the school, made some enquiries, now they are testing you, your character, personality, teaching ability and finally, and probably most importantly, whether they like you or not.

I needn't have worried, she was such a sweetie, she made me relax with her easy ways and her obvious sincerity. We went through my standard trial lesson for false beginners, and she responded to this and started to remember a lot of her lost English. The old adage, 'use it or lose it' is so pertinent in language learning. I told myself to just relax and do my best. She joined.

This student, I will call her Rie san, became very important to me, not only because she was a takarajienne but because I liked her enormously. She continued being a student at the school for about eighteen months and in that time, we developed a casual friendship as well as a teacher/student relationship. However, one of the things she often said to me was, "Jeel," her pronunciation was always, Jeel rather than Jill, "why are you always so kind to me?" I always answered, "I'm naturally kind, it's my nature, I'm not just kind to you, I'm kind to everyone." However, she never really believed me, although it was the truth. I came to understand that this is one of the drawbacks of being a takarajienne, one is always suspicious of the motives of people around you, wondering whether someone is friendly to you because of your position rather than for you yourself. I was saddened by this, but I understood it. Unfortunately, because of language difficulties, we were never really able to resolve this misunderstanding although our friendship continued on its casual basis for a long time. Rie san was an extremely confident and competent woman, who I respected and admired very much, but I often wondered where she would have been if it were not for Takarazuka which gave such women the wherewithal to have a different kind of life to one of housewife, or stuck in a menial job with little chance of advancing, which is most Japanese women's lot in life.

One day, she said, "Jeel, I have a friend, a takarajienne like me, she wants to come to your lessons, can she have a trial lesson please?"

"Of course," I said.

She told me the name, and I tried not to blink too hard. This was a really important takarajienne, a prospective top star. We arranged a date and time and at the appointed hour, she duly turned up, arriving at the door wearing a hat pulled down over her eyes, hiding her face, although you could see at a glance that she was a takarajienne by her posture and stance. They have ramrod straight backs, in a society of straight backs, and an assurance and grace that is rare. Their movements ooze confidence, iron strong muscles holding them up effortlessly with such grace and style that it is impossible to replicate if you are not a takarajienne.

"Welcome," I said, "please come in." She smiled. "Please put on these slippers," I said as I put out a pair of comfy flip flops (standard fare in Japan) for her to use. She slipped effortlessly out of her shoes and into the slippers.

"Please come this way," I led the way into my schoolroom, down the carpeted passageway. "Please sit here." I motioned to my preferred chair for students to use. I had to be careful where a student sat because as I was teaching all day, if all my students sat sideways on, I soon acquired a stiff neck. She sat down opposite me, her famous Takarazuka posture intact, and coughed, then sniffed, finishing it off with several stifled sneezes. "Do you have a cold?" I asked slowly and gently.

"Hai, cold," she replied through her sniffles. (Yes, cold).

"Are you OK? Shall we stop the lesson?" I asked her because it was obvious that she had a really bad cold. Through watering eyes she looked confused. *"Lesson wa, owarimashouka?"* I tried some of my basic Japanese.

"Ah, no. Now, time, only now." She managed to convey that she only had time right now for a trial lesson. Being such an important player in the theatre, she would be incredibly busy I knew.

So, we started to converse in very slow, easy English, and went into my trial lesson for false beginners. You don't want a student to feel they are working too hard at a trial lesson, otherwise they will not join. You also want them to enjoy themselves. A trial lesson is part coaching and part psychology. At the end of the lesson, she was speaking a lot of simple English, which she knew in her head, but couldn't get out in recognisable speech without help. Another false beginner. She joined.

My lessons with the takarajiennes progressed well, as both were fantastic students, their training enabling them to remember easily and retain what they had learnt; both of them were intelligent and quick to master things. Ideal students in fact, although it was a little tricky sorting out their lessons because they were away touring so much, so it was difficult to keep a continuity and they had no time to do any homework, but we managed between us and made good progress.

Fortunately, we all got on very well and liked each other, and it was always a thrill, albeit an embarrassing one, when my prospective top star sang to me from the stage. Often, she would spot me sitting in the stalls, and during the revue, when performers are out of character, she often sang directly to me for several seconds. I think that some of the fans got a little jealous about this as I did experience a tad of hostility sometimes, but the majority of fans took the opposite view and both Jan and I were shown nothing but kindness and great pleasure that Takarazuka was getting some foreign fans.

There are many nice things about Takarazuka and one of them is definitely the amount of parties that take place, although they are not the kind of parties we would think of in the west, with loud music, plenty of alcohol and lots of jollification. These parties are much more sedate and are more like elegant tea parties, where fans can gather and meet their star in the relaxing surroundings of a plush hotel and drink tea, eat cakes and chat a little.

Rie san, had several such parties when she retired from Takarazuka. She was of an age where she was becoming too old to be a takarajienne, She was about thirty five years old, and she had to choose a new career. She surprised me one day by inviting both me and Jan to her 'special fans' party in Tokyo which was to take place after her very last show, in the Tokyo Takarazuka theatre. This was a real honour as this party was reserved for her long and faithful fans who had proved their loyalty to her throughout the years. Ordinary fans don't get to know about these parties or what happens there. It's another secret world of Takarazuka.

I had never joined a fan club, preferring to keep a general interest in every performer, therefore, I felt honoured and delighted to be invited. Actually, Rie san would have several parties that day. One for her 'ordinary fans' one for her 'special fans' and one for her fellow performers. All this after the emotion of her last show made for a long and tiring day for her.

The day we left for Tokyo was a Saturday, a working day, but we rescheduled our late afternoon lessons and at 4.00pm rushed out at great speed to the train station to catch the shinkansen train to Tokyo from Shin Osaka station. We wanted to be in Tokyo in time for a late dinner, which is why we were in such a rush. We got our local train to Nishinomiya Kitaguchi, about 4 miles from the school, and as we were changing trains there, walking across the concourse, I happened to look down at my feet, which sub consciously must have felt a bit strange. A gasp emitted from me that made Jan stop in her tracks. "Ahhh," I yelled in dismay, "I've still got my slippers on." We both looked at my feet in disbelief, my slippers stared back. They were the only shoes I had with me. Oh dear, what to do, there was no choice but to rush back to the school and change my shoes and hope that we could just catch our pre-booked shinkansen.

I plopped a shaken looking Jan on a bench with all the bags and rushed off in my slippers, feeling silly, and threw myself into a waiting taxi. "Koutouen" I said breathlessly,

"*Sumimasen, hayaku onegai shimasu.*" (Excuse me, quick please – I never did master Japanese adverbs). He got the idea and sped off and I managed to cobble enough Japanese together to tell him that I was going to Tokyo but had my slippers on instead of my shoes. He looked at my feet and roared. I was so grateful to have a young taxi driver, who are so much more flexible and good natured than the grumpy old men one often gets. We got to the school in double quick time and he waited whilst I changed into my shoes. We then sped off back to the station and I thanked him profusely. I didn't even have to tip him as there is no tipping in Japan. We waved goodbye and I ran back to Jan, still sitting on her bench, looking grim. We ran down the stairs to the platform and just squashed ourselves into the local train for Osaka. We made it.

When a takarajienne retires, she does it publicly, on stage at the end of her final show. All retirees will be called, individually, down the grand staircase and take their applause from the audience and give a farewell speech. Rie san gave hers in a loud, confident voice as befitted an experienced takarajienne and her chin never quavered, although there were many in the audience that did. I noticed hankies coming out and sniffs were heard all around. I always knew she was a popular performer; I hadn't appreciated just how popular she was. Several other performers also retired that day and when we left the theatre, we had great difficulty making our way through the crowds of fans outside.

We went to the hotel where Rie san would have her many farewell parties and felt ourselves privileged to be included in this special world. For us, as Takarazuka fans, this was a major moment in our Takarazuka life. Normally, years of dedicated devotion to your star was the only way you could get into such a party. We were unsure what to expect and also very excited, although we had no idea how the other fans would react to us.

We needn't have worried, the other fans were very welcoming and several of them went to great lengths to make us feel comfortable and relaxed. There were about a hundred fans there and Rie san had provided a buffet but we had to buy our own drinks. You would think that would pose no problem, but unfortunately, Japanese constitutions, especially women's, are very weak where alcohol is concerned (they are missing some necessary enzyme or something equally technical) and often, wine glasses and portions are very small, looking more like eye baths than wine glasses. Being wine drinkers, this meant that Jan and I had to make many trips to the bar and consequently, I'm sure the other fans thought we were alcoholics (which we're not I hasten to add!)

As I was coming back from the bar to our table with another two eye baths, Rie san arrived. She walked down the middle of the room in her Takarazuka music school uniform of traditional Japanese clothes – dark green super wide, pleated trousers, and kimono style jacket. She stood on the stage at the front of the room and started chatting to everyone over the microphone and lots of laughter went on, although, in my usual fashion, I couldn't understand hardly a word as it was spoken too fast and was too high a level for me.

I had been studying Japanese seriously for the past four years, but still had the greatest difficulty with it. There are schools of thought that say that a brain over the age of twenty-five cannot cope with the complexities of the Japanese language and those people will never master it. I don't quite agree with that, but I can attest to the immense difficulties in mastering it for the age-challenged student.

Rie san had started to circle the room, having her photo

taken with each fan, when there was a little commotion at the door and it was announced that the rest of her troupe had arrived. We all rushed to take our places at our tables and Rie san went back to the stage area. All the eighty or so performers of her troupe walked in, one behind the other, the senior students first and so on down the line to the most junior. The performers are always called students, indicating that they are always studying and improving their performances. They all gathered around the stage and went up to Rie san a few at a time, bowed, said a few words and exchanged some anecdote or other over the microphone, so that we could all share it. It was obvious that she was as popular with her troupe as she was with her fans.

Rie san told us that the next day the whole troupe would go to a famous spa town and have a day's holiday together. This is a normal thing to do in a traditional company where the staff will often give up their small amount of spare time and gather at a spa and socialise whilst soaking away their stress in the special waters. This seems a strange thing to us westerners, but for the Japanese, it is reinforcing the group and it is supposed to bind them together to form a sticky bond so that they will honour and treasure their workmates and do their best for them in their working life.

It's a nice idea once you get used to it. The attitude between workmates in Japan is of extreme importance and becomes, for some, especially men, more important than their family. The company is family for a lot of men. The bonds created during their working life are kept and this concept runs all through life whatever group one belongs to.

Finally, all the students had chatted with Rie san and it was time for them to leave the room. They marched off again in single file, looking down at the floor, demure and serene, no one more important than the next. Importance only acknowledged within their own group by seniority of age, not popularity with the audiences. Individuality discouraged, no showing off, that's the Japanese way.

Rie san continued with her tour of the room until all fans had been spoken to and each fan had their individual photos taken with her. Then it was time for her to leave, she had another party to attend, she told us. She would now join her colleagues in a staff party. We all clapped enthusiastically as she left the room and the party broke up in quiet excitement. It was 10.00pm; it had lasted about one and a half hours. Nothing exciting had taken place, nothing extraordinary. We had just shared some time with our star and for everyone there, that was enough. A secret world Takarazuka may be, but it is all very respectable. I wouldn't have expected anything else from Takarazuka. That's its joy. It's occasionally gently risqué on stage, but off stage, all is respectability and earnest endeavour.

CHAPTER SEVENTEEN

Phuket, Sri Lanka and The Tsunami

Takarazuka can, and does, become a way of life for many fans. But for Jan and me, Takarazuka turned out to be a life saver. Literally.

It was the end of 2004 and the New Year break was looming, the main holiday time. Our school would be closed and therefore, we had time to go away. We had decided on Hawaii and went off to the travel agent's in high spirits. As we walked into our local agent's office, where we had booked many holidays before, our favourite assistant welcomed us, young, smart, always pleasant, "Where do you want to go this time?" she asked through her big smile, which always reached her eyes.

"Hawaii. We would like to fly out on December 24th and return on January 3rd"

"I'll check for you," she said sitting down at her computer and concentrating. "Ah, yes, sorry, Hawaii is full."

"Hawaii's full? Surely not." I couldn't believe it. With some difficulty, tripping over her English, she managed to explain, albeit a little painfully, "Hawaii is not full, but the plane out of Japan is full."

"Oh," was the best response I could manage as I digested this.

"How about somewhere else?" asked our assistant. "Where would you like to go?"

"Mmm," we pondered the brochures, "how about Australia?"

"No, all gone," she said softly. "How about Thailand?"

"No," we both said together, "don't fancy Thailand."

"How about Korea?" I asked.

She checked, "No, sorry, all gone. How about Phuket?"

"No," we said again, "don't fancy Thailand. How about Italy?"

She checked, "No, sorry, all flight seats booked. How about Phuket?" She asked with a cheeky grin.

We looked at each other, "No thanks," we both said again.

"Phuket is very nice, lovely beach, sea and hotels. I can give you a sea front hotel, maybe? I'll check for you. Phuket is very cheap and very beautiful. Yes, I checked, sea front hotel is OK. Shall I book it for you?"

Oh, dear, but no, we resisted.

We checked various destinations for about two hours as progress was frustratingly slow due to the language difficulties. In the end, we decided to put ourselves on the waiting list for Hawaii. You never know, someone might drop out. Several weeks went by, but nobody did. We were desperate to get away for a few days, we needed the rest. Ten days before New Year, we checked again. No new seats had become available to Hawaii. So sorry. We tried to book some hotels in Japan, but the ones we wanted were all full.

A little while later, one cold evening, the wind so strong that we had fears that our TV aerial might go walkabout, we decided that the lure of sun and warmth was too strong and we would, after all, go to Phuket, and would go back to the travel agent's the next day. Unexpectedly, that same evening, I got a phone call from a friend of ours. She was a Takarazuka friend, (you see, even I'm putting people into groups now) and she asked us if we were going to see the

250

new Takarazuka show in Osaka. The Takarazuka theatre often performs in Osaka at Theatre Drama City.

"Oh, I don't know about this show," I said. "What day are you going?"

"Christmas day and the next day," she told me. "But it will only be me this time, my sister cannot come. It would be great if you could come too. I have checked with the fan club, and they said that they would reserve tickets for you, no problem."

Masayo san and her sister Mutsumi san were from the industrial town of Nagoya. We had met them at a Takarazuka tea party some years before and always got together when they were in town. We got on so well with them that no sooner had I checked with Jan, than her eyes lit up and she nodded her head vigorously, yes, we nodded to each other. That was all the confirmation I needed. We said a mental goodbye to Phuket.

The show turned out to be superb and has now become one of my favourites, not only because it was such a good show, but because I'm convinced it saved our lives. For if we had gone to Phuket that Christmas and New Year, we would have been caught up in the Tsunami that struck Phuket so severely. If we had taken that beach side hotel, which was our intention, then it is more than likely that we would not have survived. That area, including many of the hotels were swallowed by the tsunami. Takarazuka had saved our lives as far as I was concerned.

It may sound strange, to give up a holiday just to see a show, but not if you are an ardent Takarazuka fan. We arranged to meet Masayo san on Christmas Eve for dinner in Umeda, Osaka, stay overnight in a local hotel, have a relaxing morning the next day before the 11.00am show. What we didn't bargain for was the discovery that every table in every restaurant in the Umeda area was occupied that evening. A bit like the plane seats out to Hawaii. We found out that this was because Christmas Eve is celebrated as 'lovers day'. Young couples go out for a romantic meal together, and often book themselves into a nice hotel afterwards for an exciting night of romance (hopefully!). This meant that we couldn't get into any restaurant because they were full of swooning couples.

Masayo san, a nurse, is strong and confident and took charge of the situation. She led us into the Hankyu building (the Hankyu railway company also has hotels, shops and skyscrapers) and up to the 30th floor; the restaurant floor. We felt sure we could get in somewhere here, but alas, as we left the lift, we were immediately entangled in various lines of queuing people. We chose an Italian restaurant and joined the end of the queue confident that it would go down quickly, as people tend not to linger in restaurants, but we had not allowed for the theme of the evening – romance! Half an hour later, the queue had not moved. We tried another, and another, until finally, in desperation we got a table in an old-fashioned restaurant, with a dull menu, which had one free table. At last. Even this restaurant was packed, the staff overworked but smiling and after placing our order Masayo san suddenly said, "We are single bells, right!"

"Single bells," I said, "what does that mean?"

"Oh, you don't say that in England?" she asked with an incredulous look.

"No, what does it mean?"

"It means that it is Christmas, right? And at Christmas we sing Christmas songs, right? We sing Jingle Bells, right? Well, as you now know, Christmas Eve in Japan is romance night, when most young couples go out to eat and play. Young men and women together. You don't see any families, or old couples or friends eating together do you?"

We looked around, and as expected, every table was

occupied by a young male/female couple, some gazing shyly at each other, some chatting and laughing and quaffing beer or wine (Dutch courage came to mind). While others seemed uncomfortable with each other and looked like they were on a first date and painfully conversing, or they were on their last ditch effort to save their relationship.

Masayo san continued by saying, "So, we are unusual tonight, yes? We are all women together, we don't have any men with us, therefore, we are single belles tonight."

We roared, and that is how the evening went on thereafter, but it didn't matter how loud we were because the noise level was so high, no one would have heard us anyway.

Just prior to this, two days before we met Masayo san, we got a fax from our travel agent. They had received two cancellations for Hawaii and did we want them? We could leave on Boxing Day afternoon. We checked the time of the plane and could just make it after the morning performance of the Takarazuka show. We booked it and rushed to the travel agent's to pay for it there and then.

It was during our stay in Hawaii that we first saw the news of the Tsunami on CNN. It gave me the shivers, not only because it was such a dreadful event, but on a very personal note, it could have been us. We would have been there, had it not been for Masayo san and a Takarazuka show.

As the days went by and more news of the scale of death and destruction started to come in, a little memory suddenly flickered in my mind. "Takase san," I said to Jan. "Didn't Takase san say that he was going to Phuket for Christmas?"

"Sorry, I don't remember."

But, I had a hazy memory of him telling me that he was going diving in Phuket. He had said that Phuket had the best diving and he often went there.

Takase san, our neighbour downstairs, the kind Mr. and Mrs. Takase of the Wedgewood teapot and the spare table, lent to us with gentle kindness. Oh dear.

When we arrived back in Japan, we were now presented with a dilemma. Do we knock on Mrs. Takase's door and ask her, "Is Mr. Takase OK? Is he alive? Is he missing?" Bearing in mind that Mrs. Takase had no English ability whatsoever, and couldn't understand anything we said to her, even in Japanese, this was a tricky situation. Also, bearing in mind that we were not totally sure that he had gone to Phuket.

We decided that the best way was to do nothing for a while. We didn't want to run the risk of causing more distress if the news was bad. We would wait a few days and keep a look out for him. To our utter relief, a couple of days later, we saw him getting out of his car and told him how pleased we were to see him. He looked puzzled and said that made him feel very happy, but why were we so pleased to see him?

I asked him if he had indeed, been to Phuket, and he suddenly understood. "Ah, yes, I was there, in fact, I was on the beach when the first wave struck."

"You were on the beach, and you survived?" I paused, unsure whether to proceed or not, but I asked, "Can you talk about it? Is it too painful? We would be most interested to hear your story."

"I'll come up to your flat and tell you all about it later, it's not painful for me," he said, "right now, I have to take care of grandmother."

I can see him so clearly even now, speaking to us in that calm, measured way, so beloved of the Japanese. Don't even make a molehill out of a disaster, just get on with it, make it better, don't blame anyone, work together to overcome, is their mantra. He must have been coming up to sixty, his face showing a scraping of lines, but that just added to his character rather than told you his age. I've noticed that older Japanese people are very bouncy and agile and stay that way, even into deep old age. Diet plays a big part in this, Japan being famous for its healthy food of fish, shellfish, soya, coupled with many kinds of vegetables and rice. Most of these older people would have eaten little meat and a lifetime of this diet I feel sure, has kept them supple and strong. A little bit of everything in every meal and not an overabundance of anything. You very rarely see overweight Japanese, they are pencil slim mostly, but eat plenty. Takase san was a walking model for a healthy Japanese man coming up to retirement.

We settled ourselves down with tea and he told us his tale. He said that he had been diving for several days in the waters around the bay but because one is not allowed to dive for 24 hours before flying, he was not diving that particular morning, as he was flying back to Japan later that day. Normally, at 9.00am, when the Tsunami hit, he would have already been out diving.

Whilst awaiting the time for his bus, he decided to walk down to the beach and had just arrived when he noticed a wave in the distance, it didn't look particularly large but very unusual because it was black. He thought that strange and stopped and stood on the low wall by the side of the road which runs parallel with the beach. He noticed that the local people were calling out to one another about it. He was curious, so he stayed watching the wave come nearer. When it crashed onto the beach he thought it would stop sooner or later, but it continued. He was intrigued to see how far the wave would come up and felt that he would not get wet feet because the low wall he was standing on would stop it. However, the water continued to advance rapidly and, fortunately, he decided to leave. A decision that most probably saved his life.

Another thing that saved his life was his position. He had not ventured onto the beach but had stayed on the road. He saw the wave at the same time as he reached a road junction leading back into town, away from the sea. He set off along this road with the water surging along behind him. After about 300 meters, the water slowed down and stopped. He said, "I decided to take some photos of the extraordinary scene behind me, where the street was submerged in about three foot of water and filled with all kinds of debris like chairs, baskets, tables, and the like."

At this stage, he had no idea of the tragedy that had struck or the scale of the problem. He decided to go back to his hotel as there was nowhere else for him to go. He learned afterwards that two much bigger waves came in immediately after he had left the area. Fortunately for him, his hotel was a very long way from the beach and untouched by events. Once he was back in his hotel room, he had no view of what was going on in the rest of the town.

Later, he switched on the TV, but there was very little news about what had happened because at that time, it was still happening and nobody had an overview of it all. Still in ignorance of the scale of it, he left for the airport, and the only inconvenience he found was a six-hour delay in his flight. He was able to phone his wife, becoming aware that there had been more to this wave than he had thought.

When he got back to Kansai airport in Osaka and came out of the arrivals gate, he found a mass of TV cameras and people, some shouting out to the passengers asking them if they had been in Phuket. A bit startled, he replied that he had, and found himself surrounded by reporters, cameras and microphones and being interviewed for the national news broadcast.

It was at this stage that he began to realise the full extent of the disaster and in retrospect, he felt himself to be very lucky as his decision to leave the area when he did probably saved his life. For who could ever have imagined such a disaster happening.

Naoko san, my tea teacher friend, was also greatly affected by the tsunami. She has very close links with Sri Lanka, a country she loves and visits often, and she had made many friends there. It was the day of the tsunami when she got a call from Luca, one of her Sri Lankan friends. He told her that he was OK and not to worry. It was then that she learned of the extent of the devastation Sri Lanka had suffered. He told her that he intended to do something to help the people in the stricken areas and she decided to help him. A few days later, she was on a plane to Sri Lanka, but before she went, she put a message on her webpage and contacted all her students, old and new. She explained about the situation in Sri Lanka, a country many of them had visited with her as part of their course studying tea, and most were anxious to help. By the time she flew out, she had already collected 500,000 yen, (around £2,500) which she took with her. That's a very generous amount considering that her school is small.

When she arrived, Luca and Naoko san got together with ten other volunteers. One of Luca's friends gave his container lorry for them to use and they settled down to make a final plan. They had been advised that there was a lot of help coming in for the south of the country, but virtually no help going to the east. They decided to go east.

Next, it had to be decided what to buy with the money Naoko san's students had donated and the money Luca and his family and friends had collected in Sri Lanka. Research had already been done and a list was drawn up. They had been told that people had some rice and sugar, but they had nothing to cook with. Therefore, first on the list went saucepans, followed by staples like flour, and spices, especially curry powder. Sri Lankans eat curry three times a day, it is their staple food, Naoko san told me, "I couldn't bring anything with me from Japan because it would have been too expensive, but also, the taste would have been different, we needed to bring normality back with food that people were used to, otherwise it would have been an added trauma for them. Another trauma for the women was the lack of sanitary wear. In some regions, there was literally nothing left, therefore sanitary napkins were part of the staples." I asked her how they bought the things that they wanted to take with them.

"We went to a wholesaler in Candy." Candy is a large town in the mountains and therefore unaffected by the tsunami. "We negotiated a very good price and were able to get lots of things with our money. The wholesalers were very sympathetic. We decided to make a family pack, so we got large plastic bags and put in things we thought they would need, including soya, water, milk powder, high energy dried food like biscuits, as well as soap, washing powder etc. We made up 300 family packs and loaded them into the lorry. We were working against time, the people in the East were starving, we had to get there fast. So we all worked flat out and got everything ready.

We set off for the Ampara district. I could see on the map that it was directly opposite Banda Acheh in Indonesia, where the original earthquake happened that set off the tsunami. That was why this area was so devastated."

I asked her how they had decided to distribute the food once they got there. "Well, by the time we were ready, other people with aid had managed to get through but unfortunately, it was not organized and the local people had rushed towards the food being given out. Fighting started because everyone wanted to be first to be sure to get something. It was bad for the volunteers, who got injured and the people in need, who also got injured. People in Sri Lanka don't have the nice system of queuing, as you do in Britain, and we do in Japan. It's a free for all there, and especially as these people were mostly very poor people with little education, they couldn't understand the notion of queuing in an orderly manner. Therefore, we decided that, for our own safety, and for the safety of the local people, when we got there we would try and find some reliable and trustworthy people to give the aid to, then they would decide who were the neediest. Unfortunately, some of the people who were doing the fighting to get first in the queue were not necessarily the people in most need. Therefore, we wanted to find a religious person or a professional person who we could trust."

I asked Naoko san to show me some of the pictures she took of the devastation of the area. The first picture showed a small woman, dressed in a white sari, looking lost and forlorn on a beach. She had turned around to look at the camera, which captured her look of disbelief. Naoko san explained that her house used to be where she was standing and all you could now see were thin, black rods of steel rising up from the whiteness of the sand. They were the reinforcing rods of her house; the rest of it had been swept away into the depths of the sea. Her house was one of many on that particular beach. Now, it was totally empty.

Naoko san went on to say, "The speed of the wave in this area was about 500 kilometers an hour. One cannot conceive of water travelling at that kind of speed. In Japan, the shinkansen travels at about 300 kilometers an hour, and that's considered very fast. It's just impossible to imagine." Her eyes were cast downwards, her head shaking.

"Inconceivable," she repeated in a low voice.

I know that Naoko san was greatly affected by the things she saw and did during that time. She had taken many photos to show people back in Japan, in the hope of raising yet more money for aid.

The photos showed flattened areas where once had been villages, now all that was left was the building debris of bricks, bits of walls and roofs scattered higgledy-piggledy amongst the topsy turvy palm trees.

A few people populated the photos, some of them women wearing long black robes. Naoko san said, "These are volunteers from other areas, who came to help the people here, but everyone had perished. They could only bury the dead."

The overriding feeling I got from these photos was one of silence. It seemed as if everyone was going about their grisly work cocooned inside themselves. A shocked calmness seemed to dominate.

Sometimes, as Naoko san and her friends were driving along in the lorry, they would see some children who would hold their hands out to them. At first, they stopped to give them some food, such as biscuits, but soon, adults would appear and then a fight would start as they tried to get the aid from the lorry. It was hopeless, they had to move on for their own safety and that of the refugees. They had to find their trustworthy officials soon to give their aid to.

Naoko san went on to say, "We kept traveling and we were lucky because we found a priest, or monk, I'm not sure which, who agreed to take responsibility for some of the aid and distribute it fairly. Then we found a very tired looking doctor, who was a volunteer from another district. He was a great help and we were able to leave the rest of our aid with him. So we didn't go directly into the worst of the disaster area, it would have been very dangerous for us to have done so, but we had faith in the monk and the doctor and were confident that leaving our aid with them would result in it being given out to the neediest people. We had done our best; we were only ordinary people, with no experience in this kind of thing. But we felt that we had to do something. If our aid, along with other peoples' helped to keep the refugees alive until more permanent and professional help could be found for them, then we were satisfied."

Naoko san showed me a picture of the doctor. He was about 35, tall, with a little paunch. His hair and beard were a dense black and looked disheveled and spiky. He was hollow-eyed and looked exhausted. But, tired as he was, he had taken the trouble to show them what had happened in the area. He showed them a bungalow which was still standing, and pointed to a water line just below the eaves. He said that when people had seen the tsunami coming they had run to their houses and closed the doors, that's all they had time to do, but the water came up through the foundations of the houses, from bottom to top and stayed at that level for two hours. The people were trapped inside. No one survived in this area, he added as he pointed to the foundations of the bungalow. There were none. They had been swept away, but miraculously, the house was still standing.

The day that Naoko san and her fellow volunteers will never forget was drawing to an end. They had left the town of Candy at 5.00am and arrived in the Ampara district at around 1.00pm. They stayed until dark, doing all that they could and then left again for Candy at 8.00pm. They were the lucky ones; they could go back to their lives.

But they still wanted to help and it was desperately needed. Therefore, over the next few days, they continued to collect aid and went both South and West with their lorry, distributing more aid where they could. On one such trip they were stopped by the sight of a derelict train. It was a long train, standing upright on its tracks, its many red carriages looking crushed, out of place and decidedly eerie.

The tsunami had crashed into the train, with the force of the water smashing the glass in every window. Every one of the one thousand two hundred passengers were killed. Now, the train was standing like a lost soul, unsure what to do. Its battered and bent carriages a testament to what it had endured.

The story of this train was even sadder than it seemed, because the day the tsunami hit, was a public holiday and the train was full of families going to the beach for the day. Many small children were killed along with their families.

For me, disaster on such a scale is numbing, one has difficulty relating to it, and I find it's easier to relate to personal stories. Therefore, I found the most poignant photo that Naoko san had taken, was at a graveside, one of many little mounds near the train. A volunteer happened to be painting the name of the occupant of the grave and Naoko san spoke to him. He told her that if the volunteers were able to identify the remains of the victims, their names were painted, freehand, on a piece of wood and placed at the head of the grave. He had painted, "Dr. (Miss) Sifani." That's all. That's all they had time or resources to paint but the man explained to Naoko san that the doctor was from Colombo, an area not affected by the tsunami, and he assumed that she had decided to come to the beach for a holiday. She was just twenty one years old. The scale is personal and I can relate to that.

Another personal story is the story of Naoko san's friend. He had been her tour guide for her first trip to Sri Lanka seven years previously. She told me, "He had been so kind to me and helped me so much that we became friends and I met him each time I visited Sri Lanka if I could. He was half Sri Lankan and Japanese and such a nice man. He was about thirty five or so, and when the tsunami hit, he was taking his latest charges on a tour. They had spent the morning in the mountains, which were unaffected by the tsunami, but it had been arranged that they went, briefly, to the beach for lunch. They were having lunch when the tsunami hit and he went missing. Luca and his friends tried to find him and eventually, they found his body in Colombo. Because he looked Japanese, he was assumed to be from Japan and his remains were sent to Colombo in order for them to be sent back to Japan."

Luca went to Colombo and identified his remains which were then reunited with his family in Sri Lanka. Luca said, "His body was totally black from bruising, but I could recognise him, and was able to help him one last time. He is now with his family." Naoko san added that he was such a nice person, she was desperately upset.

We were just four people in Japan who knew each other. My neighbour Takase san, Naoko san, Jan and myself. But we were all affected by the tsunami which devastated another part of the world.

Life returned to normal for all of us and Naoko san and I started our weekly visits to the Funny House restaurant again. When we walked in, the Mama San, in her usual gentle and concerned way, smiled a very small smile of sympathy and said to Naoko san, "You look older and more mature than when I saw you two weeks ago."

This was not the end for Naoko san, as she continued to raise money for relief. Her tea school takes one or two trips to Sri Lanka every year, and a trip had already been organized for March of that year. The trip went ahead as usual and they visited several tea plantations and studied how tea is grown, picked, graded, blended and processed for export. The Japanese really love their tea. After the tour and the students had returned to Japan, she stayed on and continued to help Luca with relief aid.

She had continued to fundraise in Japan, and Luca in Sri Lanka, and also to continue their research as to what was most needed by the people themselves. Unsurprisingly, toilets figured high on the list and by the middle of that same year, they had managed to provide quite a few portable toilets.

Their greatest achievement was being able to fund and arrange the building of three small bungalows in one of the devastated areas, which were given to three needy families. She showed me a picture of one of the bungalows with some of the family outside. Their grins were enormous.

CHAPTER EIGHTEEN

Earthquakes

Earthquakes are an integral part of Japanese life. It is the most earthquake prone country in the world with at least a thousand quakes every year erupting around the country. Some are so small one hardly notices them, making you think that you are suffering a dizzy spell until you realise that the earth is trembling and not your brain.

I suffered scores of such minor earthquakes and they always left me traumatized, even though they were small. It is very disconcerting to be reminded of one's complete vulnerability and that the unthinkable is possible. Like everyone else, I learned to shut my fear away and get on with life.

That was what I was doing as I visited a large furniture and electrical store near my home. Jan and I had gone to check out the kitchen cabinets, freestanding affairs reminiscent of the 1950s. Standing between two rows of cabinets, checking out their suitability, I suddenly felt my dizzy feeling again. I instinctively clutched a cabinet expecting to pass out, and then realised that it wasn't me, as the floor of the shop started to sway. Gently at first, but enough to make Jan's face ashen.

"We'd better get out from between these cabinets," I said. "If this gets worse, they could topple over on top of us." Jan agreed as the swaying intensified, and we had to clutch each other's arms to enable us to walk to the end of the row. It seemed to take an age, but we finally got free of them and found ourselves in the open display area of the furniture showroom, which was at least as big as a football pitch. It was closely packed with scores of sofas, chairs, tables, cabinets, bookshelves and the like, with the bookshelves stacked one on top of each other around the walls. The store's many hanging signs were moving disconcertingly back and forth and the floor was swaying like a ship in a storm: up one side, taking a pause, and then swaying down again. It was gaining momentum with each sway and was utterly terrifying.

The floor was shiny and glossy and I realised that if this got any worse, the furniture was in danger of taking off like skaters on an ice rink. I had visions of sofas doing the waltz and chairs hip hopping from one end to the other, of bookshelves tumbling down and my vulnerable, soft body acting as a buffer.

I grabbed Jan's arm and pointed to an outlandishly bright orange sofa about twenty feet away. "Look, that sofa is not surrounded by other furniture let's make for it as it seems the safest place to be if this gets any worse." Jan was in no condition to argue and we set off together over the large expanse of floor space in front of us, clutching each other for stability. One step this way, three the other and two back as the floor swayed even more. It was a hideously stupid thing to do I realised too late, but we were committed now and had no choice but to continue on in the vein of 'mad dogs and Englishwomen'. The staff and the other customers were frozen, hanging on to the nearest piece of furniture with their knees bent against the sway. They were absolutely still except for their eyes, which were fixed on us. Incredulity and horror at our stupidity shone out of some, while others creased with amusement.

We continued our almost impossible walk across the floor, swaying back and forth like a pair of drunken sots after a good night out. I felt stupid and ineffectual as I saw the floor in the distance continue its rise and fall with even more vigour. Finally, we reached the orange sofa and grabbed it with relief. We held on to its back as the swaying increased, but my relief in getting there buffed my confidence. Suddenly, the swaying stopped, and it was as if everyone let go of their metaphorically held breath. The relief was tangible and the Japanese started to move around as if someone had restarted the pause button on a movie. They just got on with what they had been going to do before it happened. No discussions or excited comments took place, it was back to business, it's over, forget it. I was enamoured of their stoicism as I managed to get round the sofa and collapsed on it with shaking legs. We had to sit there for a good five minutes to recover our composure. That was the worst earthquake I experienced. And it was terrifying. I don't know if I was lucky to have it happen in a large furniture store, I could have been on a train, or in a restaurant where you cook your own food in a bowl full of oil on your table, maybe that would have been more traumatic. However, I think that whatever and wherever you are, it is terrifying, the only consolation being the feeling of great relief that one has survived to experience the next one.

The area I lived in, Kansai, had been very lucky as although it suffered many minor quakes, it was thought that it was safe from any major ones. Everyone knew that – 'Kansai didn't do major earthquakes'.

That was until 17th January 1995, when the Great Hanshin Earthquake struck the Kansai area. From Kobe city centre all the way down to my town of Nigawa and on to

Takarazuka was badly hit, although none as serious as Kobe itself. Over six thousand died with more than 25,000 injured and 300,000 left homeless. The aftershocks went on for a week. People had been so confident that Kansai 'didn't do earthquakes', that very few people in the area had earthquake insurance.

A lot of my students were affected and still went pale when they talked about it. Whenever there was an earthquake it was always a talking point in class with the students telling me how frightened they were of them and that the trauma of 'the big one' had not gone away.

I was curious as to the difference between the earthquakes I had experienced and the great Kobe one, but no one could explain adequately in English until one day, a student hit on a way of explaining it that I could understand.

"There are two types of earthquakes in Japan," she told me, "the kind that sway back and forth and the kind that judder up and down. The ones that sway are not as dangerous as the juddering kinds. The Kobe earthquake was a juddering earthquake which is why it was so destructive and traumatic for everyone."

I learned the wisdom of her words not long afterwards as I went to bed one night. I had just settled myself down when, without any warning whatsoever, an immense violent judder, like a lightning strike, shot up from the ground and lifted my bed. I almost fell out. Then it was gone. Just that one judder, a second or two, but the force of it was obscene. The Kobe earthquake juddered for twenty seconds, with several serious aftershocks. I now understood why so many people were still traumatized.

Naoko san told me that after the quake the area had no water for three months, and her family had to go to Amagasaki to the public baths to bathe. "It was only ten miles away," she said, "but it took us about three hours to get there because the roads were so damaged."

During this time, the Mama san at the Funny House had a 'free table' in her restaurant. This was always stocked with food and anyone could come in and take what they needed for free. Many would come and bring something they didn't need and leave it for someone to take if they needed it. One takarajienne's mother, who lived in an unaffected area, ascertained that people were cold, so she sent the Mama san hundreds of pieces of warm underwear, long johns and the like. The Mama san put them in her restaurant for people to help themselves. Word soon got around.

The town of Takarazuka had major damage and many were killed. Fortunately, the theatre had just been rebuilt and, apart from setting off the sprinklers and ruining all the new seats and carpets, it was undamaged.

One man I met, a retired doctor, said that he was in the shower when, "All hell broke loose, and I could only brace myself with my arms against the walls and pray for it to stop. When it did, I rushed out to my wife who was still in bed. She was lying underneath a large chest of drawers. Fortunately, that chest saved her life because the top drawer fell almost fully out and wedged itself into the floor, preventing the chest falling any further. She was cocooned under it in a little pocket of space and protected from the debris of the rest of the house caving in." Their house was destroyed and they lived in a tent for two years while they waited their turn for rebuilding. They had no earthquake insurance.

It seems to me that you either survive an earthquake or you don't. No amount of forward planning can help you in the terror of the moment. If all about you is collapsing, there's nothing you can do about it. It's either your time or it's not.

*

Elizabeth Oliver is a remarkable woman. After thirty or so years in Japan, she still suffers from the 'English disease,' of having compassion and love for animals, so much so that after many years of fretting about it, she decided to open a sanctuary for homeless or cruelly treated animals. After the great earthquake, she was appalled at the situation of the many homeless and lost cats and dogs that were roaming around with no one taking care of them. She started to collect them and took them back to her sanctuary. Overwhelmed, she and her staff battled to help these animals and her sanctuary grew, which I feel sure, depressed her as it meant that more animals were in need of her.

This amazing, very English 'county' lady, had bought a plot of land in the mountains and called it ARK – Animal Refuge in Kansai, and from these small beginnings, ARK now has another two sanctuaries in Tokyo and Sasayama with hundreds of homeless and desperate animals finding their lives saved by Elizabeth, her staff and the many volunteers that she has now accrued. This is an amazing achievement in a country such as Japan which unfortunately, is a long way down the animal compassion league.

I used to go there sometimes to help walk the dogs, and my heart would melt at their plight. Always looking for funds and volunteers, and facing hostility from some of the surrounding farmers, she has been a beacon of determination and compassion, and an example of what one can achieve if you don't give up even in the direst of circumstances and animosity. I salute her.

One meets extraordinary people amongst ex-pats and I'm wondering whether they were extraordinary before they went, or whether living in such an alien culture makes one develop character and strength. Either that, or probably, you give up and go home.

*

Japan is a country of contradictions. The extraordinary kindness of its people is on a personal level, for its society, as a group, can be the personification of indifference to others' misfortune and the concept of charity is not part of their culture. I first got an inkling of this within a few weeks of arriving as I marvelled at the sight of men on bicycles balancing large sacks on either side of their bikes. I found out later that the sacks were full of squashed soft drinks cans. How they could ride with all that weight on either side was a feat in itself, as around the streets they went, following the schedule of recycle days. They would stop at each bin put out in the mornings for collection, and take the soft drinks cans out, squash them and put them into the sacks hanging from their bicycles to sell on for scrap. Many of them would be cycling around one's area each recycle day.

I found out later that these were the 'Gomi men' (rubbish men). Unemployed and homeless people, who had found a niche market, and an entrepreneurial spirit. Therefore, even though they lived on the streets, they had their gomi business to give them enough money for sustenance. (Japan does give limited state benefits to the unemployed, but presumably, these people were out of the loop, or had been unemployed for too long.)

They never bothered one, got on with their business in a calm and ordered way; they were an inspiration really, of getting off your butt and helping yourself.

Homelessness had increased enormously over the years I was there. More people would be camped out at major railway stations every year. Each person had several flattened cardboard boxes which they slept on, and each morning,

271

they would tie them up neatly and deposit them under the arches of bridges, together with their belongings in plastic bags, ready for the next night's rest. At night, they would lie on this cardboard, shoes taken off and neatly laid next to it, as they tried to get some sleep. The lights and bustle of the stations keeping them warmer than elsewhere.

No one begged or even acknowledged the other people around them. They minded their own business. They were mostly men, although I started to see several women, and at one stage, a whole family with young children camped out under the arches. But mostly they were men in later life, many were victims of the Japanese policy of a 'job for life' having gone disastrously wrong, as the long recession bit even harder.

The story goes that a lot of these men were also rejected by their wives. Now no longer of use, having lost their jobs and a drain on the household, marriage problems escalated. Couples who had spent most of their married life apart because of the long working hours and separatist society, were now thrown together 24/7 and they discovered a mutual hatred of each other, or at least the wife did. Many wives have divorced their husbands under these circumstances, an unusual thing in itself, but even more so is the fact that some of the husbands were thrown out of the marital home. With nowhere to go, many took to the streets.

As there is no tradition of charity there are no Oxfam, Shelter, Cancer Support, Mind, RSPCA or similar. There are no flag days, volunteers, charity shops; and hospices have only just reared their badly needed heads. The family takes care of you and if they don't, there is no net to catch you.

When Jan and I first went to live in Japan, we stayed in a small hotel in Kobe for a week. Every day, we would go to the railway station and pass under the railway bridge. I noticed an old woman sitting on a mattress under the bridge. She was sprightly looking and the mattress was clean. Everyone ignored her. Over the next eight months or so, we often went to Kobe and consequently saw the old lady under the bridge. Unfortunately, with every visit she had deteriorated. I wanted to do something about it, phone someone, ask them to help her, but when I asked friends about it, they told me that there were no places to ring. There was little or no official or unofficial help for people like her. Also, interestingly, they said that she probably didn't want anyone to help her. It would be too shameful. We could have given her money, but she wasn't begging. We didn't want to offend her, so passed her by as others did, doing nothing.

Finally, we saw her one April day, it was cold and wet and the old lady had aged eons. She was, in fact, almost dead. Still sitting on her, now ponging and filthy mattress, her head and body flopped one way, then the other, she was barely conscious. A young woman, dressed elegantly and expensively walked towards us, saw the old lady, did a double take with her eyes, her head remaining rigidly forward, a look of shock registered for a moment, then she walked past, expressionless. To my shame, so did we.

The next week, when I passed by, she was gone. The place where the reeking mattress lay and the stains on the pavement surrounding it were gone. Everything was scrubbed and gleaming. All trace of her had been wiped out.

I wondered about her life and what had happened to bring her to such an end. Whatever it was, it gave her a fame of sorts. So publicly living her last few months, and dying, in the full view of the passing public. A pin prick of interest on peoples' faces before they turned away and forgot her. Or did they? I didn't. She had touched me and I couldn't forget her.

The old men of the streets, for some reason, didn't touch me. I felt sorry for them, but apart from that I was indifferent. Maybe it was their look of independence and absence of any display of distress. They were living their lives and minding their own business, the Japanese way.

The one thing that always did upset me was the plight of the dogs. Medium to large size dogs almost invariably live outside in their owner's small garden with most of them tied up to a wall or kennel. Usually, they were fed and watered every day, but they would be left alone on a short chain, unable to exercise or root about. Many of the owners having no physical contact with them at all. Boredom fought with the weather to be the devil for these dogs. Left outside all through the year, many without shelter from the intense heat, and surviving that, they have to endure the bitter cold of the winter. My heart went out to them, and I know that Elizabeth Oliver and ARK are always fighting for the rights of these dogs to be treated humanely and with dignity. Unfortunately, she is mostly ignored by the masses, the rigid structure of society preferring the maxim that 'dogs are dirty' and belong outside. Few people challenge this view or are prepared to change their treatment. I suffer from the same 'English disease' as Elizabeth, and found the common sight of these dogs immensely distressing.

The one encouraging thing is that, gradually, with people like Elizabeth gaining more ground, some people are starting to change their viewpoint, especially people with smaller dogs, and they are starting to be kept inside the home, where they are pampered pets.

The Japanese don't do anything by halves; it's either the one or the other.

CHAPTER NINETEEN

A Nagoya Wedding

Masayo san didn't stay a 'Single Belle' for long. She surprised me one evening by phoning and saying that she was getting married. I said to her with great surprise, "I didn't know you had a boyfriend?"

"No, me neither," she said in that enigmatic Japanese way. "We just decided very quickly. We met at the hospital some time ago, but only just got together. I've always liked him a lot."

We were continuing our conversation about the wedding when Masayo san paused. I waited. Masayo san continued to pause and I continued to wait. Neither of us speaking for several seconds, it was getting embarrassing. I was waiting to be asked to the wedding (hopefully) and I wondered whether Masayo san, being a reticent Japanese, was unsure about asking. Deciding that one of us had to broach the subject, and knowing that hints and nuances are usually hopelessly lost in the labyrinth of the language barrier, I thought I should just come straight out with it.

Trusting that I was not breaching some unwritten social code, I ask her in simple, unambiguous English, "Can Jan and I come to your wedding?" There, it was out, and it left me feeling queasy. Had I lost my friend by being too forward? I know that it can so easily happen, the Japanese being incredibly sensitive to straightforwardness.

She gasped. I could hear it so clearly down the line. Oh dear! I feared the worst but the gasp was followed by a loud and surprised, "Oh! Do you want to come to my wedding?"

"Yes, of course."

"Really?" her voice rising even higher than before.

"Yes, really."

"Really?"

"Yes, really." (The Japanese word for really is honto, and is much more fun to say than really.)

She broke the spell, by saying, "Oh thank you, thank you for wanting to come to my wedding."

I thought that a little strange, but replied, "You're welcome, of course we would like to come."

"Oh, thank you," she said again, "I must tell my sister, she will be delighted."

I was still a little puzzled that Masayo san seemed so surprised that we wanted to go. I was to learn later of a possible reason why.

This came about in a natural way during a lesson with some of my students. We always started the lessons with free chatting, and I happened to mention that I was going to a Japanese wedding.

All three students gasped the same gasp as Masayo san had.

"Oh, that'll be expensive for you," said one student, drolly.

"Yes," said the other two, nodding their heads, "very expensive."

"Why? What do you mean, expensive?"

"Well," my most confident student started, and she had a twinkle in her eye, "don't you know about Japanese wedding presents?"

"No, I don't, please tell me."

"You always give money. Plenty of money."

"How much money?" It was now my turn to raise my voice. The students pondered and chatted together for a moment, and all nodded their heads, "Yes, we think that as you are only friends, and new friends at that, around fifty thousand yen would be about right, between you and Janet." (About £300 in British sterling at that time.)

"Oh, really?" Was all I could manage.

One student mused, "You could give less of course, but that would reflect badly on you as a person, but you are foreigners, so you could probably get away with it."

"Mmmm."

"Where will the marriage take place?"

"In Nagoya."

"Ooohhh," they all said in unison, "gorgeous wedding, yes, gorgeous, gorgeous, (gorgeous is a very fashionable word right now). I asked them why they knew it would be 'gorgeous'?

"Because Nagoya weddings are famous for being gorgeous," they said. "Nagoya weddings are always gorgeous, the most gorgeous in Japan. All Japanese women want to go to a Nagoya wedding."

"Really?"

"Yes, really."

Another student added, "Foreigners are not usually invited to Japanese weddings, so you are very lucky indeed to be invited, and to a Nagoya wedding at that. Lucky, very lucky," she finished, looking wistful.

The Shinkansen train going to Nagoya had many passengers partaking of Japan's favourite pastime, sleeping. Others were reading and a few were chatting quietly. The atmosphere was quiet and relaxed and the carriage was cool, clean and comfortable. For me, it's a train made in heaven and full of passengers made in heaven.

I was feeling relaxed and excited as we drew into Nagoya's large and interesting station. It was, as all stations, spotlessly clean and the passengers were quiet, calm and so polite it was a pleasure to pass by them. The station is situated above ground and downstairs, on the ground floor, it was all hustle and bustle with arcades of shops, restaurants, supermarkets and department stores, every one crowded. Everything you need is at this station, including the ubiquitous MacDonald's – crowded with a queue!

There was a policeman standing on a purpose made wooden plinth looking very Romanesque. He stood tall, overseeing the mall, but unlike a Roman statue, he was very real. His uniform was pressed and starched and he was holding a big stick. It came up to his shoulder and stood beside him like a third arm, thick and threatening looking, but on reflection, it was probably there to stop him wobbling or falling off his high perch.

He watched everything and everybody and could see the full length of the shopping mall. He especially watched us and studied our faces as if he was trying to memorise them. The message was very clear: don't do anything wrong, we are watching your every move. The large gun in his holster reinforcing this message. He was scary and I was duly chastised into dutiful obedience to all the laws of the mall.

We took a taxi to the hotel where the reception would be held. No one was going to the actual wedding ceremony itself except for very close family members. There is a very good reason for this – there is no actual wedding ceremony.

To get married in Japan, all that is entailed is an uninspiring trip to the local city hall. Every family must register their family details there, marriages, births, deaths, adoptions etc. and any changes to that family must be altered on the family record. Therefore, to get married, all one does

278

is to go there and instruct an employee to change your family's registration details. The bride is taken off her own family's registration and added to the groom's family details. Stamp the alteration with your *hanko* (seal) and that's it. No vows are taken, nothing is signed and you can even send someone else to do it for you. (As long as they have your hanko.) It's clinical, uninteresting and open to all kinds of ruses, but that's the legal way to get married.

Hankos are a way of life and a vital component to all official business. Basically, it is a very small seal, about the size of a large ring on a short stubby stick, overall about two inches long. It is easily lost and duplicated and you can buy them in stationary shops throughout the country. It will have your family's surname embedded into it and will become your official seal. It's quick, easy and simple to forge.

Want to change your bank account? Just stamp the alterations with your hanko. Want to transfer large sums of money, just stamp the form with your hanko. Want to seal a contract, just stamp it with your hanko. It's the traditional way, but now people are beginning to realise that this system is open to abuse as many foreigners have come into the country and played the system. Changing the bank account details of others without their knowledge or consent, creating crooked business deals and some even marrying themselves off to some unsuspecting woman who has never even met them!

The hanko system works because in ordinary life, the Japanese are extremely honest and trusting. They can't conceive of people misusing the system. But now that the world is more global and more foreigners are living in Japan, it's become a problem that wasn't there before.

Masayo san and her parents, her new husband Shinji san, and his father, would have been to city hall and altered their family registrations. They were now officially husband and wife. Married because their family records had been altered and stamped with respective hankos. But, where is the joy? I know that the Japanese love to party and what could be more unsatisfying than a marriage trip to stuffy, utility city hall, often staffed with dour, humourless old men?

I feel sure that the fashion for extravagant, cripplingly expensive wedding parties has emerged out of the pit of city halls. This wedding was no exception and I wondered what would happen. Would it live up to the reputation that Nagoya has for providing the most gorgeous weddings in Japan?

Arriving at the hotel, we found the correct floor and exited the lift into a large reception waiting room, long and sumptuously carpeted with a large gold screen placed at the far end. There were quite a few people milling around and we nodded to a few, who nodded back and we all became very shy. We knew no one here as Masayo san and her family had not arrived yet.

An announcement was made over the Tannoy, in Japanese, which we couldn't understand, and many people started to make for the lifts and disappear into the unknown. Where were they going? Had the wedding been moved? Was there a problem? We just didn't know and were probably looking confused, and were certainly feeling it.

A sweet young lady took pity on us and asked, in halting English if we had a wedding gift. I said that we did. She explained that everyone left their wedding gifts downstairs and led us to the lift where we joined several other people and went down a floor. Not knowing what to expect, I was surprised to find a large room, empty except for two medium-sized tables covered by starched white tablecloths and behind each one stood a friendly, smiling young woman, immaculately dressed, with a long queue of patiently waiting guests standing in front of them. Our friendly helper pointed to one queue and said, "Masayo san family line, other line for husband's family." She asked us if we had our envelope, and I waved it and said, "We give this here?"

"Yes, please." she reassured us and we understood that as we were friends of Masayo san, we gave our gift to her table and that the other table was for the guests and family of her husband. I had expected to give my gift to Masayo san herself, or at least to her parents. I should have known that it would be all organized and arranged in a formal setting with employees doing the hard work. (If collecting money could be considered hard work.)

I watched with interest as each guest took their turn at the head of the table and handed over their wedding gift. Each gift was, of course, money, stacked neatly into beautifully made envelopes which were a work of art in themselves. Some gold leafed, others with exquisite origami motifs, but whatever the beauty of the envelope I knew that each one contained various amounts of freshly washed and pressed pristine notes, which is a service the banks offer customers for free, it being standard practice to give gifts in voluminous amounts of cash. There was a lot of bowing and smiling between the staff and the guests and the atmosphere was very relaxed and joyful, even though most of the guests were handing over a small fortune. We were fortunate in being new friends, because if you are old family friends, close relatives etc. you are expected to increase the amount of the gift commensurate with your importance to the family. The amount of money that was stacking up on those tables must have been considerable, but no one had any thoughts of anyone trying to steal it, inside the reception or outside, or whatever happened to it afterwards. I love the honesty of this country.

Our turn came. The fashion model of an assistant, beautifully coiffed in style and manners, asked our names although it was clear enough who we were being the only foreigners there, but form must be strictly adhered to. I said our names and she checked them on her list. I handed our beautiful wedding envelope over to her with both hands, in the formal Japanese manner, and she took it from me with both hands, each of us bowing and smiling and emitting numerous thanks between the bows.

You may be wondering how much money we had decided to give, in other words, if we gave a lesser sum and disgraced ourselves as foreigners? You have probably already guessed that we didn't. We gave the recommended sum of ¥50,000 and slept easy in our beds. Actually, Masayo san had told us, in another telephone conversation, that we didn't need to worry about a wedding present. Just us being there was present enough for her, she told us. She was so delighted that we were going. It made us feel very special.

Making our way back upstairs, we awaited the arrival of Masayo san and family. We knew that they hadn't gone through a mock Christian wedding service, thank goodness, and were told that Masayo san was getting dressed for the reception after attending city hall.

Finally, a rustle and a murmur started up and my eye followed the many heads turning simultaneously, and as I turned I was confronted by an amazing sight.

Masayo san was walking slowly down the reception lobby with her new hubby, Shinji san at her side, both dressed in the traditional costumes of the Edo period (1603-1867). I had seen the kind of costume Shinji san was wearing many times in plays or in museums, but I had never seen a costume anything like Masayo san was wearing and it made me gasp, not from its beauty, but from its strangeness and other worldliness. She obviously had a kimono on but over the top of it she was wearing what I can only describe as an outer kimono, rather like a cloak which covered her from head to foot. It was made from beautiful soft silk cream brocade and was obviously meant to drag after the bride in a bridal train and therefore, was noticeably thicker and rotund around the bottom edge, like a tube. I later found out that this was indeed a kimono coat and is called an *uchikake*, a highly formal kimono only worn by a bride.

However, what really took my breath away was the strange hood she was wearing. It was part of the costume and made of the same soft cream brocade, but was, at the same time, a separate entity. It sat on her head, enormous and capacious and covered her face like a monk's hood, the sides reaching shoulder level, whilst at the back, it fell down to mid back level. It made her look as if she was ultra top heavy. It was beautifully made and striking in the extreme.

I realised straight away that this hood was so capacious because, underneath it, she was wearing the traditional Edo period wig. In those days, it was considered the coolest of cool for women to grow their hair long and then layer it over round wooden blocks to give it height and style, resulting in an oversized hairdo, pulled, waxed and immovable. Consequently, if you wore a hood, it had to be big enough to go over this immense hair style.

Making their way down the room, people clapping them as they passed, the bride and groom slowly walked towards us. Masayo san was demure, with eyes cast downwards as befits a Japanese bride, but even though her eyes were looking downwards, in true Japanese fashion she didn't miss a thing, and suddenly spotted us. Never a one to be too kowtowed by form, she broke rank and glided over to us (one always glides in a kimono, it's the only way one can walk in them).

Her smile was huge and infectious as she said, "Oh, thank you, thank you for coming to my wedding. I'm so happy." I said something vague about her hood, not wishing to sound, for my part, ignorant and for her part, rude. Her eyes lighted up and with great glee, she said, "This hood is hiding my 'devil's horns'."

"Your what?" I said, totally taken aback, and Masayo san, not at all worried that she was holding up the formal celebrations went on to say, "In Japan, in olden times, women were said to be wicked creatures and have the horns of the devil, but they hid them from men until they married. So, at her marriage, a woman would wear a hood to hide her horns." With that, leaving us both dumbfounded, she glided back to her new hubby, who was looking decidedly nervous and uncomfortable with all the attention. Masayo san was just reveling in it.

Having never even seen her new husband, Shinji san, before, let alone met him, I took particular interest in him. Tall, slim and well muscled, he had the statuesque posture of the Japanese. In his mid thirties, straight black hair parted in the middle in the latest fashion, he was good looking in a not too blatant way. I liked him on sight and got good vibes from him, even if he did look terrified.

He wore his costume well and looked comfortable in his *hakama* trousers, which are more like a skirt, being very wide with a seam dividing them in the middle. They were voluminous in the extreme, made of grey linen and ended just above the ankles to show off his white *tabi* (toe) socks and geta shoes. Over the top he wore a *haori*, a traditional kimono jacket, which is worn by both men and women. It was black with a white trim at the collar and had the traditional wide sleeves. Most importantly, it is worn open at the front and kept neatly together by a tied tassel. This was important in the olden days because men would have kept their swords tucked into the front of their waistbands and because they needed quick access, they needed an open haori. Too bad if it's snowing, but then, the Japanese don't seem to feel the cold. Fortunately, the only weapon Shinji san was carrying today was his fan, which he held delicately and respectfully.

The new husband and wife, together with their parents, arranged themselves in front of the high gold screen at the end of the room and all the guests started to file slowly in front of them. Guests and the wedding families bowed to each other, as the guests then passed by into the reception room proper.

We took our turn and bowed, first to the bride and groom and then to their parents. Being brought up in postwar Japan, their parents were small compared to us and Jan and I both towered above them. I felt like Gulliver as I turned and entered the reception room.

The room was large with about a dozen round tables, each seating eight people. It was elegant and expensive with a high ceiling and lots of mouldings. European in style, we could have been in any city in Europe rather than in the middle of industrial Japan. The thing that caught my eye the most was what I assumed to be the bride and groom's table. It was set apart, raised up on a small stage. It had the same gleaming white tablecloth as the rest of the tables, but with the added glory of a cascade of small pink flowers, like a waterfall covering the edges. Baskets of strategically placed flowers gave it the finishing touch. It was very effective.

I was excited and a little nervous because Jan and I were the only foreigners here and we had no idea what was going to happen. I was constantly being surprised by the unexpected and therefore, I was a little apprehensive as I looked for my place card.

My first surprise was that Jan and I were seated at one of

the tables opposite the bride and groom's. A place of honour as the rules of wedding etiquette are, I discovered, that the most valued guests, i.e. friends and business colleagues, sit near the bride and groom and, in true self deprecating Japanese style, the 'humble' family members fan out further away until, getting out your binoculars, you finally find the parents and grandparents, the most humble in the family's eyes, in a far flung corner of the room. The other people on our table were friends of Masayo san, all of them women in their thirties, who welcomed us in a friendly manner, all of us nodding to each other in informal bows. Shinji san's friends were all male and seated together on a separate table nearby, continuing the concept of separation of the sexes.

Finally, everyone was seated and chatting away, when suddenly the lights dimmed and soft music wafted into the air making everyone shut up instantly. A spotlight came on and lit up the large double doors at the end of the room. They opened slowly, (it was all very dramatic) and finally in stepped the bride and groom, in seemingly slow motion.

Masayo san and Shinji san made their slow winding way through the tables, visiting each one and nodding and smiling at everyone, until, by a circuitous route, they reached their own table, with everyone clapping them on their way.

After they had made themselves comfortable, the MC started her spiel. MCs are popular in Japan and most occasions have a professional MC to help things along. The Japanese love of doing things in the correct way and following orders is probably one of the reasons for this. This MC was very good, not too intrusive and kept up a jolly patter in her high pitched voice.

Speeches ensued by various men in suits, work colleagues I assumed, and many jokes were made. Masayo san looked radiant, whilst Shinji san still looked nervous.

It was time for the bride and groom to do official things, and following the tradition of western culture, they stood up and went over to cut the wedding cake, although it was not the traditional wedding cake I expected, but seven separate cakes, arranged on a spiral cake stand. I recognised a sponge cake, a mousse, a fruit tart, a cheesecake amongst others. It was all very pretty with something there for every taste, and one delight in a day of delights.

Then, one of those little Japanese moments happened, that so endear one to the country and people, when a staff member came and took the knife from them with supreme delicacy and elegance. She picked up one of the dazzlingly white table napkins, and wrapped it around the blade of the knife, with the same grace as if she were performing in a ballet. This was to ensure that no one would stand the chance of an inadvertent nick, then, with the same grace, she took the handle of the knife out of their hands, supporting the blade as she did so and gently put it down in a safe place and then guided them back to their table. It was a work of art. So simple and effective.

I noticed that another staff member was holding Masayo san's kimono coat off the floor so the she could walk up the steps back to their table. When seated, the staff member knelt beside her and arranged her kimono and coat around her feet in a comfortable position. I guessed that Masayo san would not be able to move at all if these were not so adjusted.

The MC started up again and the food arrived, the first of many courses expertly delivered to us by waiters in black waistcoats and dickey bows. In seven years I never experienced a bad waiter (or waitress). Unfailingly professional, discreet, polite and helpful, they are such a pleasure. Waiters are generally treated with respect by the customers and they treat the customer with respect too, no tipping is allowed, or bad temper or attitude, you have to do the job, so why not do it pleasantly and politely. It makes for a much better atmosphere and everyone stays calm and polite, which helps keep one's health on an even keel. By the way, Japan has the highest longevity in the world.

The food was 'gorgeous'. It was exquisitely presented and absolutely delicious. Course after course came along and our wine was discretely replenished without fuss or delay. The noise level rose as the wine (or beer) glasses emptied. People were relaxing and losing their inhibitions, and even the groom was looking more at ease.

The MC made an announcement and the bride and groom rose from their table and left the room slowly, Masayo san being incapable of moving any other way with the weight and tightness of her clothes. Everyone politely clapped again until they left the room by the double doors at the other end of the room this time. Obviously one for entrances and one for exits. They both bowed formally towards the room and the doors slowly closed behind them, the spotlight faded and the serious business of eating and drinking really got underway. Within seconds, the noise level rose fourfold, cigarettes were lit, scores of them as Japan has almost zero no smoking laws.

We spent some time getting to know our table mates, and other people started to mingle big time, table hopping, and the noise level increased to yet louder decibels. Jan and I were delighted to be gently accosted by a semi-drunken uncle. He knelt down between us in that uniquely Japanese way, so that he was on the same level as us, making us feel comfortable, and he started a slow and tortuous conversation in English. He was a joy and so unthreatening and happy with life, not an ounce of aggression or attitude, he chatted to us for a good five minutes until he decided that he needed another beer. He took his departure with lots of bowing and smiles and good grace. All of us on our table were utterly charmed.

Mutsumi san, Masayo san's sister, came over to chat to us next. She was very happy and relaxed, and made lots of jokes. We asked her to show us her kimono and she twirled around like a model explaining the design as she went. She said, pointing to her sleeves, "Long sleeves, I have long sleeves, that is because I am an unmarried woman. Unmarried women always have long sleeves on their kimono. But, I am not a *young* woman (She pronounced 'young' with vigor and emphasis, making us laugh) I am an *old* woman (she's about 40) so my sleeves are not so long. Very young women have sleeves to the floor, but mine are just half way, down to my hips." She looked around, "You see my sister-in-law over there, she is a married woman and therefore, she is wearing a black kimono which is very formal and she has short sleeves that only come to her wrists, denoting that she is married."

She called her over and sister-in-law glided over so elegantly, but the look was ruined somewhat by the large bottle of beer she was clutching to her midriff. She was not drinking the beer, but was serving it to valued guests in the traditional way the Japanese have of always pouring someone else's drink for them. She was an astoundingly beautiful woman with soft laughing eyes and upon request, she too twirled and showed off her kimono. As is dictated in the formal style she was wearing, it was totally plain above the waist, but below were a few designs of such delicacy and understatement one almost didn't notice them, but when one did, it was like one of those shocks of delight that the Japanese do so well.

One of the things I love so much about Japan is that you are continually getting these little shocks of delight. Unexpected, innocent little happy instances. It could be a child and its mother interacting in such a calm, respectful way. It could be the cuteness of the children (and they are especially cute). Kids together, being sweet with each other. The kindness of strangers. Turn a corner and get faced with an hotel covered in Father Christmases and Reindeers (life size) (in June). Teenagers, covered in heavy makeup and studs, just experimenting with a little bit of attitude (Japanese style) who suddenly realise they have got in your way and bow and apologise profusely. Turn another corner and find yourself looking at several women in kimono, gliding along and laughing together in such a soft and delicate way. Drunken salary men on the train at midnight, going home from work, exhausted and drunk from business meetings in restaurants or bars. Unthreatening, minding their own business, no trouble to anyone, they unsteadily make their way home. Priests from temples, in all their ritual finery, on the local train. Buddhist monks on scooters, their robes flying behind them, as they go about their business. Patient car drivers, who don't react when another driver does something silly, no road rage, they are more likely to smile an understanding smile than get angry. I could go on. I love it all.

Masayo san's father appeared next, small and dapper, he had been a professional *enka* singer for a number of years and has many prizes for his singing. But everything was put on hold as, suddenly, the lights went down again and the music changed to a Japanese love ballad, the spotlight lit the doorway which slowly opened and in stepped Masayo san and Shinji san again. A gasp of delight went up and everyone clapped again as Masayo san entered denuded of her kimono coat and 'devil's horns' hood, and now in the full glory of her Edo style kimono and wig.

The kimono was stunning. It was a deep, vibrant purple, patterned in all the colours of the rainbow, but so expertly designed and put together that it looked but a mere trifle when in fact, it was a feast. Shinji san was still wearing his same Edo period costume, and the bride and groom did another slow walk around the tables and nodded and paraded. He looked much more relaxed now and even managed some mega smiles.

Putting on a kimono is a major and skilled task. Its main part is made from a single piece of material and can fit any size from small to big. Therefore, it has to be tucked and fastened in all sorts of inaccessible places around the body. Then there is the belt. Actually, to call it a belt is an insult, but that's its purpose. It is often the most expensive part of the kimono and is its crowning glory. It's called an *obi*, which is a rather unattractive name for such a work of art. Obis are sumptuously decorated and can cost thousands of pounds. It is wrapped around the body several times, just under the bust line; it has to be tight to stop it from slipping and friends have told me that it is incredibly uncomfortable, especially for sitting because it is tied in the back in a huge, rounded, monstrous knot. It can take anywhere between one to four hours to put the whole ensemble on, (depending on its complexity) and women today usually only wear a kimono for special occasions, which means of course, that many have lost the skills needed to put one on. This has produced a whole industry of professional kimono dressers. Kimono are very expensive, going up in stages of quality, which dissuades many from buying one, preferring instead to wear their mother's, or go to a professional dresser, where they can usually hire one for the day as well as getting it put on for them.

All kimono are designed to be worn off the neck. It dips deeply at the back exposing the nape of the neck and a tiny part of the upper back. This is because in olden times, men thought this area was the most provocative part of a woman's body. Mmmm, try telling that to today's *Playboy* reader!

I was really enjoying myself, having such a good time, but I've noticed that there's always a price to pay for happiness and it was as true that day as any other. My suffering was about to begin in earnest, as a male guest got up and went to the karaoke machine and started to sing an enka song. Enka, for the uninitiated, is the traditional way of singing and its closest comparison for many, is to the wailing of cats. Think of tightening your vocal cords and screeching as loudly as you can through the tiny gap that is left at the back of your throat. Its high pitched tones can leave ones ears ringing and it takes a lot of practice to do this at full volume, especially to master the dramatic warbles so important in enka. I've spoken to many people about the idea behind enka and the consensus was that – yes indeed – it should resemble the wailing of cats as much as possible. It blends an overwrought style of singing with lyrics that are always maudlin and sentimental. In fact, the more melodramatic it is the better. One doesn't want to distract from the story being sung so distinctive melodies or arrangements are not encouraged. One needs to concentrate on the singer's performance where histrionics and real tears are admired.

For a foreigner, to sit and listen to enka can be a painful experience, (and many Japanese agree) but it is traditional and I am all for preserving the traditions, so I didn't mind so much, especially when everyone got the giggles because the singer was so bad. I had never thought before that an enka singer has to sing in tune, but I realised then, that it is just as important to wail in tune as to sing sweetly in tune. As he started to wail – sorry – sing, I noticed that Masayo san looked astounded and then she exchanged looks with Shinji san and they had a very intimate couple moment with a discreet fit of the giggles. But everybody clapped politely, in a most appreciative manner at the end because taking part is the thing. The fact that he did his best, even though it was so bad, was worth encouragement and appreciation.

Three little kids got up next to sing, and thankfully, they sang an ordinary, mundane pop song albeit delivered in such a high register that it could just qualify for enka. Two little girls, sisters I guess as they were dressed in identical pink fluffy dresses, aged about five and seven, flanked a little boy aged about three who looked very cute in his short trousers, waistcoat and dickey bow. The girls launched into their song, doing all the actions necessary for a professional performance, their eyes fixed to the karaoke screen as if mesmerized, while the little boy mouthed the words in a fishlike manner and looked desperate to emulate the girls, but finding it too hard for him. The other little kids were gathered around watching, jigging about to the music, aunts and uncles on their knees, getting down to their level, and jigging beside them. It was all so sweet. The singers got a present each from the bride and groom afterwards and a huge round of applause.

The food kept coming. Pretty little dishes of the most elaborate concoctions, beautifully presented. Every dish different in what seemed like an endless display of the chefs' imaginations. Vegetables cooked in various styles and cut and presented as works of art. Meat and fish in delicate bite-size pieces, mixed with grated root vegetables and salads in sensational sauces. My palette exploded so many times I started to get blasé about it – until the deserts arrived, and I discovered whole new taste buds I didn't know I had. It was an experience to cherish, and must have cost a fortune.

To accompany all this, the wine kept being replenished, which was just as well as it was now time for Masayo san's father to give us a sample of his skills in enka singing. He had retired, but still kept his hand in on occasions such of these.

He was a very skilled singer, his imitation of cats wailing was sensational as he lived his song. I noticed that he hardly opened his mouth to sing, keeping his lips and teeth in close proximity, even when he hit the high notes. He was a master craftsman and got a huge round of applause. Great. He had finished. I was so relieved to get it over.

The atmosphere was delightful. I was in a strange country, with people I had never met before, but I felt totally relaxed, safe, and welcome, even though the drink was flowing and inhibitions were getting drowned, no one got drunk or raucous and everything and everyone remained elegant. Although one could get drunk just on the good will and bonhomie of the atmosphere.

The little kids were treated as equals and many of the adults gave them lots of their time to ensure they enjoyed this party as much as everyone else. I didn't hear a single child cry the whole six hours the party lasted. Parents want to be friends with their children throughout their lives, therefore they are usually treated with respect and very carefully. I remember one time, Ryoko and I had a badly behaved child in our class and I was getting very annoyed at his continued bad behavior. Ryoko said to me, "It is our job to help him understand that there are better ways to behave, and we will do that through example, don't tell him, show him. We should help him become a better person, show him a better way, not just tell him to behave." It worked too. Generally, children are treated with lots of patience and understanding and special relationships often form between them and their mothers.

I don't know if all Nagoya weddings are like Masayo san's, but I hope so, because this was one of the most treasured moments I have of Japan and its people. Masayo san's sister-in-law (of the black kimono and the beer bottle) was playing kissing games with a little boy of about two, who was sporting the most irresistible little top knot, which looked like a mini chimney sweeps' brush. His daddy was holding him up and sister-in-law and little boy were kissing and parting, kissing and parting. Big smackeroos on the lips and both were enraptured with each other. I think that she must have been his mother as love certainly shone out of her eyes.

More food arrived, *sashimi* this time (raw fish). It was presented beautifully, but I decided to just stick to the wine! I soon found that I needed it too as a thick set woman in a kimono suddenly appeared in front of the karaoke machine. Large glasses perched squarely on her face, hair swept up, middle aged, she looked like someone's aunt. She did a fair rendition of cats wailing, but her voice was weak so it sounded more like cats dying. And then, she gave a melodramatic warble at the end of one note that brought cheers and applause from around the room. I really must get more educated about enka I thought. Several more people fancied themselves and murdered an enka song or two over the next half an hour and do you know what? By the end, I was just beginning to enjoy it!

I'd just realised that the bride and groom had been missing again, when all the lights went down and it was time for another grand entrance. The spotlight lit the doorway, the doors slowly opened, everyone was agog. They stepped inside in unison and everybody gasped and clapped and a cheer went up. Both were dressed completely in white. Masayo san in a fairytale wedding dress, like a princess, and Shinji san in a white Regency style suit, with white pleated silk waistcoat and matching tie, finished off perfectly by white, winkle picker shoes and a pink flower in his buttonhole. Both looked like film stars on a Jane Austen set, and of course, both had the beautiful straight-backed posture of the Japanese which added to the elegance of the scene.

Masayo san's hair was now her own and was swept up and held in place by her short veil and a sparkling tiara, tendrils of hair sweeping down her face. Her dress was off the shoulder and circled with hoops of delicate frills right down to the floor where at the back it turned into a thick, sumptuous train. They looked the epitome of a fairytale prince and princess.

However, don't rest on your laurels, this was a Nagoya wedding and the surprises were not over yet, as bride and groom proceeded to do an extraordinary thing. Firstly, a staff member appeared with a long silver poker. She lit the end, which jumped into a flame of gas about two inches long. The other end of the poker had been decorated with a pink ribbon extravagantly tied, and the bride and groom held this end as they walked slowly to the nearest table, leaned over it and lit a candle that had been waiting patiently there all afternoon. A soft cheer went up around that table when it was finally lit after a little trouble, and they then moved to the next table and repeated the process. The room was dark, as the lights were still dimmed and the spotlight followed them around while the calming music continued to play. It was fascinatingly dramatic and entertaining, and everyone's eyes were focused on each movement made and candle lit as they made their way around the room. It was a simple and innocent process, but it packed a punch of pure enjoyment.

I noticed that Shinji san had his arm very securely placed around Masayo san's waist in case of a stumble in her abundance of wedding dress. It all looked incredibly dangerous to me, with all those frills Masayo san was wearing and that large, naked flame only a couple of feet away, but health and safety laws are very different in Japan, where people are not afraid to do fun things just because there is a slim chance that something could go wrong.

This process continued around the room, until they got to Shinji san's work mates' table, where having consumed several bottles of beer each, they had become very happy, mellow fellows. One of them picked up the candle and, laying himself across the table, placed the candle on his stomach and invited them to light it. They hesitated momentarily, and after confirmation from the happy-go-lucky candle holder, leaned forward and lit it with everyone having a jolly good laugh. As I said, health and safety laws are tucked away in a safe place here.

After the last candle was lit, the bride and groom made their way, still clutching the flaming gas poker, to their own table, there to light their own candle, placed in the middle of a red heart. A big "Ah," went up with a round of applause. We all laughed. The heart of love was alight and burning brightly. It was magical. I was on a cloud of pleasure and, by their faces, so were the bride and groom as they posed for photos beside their burning heart.

A bouquet of flowers suddenly appeared in Shinji san's hands, where had it come from? I hadn't noticed. Bride and groom made their way over to a table next to the far wall. They approached Masayo san's grandmother, a very small woman of about ninety, and presented her with the flowers and chatted with her for several minutes. Many bows later, they parted company and we had to return to reality. It was enka time again!

The food and drink just kept on coming, hour after hour, keeping our energy levels up and our taste buds bouncing. Which is more than can be said for the enka. Masayo san's father was up on stage again, this time dressed in a ship's captain's uniform, looking very dapper. Fortunately, the wedding cakes, now cut into slices, appeared and we were asked to help ourselves, and this took our minds off his tortuous renditions from the stage. After a while, I looked around our table and all of us had pained expressions of resignation, oh dear, he did wail superbly, but everyone cheered up at the end of the song and the disappearance of Papa. It was not to last, as Papa reappeared some minutes later, this time dressed in a velvet sequined jacket. Each costume change seemed to bring more angst and wailing (if that was possible) and by the end of that song, we were all drained. Even I, who couldn't understand the words, understood his anguish. Many of his warbles got appreciative applause and even a cheer or two. At the end, he enjoyed sumptuous applause, and he deserved it. He was a superb enka singer.

He took his bows and was presented with a bunch of flowers. Then the lady enka singer – of the glasses and kimono, who had warbled so well herself – approached him and carefully placed a ¥10,000 note into his top pocket, leaving it half in and half out. Everyone laughed and appreciated the joke. Especially Papa.

Small speeches of thanks were given by Masayo san and Shinji san to thank everyone for coming. The staff came around and gave everyone two presents from the bride and groom. A large wooden box of specially cooked celebration rice, full of all kinds of mysterious ingredients (at least to me) and a beautiful box which when opened, revealed two white cups and saucers from a special pottery commemorating the day.

It was finally coming to an end at 8.00pm. The atmosphere was winding down, curling itself up for a well earned sleep, as were the little kids. We had all sipped at the edges of the bride and groom's obvious happiness. Thank you Nagoya. Your weddings are truly worth their reputations. Thank you to Masayo san, Shinji san and their families, who welcomed us so warmly and generously. Both Jan and I felt incredibly privileged.

CHAPTER TWENTY

It All Comes to an End

Japan had been a country of contrasts and contradictions for me. Whenever I discovered one solution to a cultural mystery, several others popped up in its place. Foreigners are always at a disadvantage, and Japanese culture really is inscrutable. I'm not sure that even the Japanese understand it. But it's fascinating and never dull. If you're bored with Japan, you're bored with life, to plagiarise Dr. Johnson.

However, incredible kindness holds hands with, what I would call, a nationalised cruelty to those who do not conform, but I don't think the Japanese notice. It's just their culture and their way. It's up to the Japanese themselves to alter things if they want to. It's not up to me or to any of the other foreigners who go there and want to 'educate' the people they meet in western ways – and there are many that do. Vivre la difference I say, and what will be will be up to the Japanese. I grew to respect the country and would ponder on many of the mysteries of its culture. When understanding dawned from time to time and I learned to change my thinking, turning it upside down and inside out, I found logic and attraction in their unique ways of living and thinking. When I returned home to England, I was the odd one out. Unexpectedly, I got culture shock in reverse. It was enormous and I felt an outsider. I didn't belong anymore. I hadn't realised how 'Japanese' I had become. I had to change my thinking back to British ways and I wasn't always happy doing that. I found I preferred the Japanese way.

Japan was a fascinating and tantalising journey, but it was coming to an end. I knew it when I took a holiday in Canada. Jan and I went for a month's holiday to recoup our energy levels, getting in temporary teachers to cover us. The students were very understanding and didn't mind, wishing us a happy time.

Whilst in Canada we did a lot of serious thinking and talking about my health and energy levels, which had plummeted over the previous year. Success was one of the problems. We had an average of between sixty to seventy students, peaking at eighty two. This meant a lot of work for us and was also my downfall. I became exhausted, not only from hard work, I was never afraid of that, but I had started to experience ill health which dragged me down and sapped my energy even more. I never really recovered from a severe bout of shingles which erupted during a holiday in Australia three years before and I realised that I was doing too much. It took me about six months to recover my strength after the shingles because I didn't want to stop working, maybe I should have taken a break, but the Japanese ethos of work whatever your personal circumstances had got itself ingrained in me. I couldn't comprehend taking a few weeks off. Looking back on it, I realise that would have been the best option but I had become a bit of a workaholic, like most Japanese.

In Canada, we took the difficult decision to sell the school and return to England. We couldn't afford to stay in Japan without working and even though the work was still very enjoyable, it was becoming too difficult. My health was in crisis. Jan too was feeling the strain of working too hard. She was 67 by this time and starting to slow down and each weekend of rest was eagerly looked forward to. Therefore, she was in accord and gently muttered something about, "Giving out flyers at the station gets harder every time."

Strangely, when we returned to Japan, a marvellous thing happened. We found that we were incredibly pleased to be back in Japanese society. Again, it worked its magic on us both, enfolding us under its calm but energetic wing. I just loved the people and atmosphere so much that I got a second wind. I appreciated anew what a great little country it is, and my heart sang and my spirits and energy rose. Jan concurred and we changed our minds and decided to stay until I reached the age of sixty in two year's time.

I could have made it too, but my health continued to decline rapidly. For the past year or so, I had suffered from a persistent pain in my groin area. Walking, sitting, sleeping, it didn't matter what position I was in, the pain persisted and continued to get worse, until I was almost unable to move without great effort. I should have gone to the doctor earlier, but I had thought it was a problem with a trapped nerve and would get better. The body's a wonderful thing and you adjust to changes in it, sometimes without realising the extent of its progression – or you are in denial! Looking back, I think I was doing my imitation of an ostrich and not facing up to the bare facts. Struggling on and hoping it would go away – I'll deal with it tomorrow, it's not so bad, I'm fine! Yes, really, I am!

Finally, I went to the doctor just before Christmas of that year and he sent me for an X-ray at the local hospital. They diagnosed a problem with two discs in the lower spine which had deteriorated from the wear and tear of life, but with the added complication of two scoliosis (curvatures of the spine.) Not such an uncommon complaint and with care and attention, not too serious. They advised me that the pain was coming from the back problem where nerves from the back went around the groin area and down the legs. The immobility problem was due to the fact that I had stopped using many of my muscles and tendons due to the pain. A classic catch 22.

I was given a course of physiotherapy treatment for three months to loosen up the muscles and ligaments in my legs and back which, by all accounts, had started to atrophy because of lack of use. I was also given a course of exercises to do every day, which I did religiously.

If I could have married my physiotherapist I would have. What a pair of hands that man had. He made me semi mobile again as he soothed and softened my muscles dangerously near personal places, groins meaning nothing to him as he massaged my inner thighs. I felt like I could jump over the moon after each session, but unfortunately, that feeling didn't last for long and I was always looking forward to my next session with him. I saw him twice a week for three months. He didn't speak English and he couldn't understand my Japanese, but we didn't need words. Grunts and sighs said it all.

Regrettably, I didn't really get any better and by now it was really hard for me to walk and move around. The life of teaching was making things worse as I was sitting down most of the day, and as the school rooms were small there was no room to walk around during lessons. I tried standing up a few times, but we were all in such close proximity that my students were getting stiff necks looking up at me. It was not a good situation.

I carried on for as long as I could, but I finally had to admit defeat and, with Jan's agreement, made the difficult decision to return back home to England. I was exhausted and I was truly worried about my back and Jan was recognising that she couldn't keep up teaching full time, posing even more difficulties if we stayed on. We didn't want to go down the road of employing teachers as one just swops one lot of stress for a different kind as English teachers in Japan tend to be transient, young and to go where the wind blows them. All I could really think about at this stage was that the lifestyle was making my physical condition worse and I didn't know how to improve my health and stay in Japan. The Japanese doctors were helpful, but I couldn't understand why the treatment had not started a recovery. When one is in constant pain, most of one's energy goes into basic body functioning and concentrates on alleviating that pain. There is little energy left for challenges and ambition. I had no choice in the end and decided to close my school. If I'd been younger, it would have been different, but I was finding it incredibly hard to keep my energy levels going.

I contacted the boss of my franchise system and told him the bad news. "I can't go on," I told him. "I'm sorry, I should have stopped earlier, but I was hoping that I would get better. I want to close the school down and return to Britain within the next month if possible." He was very sympathetic but refused to let me close the school down. "Wait a few more months," he advised, "this is such a good school, I'm sure that you can sell it very quickly."

Surprisingly, within a few weeks, it was indeed sold. It was so fast and I was so busy clearing everything up, that together with my weakened health, the last few weeks were a blur and a huge stress. In fact, I've never done anything so stressful in my life. Telling the students that the school was changing hands was a great trauma and many of them cried because they were so upset that Jan and I were leaving Japan and giving up the school.

Finally, it was sorted out, and I felt both dissatisfied that it was all done so quickly, which upset the students, and at the same time, very relieved that I could now concentrate on myself and my health.

When I did get back to England I was finally diagnosed with osteoarthritis in both hips and lower spine, which of course, explained everything. Osteoarthritis of the hip is very common in Britain, although in Japan, it's the knees that get it and as far as I can judge, arthritis of the hip does not seem to be common, but whatever, the doctors in Japan failed to diagnose arthritis, even though I had asked them to check for it. To be fair to the Japanese doctors, the specialist in Britain told me that it can sometimes be difficult to diagnose osteoarthritis of the hip in its early stages. The Japanese doctors did their best and they were very kind to me, I'm not criticising them, it was just one of those things.

The sedentary lifestyle of my teaching methods and conditions were making the problem worse. In retrospect, I could possibly have changed those conditions, but it would have meant a change of premises, which meant much more work and effort than I was able to gather the energy for. My physical condition had sapped my strength, both physically and mentally. I was exhausted and with a heavy heart and a sense of unreality, Jan and I prepared to leave Japan.

Much to my joy, many of our students gave goodbye parties for us and the next month was spent packing up our lives into boxes for shipping back home; interspersed with four or five parties every week during that month. There was no time for reflection, or even to feel sad, that came later, I was too busy to think of anything but the immediacy of the moment as Jan and I made all our arrangements and said goodbye to our friends. So many of our students had turned into friends, who we still keep in touch with today.

Tea parties, dinner parties, general goodbye parties, we went through them all with emotion and sadness. I invited twenty of our very special friends to a party at the Funny House restaurant. These were the people who had helped me the most, unselfishly giving me their wisdom, time and goodwill to make everything possible. It was an emotional party and many tears were shed, especially by Ryoko who was so shocked by our sudden departure.

*

So where did this leave me, after seven years in Japan? What had I achieved? Had it been worth it? I would say a resounding yes. Japan changed me and made me a better person. I learned from their culture and applied it to my own ingrained Britishness, rubbing off the edges of one and learning a new way of being, and I emerged on the other side a more well rounded, confident, patient, and tolerant person.

I've tried to show the Japan which exists under the surface, not the 'face' the Japanese present. The 'real Japan' as I saw it, through the people and the things that happened to me. Ryoko once told me that one can only truly understand Japanese society if one is born Japanese. She may be right. But that doesn't stop one from trying.

It was Ryoko who gave me the best leaving present she could possibly give me. In a farewell speech she had prepared she told me that meeting me changed her life and way of thinking dramatically, saying, "If I hadn't met you, I would still be an ordinary Japanese housewife, timid and shy and working for an employer, rather than owning my own school, creating my own curriculum and running my own culture salon. You gave that to me. I had always been a follower, you gave me the courage to be a leader. I was able to throw away the Japanese mantra for women; don't complain, don't disagree, don't get angry, never say anything although you have strong opinions. You showed me a new way to think and behave and I grabbed it with both hands like a lifebelt and revelled in my new found power. I needed you, I couldn't have done it without you. Thank you, Jill."

Tears filled her eyes: mine too. I had not realised that I'd created such a dramatic change and been such an important influence on her. As she had on me.

Thank *you* Ryoko.

Life is strange and fate is a conundrum – even more so in Japan.

Japan, oh, how I miss you.